The Study of Primary Education
A Source Book — Volume 4:
Classroom and Teaching Studies

Second edition compiled by
Marion Dadds
with
Brenda Lofthouse

(First edition compiled by
Colin Richards
with
Brenda Lofthouse)

 The Falmer Press

(A member of the Taylor & Francis Group)
London · New York · Philadelphia

UK	The Falmer Press, Rankine Road, Basingstoke, Hampshire, RG24 0PR
USA	The Falmer Press, Taylor & Francis Inc., 1900 Frost Road, Suite 101, Bristol, PA 19007

First published 1990

British Library Cataloguing in Publication Data
The study of primary education: a source book. — 2nd ed. Vol. 4,
  Classroom and teaching studies
  1. Great Britain. Primary education
  I. Dadds, Marion   II. Lofthouse, Brenda
  372.941

  ISBN 1-85000-737-3
  ISBN 1-85000-738-1 pbk

Library of Congress Cataloging in Publication Data
(Revised for Vols. 2–4)
Main entry under title:
The Study of primary education: a source book — /Volume 1:
  Perspectives — 2nd ed.

  Vol 1 compiled by Colin Conner with Brenda Lofthouse
  Vol 2 compiled by Brenda Lofthouse
  Vol 3 compiled by Geoff Southworth with Brenda Lofthouse
  Vol 4 compiled by Marion Dadds with Brenda Lofthouse

  Includes bibliographical references.
  Contents: Vol. 1 Perspectives — v. 2. The curriculum —
v. 3. School organization and management — v. 4. Classrooms and
teaching studies.

  1. Education, Elementary.   2. Education, Elementary — Great
Britain.   I. Conner, Colin.   II. Lofthouse, Brenda.   III. Marion
Dadds.   IV. Geoff Southworth.
  ISBN 1-85000-734-9 (v.1)
  ISBN 1-85000-735-7 (pbk. v.1)
  ISBN 1-85000-718-7 (v.2)
  ISBN 1-85000-719-5 (pbk. v.2)
  ISBN 1-85000-735-7 (v.3)
  ISBN 1-85000-736-5 (pbk. v.3)
  ISBN 1-85000-737-3 (v.4)
  ISBN 1-85000-738-1 (pbk. v.4)
  LB1555.S887   1990   90-33099
  372—dc 20   CIP

Jacket design by Caroline Archer

Typeset in 10/12 Times
by Graphicraft Typesetters Ltd Hong Kong

The Study of Primary Education
A Source Book — Volume 4:
Classroom and Teaching Studies

The Study of Primary Education Source Books

The four volumes in this series are:

The complete contents for each volume are included at the end of this book.

Contents

Contents

Contents

Contents

Contents

The Study of Primary Education — A Source Book: Contents of Volumes 1,
2 and 3

General Introduction

The nature of primary school teaching is difficult to appreciate for those who have no experience of it, except as a pupil. From a child's view, it seems straightforward enough. In reality, the task of the teacher is a complex and demanding one, requiring a wide range of skills and personal qualities, as well as extensive knowledge. The four volumes of these source books have been compiled to help in the professional development of primary school teachers, but the nature of the help they can give needs to be appreciated by potential readers.

In the report, *Postgraduate Certificate in Education Courses for Teachers in Primary and Middle Schools: A Further Consultative Report* (1982), the Universities Council for the Education of Teachers spelt out five elements in the professional 'equipment' of teachers of younger children: (1) techniques; (2) curricular knowledge; (3) professional knowledge; (4) personal and interpersonal skills or qualities; and (5) constructive revaluation. The compilers of these source books acknowledge the importance of all five elements but do not believe that any book can do justice to all of them. The source books focus on two: they contribute both to primary teachers' professional knowledge and to the development of their ability to re-evaluate their own experience and the enterprise of primary education itself. They do this by introducing readers to extracts from 'official' publications and from academic material which put primary education in context and which introduce readers to many of the important theoretical, yet professional, issues that need to be considered by practitioners. Most of the extracts focus directly on primary education or on primary-aged children; this was a major criterion used in selecting material for inclusion in the source books. The four volumes are not intended to provide a complete course of study; they need to be supplemented, where possible, by students' general reading in educational and professional studies: psychology, sociology, history, philosophy, curriculum studies and management studies. However, though not intended as a substitute for students' reading of a wide range of original material, the source books acknowledge the constraints of time and of availability of such material, under which students have to study.

The four books are intended to be used by students taking BEd or PGCE courses and by teachers in service, taking diploma or higher degree courses in primary education. The material extracted can be used by tutors as a focus for seminars or as reading to back up lectures, and by students as a source for essays or as a starting point for further reading. The books are not intended to be read straight through from cover to cover but can be used selectively and flexibly at various stages in the course. For convenience, the extracts have been organized into a number of sections.

Volume 1 comprises extracts which examine primary education from historical, ideological, philosophical, sociological and psychological perspectives. Volume 2 deals with curriculum studies, Volume 3 with school organization and management and Volume 4 with teaching and classroom studies. Because of limitations of space, primary education has been confined to the education of children aged 5 to 11, though the compilers acknowledge that in doing so they may offend those teachers in nursery or middle schools who regard themselves, justifiably, as primary practitioners.

The contents of these four source books indicate the demands made on primary teachers in just two of the five elements outlined above. They also illustrate that the professional development of teachers is almost as complex and demanding a task as primary teaching itself.

The Compilers
Spring 1990

Compilers' Notes

In editing the material the compilers have:

1 provided their own title for each extract;
2 standardized the format of the references;
3 deleted all cross-references in the original text;
4 placed editorial insertions in square brackets within the extract itself.

Immediately beneath the heading of each extract, the source of the material is given in detail. The page numbers in the detailed reference refer to each of the pages in the original text, from which passages making up the extract have been taken. For example, if the reference refers to pages 2, 2–3 and 3, then one of the passages making up the extract has been taken from page 2 of the original text, one passage has been taken from a piece beginning on page 2 and running on to page 3, and a third passage has been taken elsewhere on page 3.

In the editorial material introducing each section and each extract, all the page numbers in brackets within the text refer to other pages within the source book, so as to aid cross-referencing. Any quotation used in the editorial material, unless otherwise referenced, can be found in the text from which the extract has been taken.

Acknowledgments

The publishers are grateful to the following for permission to reproduce copyright material:

Allen and Unwin for BASSEY, M. (1986) 'Does action research require sophisticated research methods?'; GROARKE, J., *et al.* (1986) 'Towards a more open classroom'; CUMMINGS, C. and HUSTLER, D. (1986) 'Issues in action research'; ROWLAND, S. (1986) 'An approach to understanding children'; all in HUSTLER, D. *et al.*, *Action Research in Classrooms and Schools*.

Batsford for SIMON, B. (1981) 'Why no pedagogy in England?' in SIMON, B. and TAYLOR, W. (Eds) *Education in the Eighties: The Central Issues*.

The editor and publishers of the *British Journal of Educational Psychology* for BOYDELL, D. (1975) 'Pupil behaviour in junior classrooms'; AITKEN, M. *et al.* (1981) 'Teaching styles and pupil progress: A re-analysis'; GRAY, J. and SATTERLEY, D. (1981) 'Formal or informal? A re-assessment of the British evidence'.

Cambridge Institute of Education for ELLIOTT, J. (1981) 'A framework for self-evaluation in schools'; DAY, C. (1986) 'Sharing practice through consultancy: Individual and whole staff development in the primary school', in HOLLY, P. and WHITEHEAD, D. *Classroom Action Research Bulletin 7*; HULSE, Y. (1988) 'Discovering discovery learning', in CONNER, C., *Topic and Thematic Work in the Primary and Middle Years*.

The editor and publishers of the *Cambridge Journal of Education*, 17, 3 for SOUTHWORTH, P. (1987) 'Happy talk'.

Cassell for POLLARD, A. and TANN, S. (1987) *Reflective Teaching in the Primary School*.

The editor and publishers of *Forum* for SIMON, B. (1980) 'Inside the primary classroom'.

Grant McIntyre for ARMSTRONG, M. (1981) 'The case of Louise and the painting of the landscape'; ENRIGHT, L. (1981) 'The diary of a classroom', both in NIXON, J., *A Teachers Guide to Action Research*.

Heinemann for CALKINS, L.M. (1983) *Lessons from a Child*; STENHOUSE, L. (1985) 'Research as a basis for teaching' in RUDDUCK, J. and HOPKINS, D., (Eds) *Research as a Basis for Teaching: Readings from the Work of Lawrence Stenhouse*.

The Controller of Her Majesty's Stationery Office for extract from (1978) *Primary Education in England: A Survey by HM Inspectors of Schools*.

Holt Educational for ALEXANDER, R.J. (1984) *Primary Teaching*; POLLARD, A. (1985) *The Social World of the Primary School*.

Lawrence Erlbaum Associates for BENNETT, N., DESFORGES, C. *et al.* (1984) *The Quality of Pupil Learning Experiences*; TIZARD, B. *et al.* (1988) *Young Children at School in the Inner City*.

Longman for the Schools Council for PICKOVER, D. (1984) 'Recognising individual needs'; SIEGAN-SMITH. N. (1984) 'Talking counts'; WATERSON, M. (1984) 'However do they do it?', all in THOMPSON, A. and L. (Eds) *What Learning Looks Like*.

Methuen for BERLAK, A. and H. (1981) *Dilemmas of Schooling: Teaching and Social Change*.

NFER for BARKER-LUNN, J. (1970) *Streaming in the Primary School*.

The editor and publishers of *New Society* for FRENCH, J. (1986) 'Gender in the classroom'.

Open Books for BENNETT, N. *et al.* (1976) *Teaching Styles and Pupil Progress*; MORTIMORE, P., SAMMONS, P., STOLL, L., LEWIS, D. and ECOB, R. (1988) *School Matters*.

Routledge and Kegan Paul for GALTON, M. and SIMON, B. (Eds) (1980) *Progress and Performance in the Primary Classroom*; CROLL, P. and MOSES, D. (1985) *One in Five: The Assessment and Incidence of Special Educational Needs*; NIAS, D.J. (1989) *Primary Teachers Talking: A Study of Teaching as Work*.

University of East Anglia for BARRETT, C. (1986) *Starting School: An Evaluation of the Experience*.

Introduction:
Classroom and Teaching Studies

The study of primary education has been given an added dimension in recent years by empirical work focusing on schools, on classrooms and, in particular, on pedagogy — the complex of teaching approaches, skills, strategies, tactics and forms of organization through which the curriculum is transacted by teachers and children. Such studies are in their infancy, and though their pay-off in terms of increasing the effectiveness of work in primary classrooms cannot be demonstrated, they have been useful in helping to dispel some of the myths surrounding primary practice and in raising important questions for teachers and teacher trainers alike. Their contribution has been more a form of consciousness-raising than the provision of definitive answers to questions of appropriate organization and technique.

Selections from some of the larger scale statistical studies represented in parts one and two of this volume attempt to illustrate the major themes on classroom research which have emerged since Neville Bennett's contentious work on teaching styles and pupil progress in 1976. These include studies of teaching styles and pupil learning; studies of the way in which teachers match tasks to children; the time children spend on different tasks and how this relates to achievement; the relationship between quality of learning experience and quantity of time on task; and, more recently, in the work of Peter Mortimore and his colleagues, factors at school and classroom level which seem to have a bearing on children's progress through school. The latter has generated a new interest in developing the concept of school and classroom effectiveness, in which children's progress, not just attainment, has become a key criterion. Selections from smaller scale, qualitative studies, contribute to some of these themes.

In addition to these major research projects there has been a richness and diversity of smaller scale studies. They have contributed significantly to our understanding of other important classroom issues. The work of Charles Desforges and Ann Cockburn, for example, takes a much needed look at the problems presented to teachers by information processing and decision-making in the modern primary classroom. A number of contributors ask why the ideals of such major reports as Plowden and Cockroft have not been fully realized in practice. Several credible hypotheses are offered and the work of Desforges and Cockburn may have much to teach us in this area. What kinds of external pressures, attitudes and constraints affect teachers' classroom and curriculum decision-making? Do the kinds of classroom organization advocated in progressive ideology simply become too complicated and stressful for many teachers to handle? Contributions by Maurice Galton and Brian Simon have also explored some of these areas, and, at a common sense level, many primary teachers would have sympathy with their insights. Adopting a less simple form of organization, plus a broader curriculum catering for individual differences in children, may require complex change processes for the teacher, as well as highly sophisticated classroom management skills. Changing from a more traditional to a more progressive style can be a slow, and highly demanding process. The extract from Lucy Calkin's work on teacher change and curriculum innovation illustrates the nature and pace of change which is possible for the teacher if it is to be handled well. Peter Mortimore's study suggests that the most effective teachers have a more simplified classroom and curriculum organization than that envisaged in certain types of integrated day. Brian Simon argues that the concept of individual differences, in itself, is unhelpful to the class teacher catering for the needs of such large groups of children. He suggests that this notion needs re-thinking if classroom effectiveness is to be improved. It is far from clear, yet, whether the kinds of expectations on teachers which various versions of progressive philosophy have generated are realistic.

A further topic of current interest concerns the way in which schools and classrooms socialize children into roles, some of which may be of benefit to the child, some of which may depress achievement and fulfilment. Andrew Pollard has made a valuable contribution to our thinking in this. Extracts from his work are supported by others which look at gender roles and stereotypes, and at the early socialization which goes on for young children starting school. This is a crucial time for children. Their experience in the early stages of schooling can have a significant long term effect, as the extract from the large scale study by Barbara Tizard and her colleagues suggests. Gill Barrett's work shows the range of issues confronting children, teachers and families as the first transition is made, from home to school.

The division which has been made between teaching and learning in parts one and two of this volume is, obviously, an arbitrary one. Teaching cannot be studied without relating it to the style and quality of learning experiences which arise for children. Similarly, the kinds of learning experiences for children to which a teacher aspires may affect the teaching style and classroom environment to be adopted. Most contributions in parts one and two, therefore, have inseparable insights to offer on teachers and children.

Part three looks at the 'teacher as researcher' movement, a movement which has evolved in recent years as a reaction against the limited use, by teachers, of much traditional research. Many teachers and teacher educators alike have worried about the inaccessibility, for teachers, of much traditional, externally conducted research. Research which is not read or known by teachers clearly cannot affect classroom practice or aid teacher development. Even if larger scale research projects influence educational policy making this is no guarantee that teaching and learning will automatically and immediately benefit. The teacher researcher movement evolved in an attempt to give teachers a more central role in the research process, encouraging them to focus on, and research, their own concerns and understandings. It also aimed to feed research outcomes back into practical classroom improvements. Several of the contributions selected for part three explore the rationale behind the movement. Other selections are drawn from the work of teacher researchers themselves. They come from teachers' own accounts of their small scale research studies, studies which are rooted in an examination of teaching and learning in their daily professional lives. These extracts give a flavour of the relationship between research, teacher thinking, curriculum development and classroom improvement. Though very different in style and scope from most of the studies selected in parts one and two, this approach to the study of classrooms and teaching has generated a great deal of interest amongst teachers and teacher educators alike. As a result, it has had a profound effect on pedagogy within some initial and in-service training courses. More recently, similar work has been evolving within the context of developmental teacher appraisal. It is probable that the profession will see more of this approach to small scale educational research in the next few years.

1   Teachers and Teaching

Towards a Revitalized Pedagogy

(From Simon, B., 1981, 'Why no pedagogy in England?', in Simon, B. and Taylor, W. (Eds) *Education in the Eighties: The Central Issues*, London, Batsford, pp. 137–8, 139–40, 141–3.)

In the paper from which this extract has been taken Brian Simon explores why pedagogy (the scientific approach to the practice of teaching) has been neglected in England, despite promising beginnings about a century ago. In this particular passage he argues strongly for a renewed attempt at developing pedagogic science rooted in two general principles (the recognition of the human capacity for learning and the similarity of the process of learning across the human species), leading eventually to the determination of general principles of teaching. Provocatively, he contends that concern with individual differences (exemplified by the Plowden Report) has prevented pedagogic progress. We need to start 'from what children have in common as members of the human species; to establish the general principles of teaching and, in the light of these, to determine what modifications of practice are necessary to meet specific individual needs.'

What, then, are the requirements for a renewal of scientific approaches to the practice of teaching — for a revitalized pedagogy?

First, we can identify two essential conditions without which there can be no pedagogy having a generalized significance or application. The first is recognition of the human capacity for learning. It may seem unnecessary, even ridiculous, to single this out in this connection, but in practice this is not the case. Fundamentally, psychometric theory, as elaborated in the 1930s to 1950s, denied the lability of learning capacity, seeing each individual as endowed, as it were, with an engine of a given horse-power which is fixed, unchangeable and measurable in each particular case, irrevocably setting precise and definable limits to achievement (or learning). It was not until this view had been discredited in the eyes of psychologists that serious attention could be given to the analysis and interpretation of the *process* of human learning.

The second condition has been effectively defined by Professor Stones in his helpful and relevant book *Psychopedagogy*, sub-titled 'Psychological Theory and the Practice of Teaching' (1979). It is the recognition that, in general terms, the process of learning among human beings is similar across the human species as a whole. The view on which Stones's book is based is that 'except in pathological cases, learning capability among individuals is similar', so that 'it is possible to envisage a body of general principles of teaching' that are relevant for 'most individual pupils'. The determination, or identification, of such general principles must comprise the objectives of pedagogical study and research (Stones, 1979, p. 453).

One further point may be made at the start. The term 'pedagogy' itself implies structure. It implies the elaboration or definition of specific means adapted to produce the desired effect — such-and-such learning on the part of the child. From the start of the use of the term, pedagogy has been concerned to relate the process of teaching to that of learning on the part of the child. It was this approach that characterized the work of Comenius, Pestalozzi and Herbart, and that, for instance, of Joseph Priestley and the associationist tradition generally. . . .

The work and thinking of both Luria and Bruner (as representatives of their respective traditions) point in a similar direction — towards a renewed understanding both of the power of education to effect human change and especially cognitive development, and of the need for the systematization and structuring of the child's experiences in the process of learning. And it is precisely from this standpoint that a critique is necessary of certain contemporary standpoints, dichotomies and ideologies, and, in particular, of the whole trend towards so-called 'child-centred' theories, which have dominated this area in Britain basically since the early 1920s, to reach its apotheosis in what is best called the 'pedagogic romanticism' of the Plowden Report, its most recent, and semi-official expression. . . . Plowden takes the child-centred approach to its logical limits, insisting on the principle of the complete individualization of the teaching/learning process as the ideal (even though, from a pedagogic standpoint, this is not a practical possibility in any realistic sense). In their analysis the hereditary/environmental interactional process is interpreted as exacerbating initial differences so greatly that each child must be seen to be unique, and be treated as such. The matter is rendered even more complex by their insistence that each individual child develops at different rates across three parameters, intellectual, emotional and physical; and that in determining her approach to each individual child each of these must be taken into account by the teacher. The result is that the task set the teacher, with an average of 35 children per class when Plowden reported, is, in the words of the report itself, 'frighteningly high' (Plowden, 1967, I paras 75, 875).

I want to suggest that, by focusing on the individual child ('at the heart of the educational process lies the child'), and in developing the analysis from this point, the Plowden Committee created a situation from which it was impossible to derive an effective pedagogy (or effective pedagogical means). If each child is unique, and each requires a specific pedagogical approach appropriate to him or her and to no other, the construction of an all-embracing pedagogy, or general principles of teaching becomes an impossibility. And indeed research has shown that primary school teachers who have taken the priority of individualization to heart, find it difficult to do more than ensure that each child is in fact engaged on the series of tasks which the teacher sets up for the child; the complex management problem which then arises takes the teacher's full energies. Hence the approach of teachers who endeavour to implement these prescripts is necessarily primarily didactic ('telling') since it becomes literally impossible to stimulate enquiry, or to 'lead from behind', as Plowden held the teacher should operate in the classroom. Even with a lower average of 30 children per class, this is far too complex and time-consuming a role for the teacher to perform.

The main thrust of the argument outlined here is this: that to start from the standpoint of individual differences is to start from the wrong position. To develop effective pedagogic means involves starting from the opposite standpoint, from what children have in common as members of the human species; to establish the general principles of teaching and, in the light of these, to determine what modifications of practice are necessary to meet specific individual needs. If all children are to be assisted to learn, to master increasingly complex cognitive tasks, to develop increasingly complex skills and abilities or mental operations, then this is an objective that schools must have in common; their task becomes the deliberate development of such skills and abilities in all their children. This involves importing a definite structure into the teaching, and so into the learning experiences provided for the pupils. Individual differences only become important, in this context, if the pedagogical means elaborated are found not to be appropriate to particular children (or groups of children) because of one or other aspect of their individual development or character. In this situation the requirement becomes that of modifying the pedagogical means so that they become appropriate for all; that is, of applying general principles in specific instances.

What is suggested here is that the starting point for constructing the curriculum, or children's activities in school, insofar as we are concerned with cognitive development (the schools may reasonably have other aims as well) lies in definition of the objectives of teaching, which forms the ground base from which pedagogical means are defined and established, means or principles which underlie specific methodological (or experiential) approaches. It may well be that these include the use of co-operative group work as well as individualized activities — but these are carefully designed and structured in relation to the achievement of overall objectives. This approach, I am arguing, is the opposite of basing the educational process on the child, on his immediate interests and spontaneous activity, and providing, in theory, for a total differentiation of the learning process in the case of each individual child. This latter approach is not only undesirable in principle, it is impossible of achievement in practice.

In a striking phrase Lev Vygotsky summed up his outlook on teaching and learning. Pedagogy, he wrote, 'must be oriented not towards the yesterday of development but towards its tomorrow'. Teaching, education, pedagogic means, must always take the child forward, be concerned with the formation of new concepts and hierarchies of concepts, with the next stage in the development of a particular ability, with ever more complex forms of mental operations. 'What the child can do today with adult help', he said, 'he will be able to do independently tomorrow'. This concept, that of the 'zone of next (or "potential") development' implies in the educator a clear concept of the progression of learning, of a consistent challenge, of the mastery by the child of increasingly complex forms — of never standing still or going backwards. 'The only good teaching is that which outpaces development', insisted Vygotsky. Whether the area is that of language development, of concepts of number and mathematics — symbolic systems that underlie all further learning — or whether it covers scientific and technological concepts and skills as well as those related to the social sciences and humanities, appropriate pedagogical means can and should be defined, perhaps particularly in areas having their own inner logical structures. In this sense, psychological knowledge combined with logical analysis forms the ground base from which pedagogical principles can be established, given, of course, effective research and experiment.

[Here I am] strictly concerned with cognitive development, since it is here that technological/scientific and social changes will make their greatest impact and demands. But for successful implementation of rational procedures and planning, in the face of the micro-processor revolution, more than this needs consideration. There is also the question, for instance, of the individual's enhanced responsibility for his own activities; the development of autonomy, of initiative, creativity, critical awareness; the need of the part of the mass of the population for access to knowledge and culture, the arts and literature, to mention only some aspects of human development. The means of promoting such human qualities and characteristics cannot simply be left to individual teachers, on the grounds that each individual child is unique so that the development of a pedagogy is both impracticable and superfluous. The existing teaching force of half a million have, no doubt, many talents, but they need assistance in the pursuit of their common objective — the education of new generations of pupils. The new pedagogy requires carefully defined goals, structure, and adult guidance. Without this a high proportion of children, whose concepts are formed as a result of their everyday experiences, and, as a result, are often distorted and incorrectly reflect reality, will never even reach the stage where the development of higher cognitive forms of activity becomes a possibility. And this implies a massive cognitive failure in terms of involvement and control (responsible participation) in the new social forms and activities which the future may bring.

References

BRUNER, J.S. (1972) *The Relevance of Education*, London, Allen and Unwin.
CENTRAL ADVISORY COUNCIL FOR EDUCATION (England) (1967) *Children and Their Primary Schools* London, HMSO.
LURIA, A.R. (1962) Voprosy Psikhologii 4.
STONES, E. (1979) *Psychopedagogy: Psychological Theory and the Practice of Teaching*, London, Methuen.
VYGOTSKY, L.S. (1962) *Language and Thought*, Wiley.

Teaching Styles

(From Bennett, N. *et al.*, 1976, *Teaching Styles and Pupil Progress*, London, Open Books, pp. 44–5, 45–7.)

As an art, teaching is to some degree idiosyncratic; individuals approach the task in rather different ways. Nevertheless, for the purpose of analysis it has proved possible to categorize the teaching approaches of primary teachers into a smaller number of 'styles'. A number of classifications have been advanced since the mid-seventies, the earliest and most controversial being that identified by Bennett as a result of an analysis of *questionnaire* responses by third and fourth year junior teachers in over 700 schools in the north-west of England. The passage below provides short descriptions of the twelve-styles so identified. The characterization of teaching in such terms has been strongly challenged. Alternative typologies are presented in later extracts (p. 16).

In order to isolate the variety of these styles a cluster analysis was undertaken. This is a useful technique since it allows people to be grouped together who have similar characteristics, in this instance teachers who had a similar profile of responses to all the questionnaire items. . . .

Twelve teacher types or styles were extracted from the cluster analysis, and can be described as follows:

Type 1
These teachers favour integration of subject matter, and, unlike most other groups, allow pupil choice of work, whether undertaken individually or in groups. Most allow pupils choice of seating. Less than half curb movement and talk. Assessment in all its forms — tests, grading, and homework — appears to be discouraged. Intrinsic motivation is favoured.

Type 2
These teachers also prefer integration of subject matter. Teacher control appears to be low, but the teachers offer less pupil choice of work. However, most allow pupils choice of seating, and only one third curb movement and talk. Few test or grade work.

Type 3
The main teaching mode of this group is class teaching and group work. Integration of subject matter is preferred, and is associated with taking their pupils out of school. These teachers appear to be strict, most curbing movement and talk, and offenders are smacked. The amount of testing is average but the amount of grading and homework is below average.

Type 4

These teachers prefer separate subject teaching but a high proportion allow pupil choice of work both in group and individual work. None seat their pupils by ability. They test and grade more than average.

Type 5

A mixture of separate subject and integrated subject teaching is characteristic of this group. The main teaching mode is pupils working in groups of their own choice in tasks set by the teacher. Teacher talk is lower than average. Control is high with regard to movement but not to talk. Most give tests every week and many give homework regularly. Stars are rarely used, and pupils are taken out of school regularly.

Type 6

These teachers prefer to teach subjects separately with emphasis on groups working on teacher-specified tasks. The amount of individual work is small. These teachers appear to be fairly low on control, and in the use of extrinsic motivation.

Type 7

This group are separate subject orientated, with a high level of class teaching together with individual work. Teacher control appears to be tight, few teachers allow movement or choice of seating, and offenders are smacked. Assessment, however, is low.

Type 8

This group of teachers has very similar characteristics to those of type 3, the difference being that these prefer to organize the work on an individual rather than a group basis. Freedom of movement is restricted, and most expect pupils to be quiet.

Type 9

These teachers favour separate subject teaching, the predominant teaching mode being individuals working on tasks set by the teacher. Teacher control appears to be high; most curb movement and talk, and seat by ability. Pupil choice is minimal, regular spelling tests are given, but few mark or grade work, or use stars.

Type 10

All these teachers favour separate subject teaching. The teaching mode favoured is teacher talk to whole class, and pupils working in groups determined by the teacher, on tasks set by the teacher. Most curb movement and talk, and over two thirds smack for disruptive behaviour. There is regular testing and most give stars for good work.

Type 11

All members of this group stress separate subject teaching by way of class teaching and individual work. Pupil choice of work is minimal, although most teachers allow choice in seating. Movement and talk are curbed, and offenders smacked.

Type 12

This is an extreme group in a number of respects. None favour an integrated approach. Subjects are taught separately by class teaching and individual work. None allow pupils choice of seating, and every teacher curbs movement and talk. These teachers are above average on all assessment procedures, and extrinsic motivation predominates.

The types have been subjectively ordered, for descriptive purposes, in order of distance from the most 'informal' cluster (type 1). This suggests that they can be represented by points on a continuum of 'informal-formal', but this would be an over-simplification. The extreme types could be adequately described in these terms, but the remaining types all contain both informal and formal elements.

Exploratory and Didactic Teaching

(From DES, 1978, *Primary Education in England: A Survey by HM Inspectors of Schools*, London, HMSO, pp. 26–7, 27, 27–8, 95.)

As part of a survey of over 1100 primary classes conducted in the mid-seventies, HM Inspectorate categorized the teaching seen in terms of two broad approaches: 'mainly didactic' and 'mainly exploratory'. In the passage below these two terms are explained and relationships established between teaching approaches and (1) match of work to children's capabilities, and (2) children's attainment on standardized reading and mathematics tests.

3.19   Teachers varied their own approach to teaching according to the circumstances, and in the course of one lesson a variety of approaches might be used. For this reason it can be misleading to categorise teaching methods. Nevertheless, for the purpose of this survey two broad approaches to teaching were postulated. They were defined as 'mainly didactic' and 'mainly exploratory'. A didactic approach was one in which the teacher directed the children's work in accordance with relatively specific and predetermined intentions and where explanations usually, though not always, preceded the action taken by the children. An exploratory approach was one in which the broad objectives of the work were discussed with the children but where they were then put in a position of finding their own solutions to the problems posed and of making choices about the way in which the work should be tackled. The scope and timescale of the tasks involved were likely to be flexible and the path of the work was likely to be modified in the light of events; explanation by the teacher more often accompanied or followed action taken by the children.

3.20   In the survey classes about three-quarters of the teachers employed a mainly didactic approach, while less than one in twenty relied mainly on an exploratory approach. In about one-fifth of the classes teachers employed an appropriate combination of didactic and exploratory methods, varying their approach according to the nature of the task in hand, and could not be said to incline to either approach....

3.22   The impetus for extended studies which involved children over a period of time could arise from the children or be introduced by the teacher.... A good example of an extended study by a group of children, introduced by the teacher, was seen in a 7 year old class where the teacher had introduced a topic on water, following the interest aroused in the children by a burst water main outside the school gate. In the course of the work, children examined a number of different aspects of the subject including rusting, floating, sinking, water levels, rates of flow, the importance of water to plant and animal life, and where their own supply of drinking water came from. The work involved discussion, writing, drawing and practical experiment, and culminated in a visit to a local reservoir.

3.24   In this case the teacher used a combination of didactic and exploratory approaches, sometimes introducing the work with discussion and explanation, occasionally following up a point of interest raised by a child and sometimes presenting the children with a practical problem to be investigated. The problems posed were usually specific and predetermined, concerned, for example, with the investigation of properties of corrosibility and buoyancy or the effects of water pressure; explanations preceded, accompanied or followed the children's activities, with the teacher varying her approaches according to the needs of the moment.... Teachers in a minority of classes employed a combination of didactic and exploratory approaches; in these classes the work children were given to do was better matched to their capabilities for the least, average and most able than in those classes using mainly didactic or mainly exploratory methods.

7.26   In the smallest group of classes, one in twenty, which relied on a mainly exploratory approach the children scored less well in the NFER tests in reading and mathematics. There was also some indication that the work was least well matched to the children's abilities in these classes although the number of classes involved was too small for formal analysis.

7.27   In classes where a didactic approach was mainly used, better NFER scores were achieved for reading and mathematics than in those classes using mainly exploratory approaches. The NFER scores for the group of classes using mainly didactic approaches were only marginally lower than for the children in the classes using a combination of exploratory and didactic methods; the difference was not statistically significant.

Teaching Styles: An Alternative Typology

(From Galton, M., 1982, 'Strategies and tactics in junior school classrooms', in Richards, C. (Ed.) *New Directions in Primary Education*, Lewes, Falmer Press, pp. 198–9, 204–6.)

A typology of teaching styles was proposed by the ORACLE research team as a result of their observation of teachers and pupils in fifty-eight classes containing children of junior age. The theoretical framework which the team used to think about teaching is summarized in the first part of the extract below. The second part describes the teaching styles resulting from a cluster analysis of the mass of data recorded on the Teacher Record (the observation schedule whose main headings are summarized on Table 1). From the analysis three 'primary' styles are derived; a fourth is less clearly delineated and seems more accurately described as a 'secondary' style comprising varied mixtures of the three 'primary' ones. The team claim to have broadly replicated their findings through the systematic observation of a further sample of teachers. The classification offered is more firmly based on observational data and less simplistic than that offered by Bennett (p. 26), but its validity across both infant and junior teachers and in a wide range of contexts has not been established. It does, however, provide a more useful way of discussing primary school teaching than the 'formal-informal' dichotomy often used.

There appear to be three key strategic decisions that any teacher has to make when confronted with a new situation such as starting a fresh year with a new class. The first concerns the *organizational strategy*, how to manage the learning environment, the second the *curriculum strategy*, what to teach and the third the *instructional strategy*, how to teach it.

The organizational strategy is largely directed towards seeing that each pupil is allowed the maximum opportunity for learning. It will concern decisions such as whether to teach the class as a whole or whether to organize group work or to provide for individualized instruction. When groups are used then there are decisions involving their composition (their size, balance between sexes, mixed ability, etc.). Such strategies are largely directed towards maintaining control and to producing an efficient working atmosphere. The curriculum strategy is concerned with the content and balance of the curriculum. At junior school stage, when separate subject teaching is preferred to an integrated approach, then the different degree of emphasis given to different subject areas will be reflected by the time-table. Within any subject area, however, there will be considerable room for each teacher to emphasize different aspects in her teaching. For example a study by Ashton[1] of primary teachers' aims showed that many teachers wished to give equal emphasis to applying basic skills to every-day practical situations as to using the four rules. Such teachers would presumably give as much time to such activities as measuring and shopping games as they would to learning tables and doing formal sums.

The instructional strategy corresponds to what is often loosely called teaching methods and may include a combination of lecturing, demonstrating, class discussion, using work cards or project activity. For Taba[2] the instructional strategy is the most important and she argues that the main function of teaching is to develop the pupils' capacity for thinking. Her instructional strategies are aimed at developing correct thinking in pupils and emphasize a questioning rather than a telling approach during class discussion. The ultimate aim is to allow pupils to manage their own learning so that they will make use of these questioning techniques even when the teacher is not present. It is clear that all three elements in the overall teaching strategy must be linked. A decision to engage in, for example, a discussion strategy would also involve decisions about organizational and curricular ones such as the nature of the groups and the selection and structuring of appropriate content in order to promote discussion among the pupils.

Teaching Tactics and Teaching Style

Once the lesson has begun the strategies have to be worked out by means of the exchange between the teacher and her pupils — the teaching tactics. It is here suggested that each tactical exchange will seek to emphasize either an aspect of class *control*, the development of social and personal skills in the pupils or the pupils' *cognitive* development. Thus when a teacher asks a pupil a question 'two times two?' and receives the reply 'four' she is mainly concerned with a cognitive outcome but if she tells pupils, in a normal tone of voice, to 'carry on working and wait until I come to you' she is primarily exercising a management function designed to keep control of the teaching situation. The third type of tactic relating to social and personal development is not directly monitored by the observation schedules used in the ORACLE research,[3] although it is reflected in some exchanges which give rise to teacher praise or criticism. . . .

After a settling down period with the class a state of equilibrium is established where the teacher begins to make use of *a consistent set of tactics* and it is this which is here defined as her *teaching style*. According to Strasser[4] the use of a set of tactics evolves mainly as a result of careful observation of pupil behaviour and less immediately because of previous knowledge about the pupils' attainment, but as the teacher and her pupils adjust to one another the latter's performance becomes an increasingly important factor in determining the relative success of the overall aims and strategy. Typically, however, researchers interested in teacher effectiveness have sought to define good and bad teaching mainly in terms of test results and to ignore pupil activity in the classroom. The ORACLE research

Figure 1.   A description of the teaching process

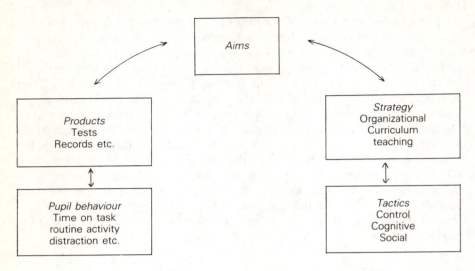

programme is designed around the principle that a complete evaluation should concern itself with five elements in the teaching process listed in figure 1.

For simplicity only the outer links are joined although some elements of teaching strategy may have a direct effect on pupil behaviour so that inner links may be appropriate in certain cases. The arrows are double headed because there is as yet little research evidence clarifying in which direction these links should operate. ORACLE is one of the few studies to investigate whether there is even a relationship between certain kinds of teaching tactics and different types of pupil behaviour. Studies using naturalistic rather than experimental designs must introduce an element of replication if evidence is to be obtained about the direction of such relationships. Pupils in the ORACLE study will have been observed, in some casses, over three years. This will enable behaviour of pupils who move from one teacher to another of different style to be investigated. . . .

Style 1

This group accounted for 22.4 per cent of the sample and was characterized by the low level of questioning and the high level of silent interaction. The teachers engaged in a large number of short-lived interactions which were usually concerned with telling pupils what to do (task supervision S3). The general impression gained, from a variety of accounts provided by the observers, was of pupils working mainly on individual tasks with teachers

Table 1   Cluster characteristics as percentage of total observations

		1 Individual monitors	2 Class enquirers	3 Group instructors	4 Style changer
Questions	Q1 Recalling facts	3.9	4.1	2.4	3.4
	Q2 Solution (closed)	1.1	3.3	2.0	2.4
	Q3 Solution (open)	0.3	1.0	0.9	0.6
	ask questions	5.3	8.4	5.3	6.4
	Q4 Task supervision	2.9	4.1	3.2	4.5
	Q5 Routine	1.3	2.2	1.5	2.0
	All other questions	4.2	6.3	4.7	6.5
Statements	S1 Of facts	5.6	8.0	11.9	6.0
	S2 Of ideas	2.1	4.2	1.0	2.6
	All task statements	7.7	12.2	12.9	8.6
Task supervision	S3 Telling	15.8	11.2	11.6	11.8
	S4 Praising	1.0	1.3	0.6	1.1
	S5 Feedback	8.7	10.9	15.9	8.7
Routine	S6 Information	5.6	7.0	6.7	6.8
	S7 Feedback	1.8	2.3	2.3	2.0
	S8 Critical control	2.0	1.5	2.4	2.6
	S9 Small talk	1.3	1.7	0.6	1.4
	All other statements	36.2	35.9	40.1	34.4
Silent interaction	Gesturing	1.8	0.9	3.7	1.8
	Showing	2.4	3.3	2.0	2.6
	Marking	16.4	5.7	7.4	9.4
	Waiting	1.7	1.6	2.1	2.0
	Story	0.6	1.8	1.0	0.7
	Reading	3.0	3.4	2.2	3.8
	All other interactions	25.9	16.7	18.4	20.3
Audience	Individual	66.9	42.5	52.3	55.3
	Group	5.5	5.8	17.7	6.3
	Class	6.9	31.2	11.4	14.6

under a considerable amount of pressure. The observers describe some teachers moving rapidly from table to table but others sitting at their desks with pupils queuing up either for information or for some clarification of the instructions in the text-book or worksheet. The pupil-adult categories on the Pupil Record indicate that most of these interactions were brief. Some pupils wished to know how to spell a word, others wanted to know whether they should go on to the next exercise. Any attempt by the teacher at prolonged interaction with a pupil was usually prevented by the pressures resulting from the demands of the other pupils and from her concern to keep waiting time to a minimum.

Within such a complex organization the task of monitoring the pupils' work takes on a high priority. It is important not only to correct books but also to record progress so that where pupils are involved in planning their own time-tables regular checks can be carried out to see if each has fulfilled his quota. There was thus a very high level of interaction concerned with marking. Under the ground rules of the observation schedule, marking consists of the teacher giving feedback by writing corrections on pupils' work rather than by making oral comments. It is this particular characteristic which suggests that Style 1 teachers should be labelled as *individual monitors*.

Style 2

This group comprised 15.5 per cent of the sample and was defined by the emphasis given to questioning, particularly questions relating to task work. The level of statements made was also relatively high which suggested, in keeping with the amount of class teaching, that much of the learning was 'teacher managed'. However, when examining the sub-categories of teacher talk it can be seen that much of the conversation related to the higher cognitive levels. Although the level of cognitive discourse in junior school classrooms appears, for the most part, to be concerned with the transmission of information, the teachers under Style 2 used a much higher proportion of both closed and open questions (Q2, Q3) and made more statements of ideas and problems (S2) than did the remaining groups.

The picture which came from the observers' impressionistic accounts was of teachers who introduced new topics to the whole class and then engaged in question and answer routines with individual pupils, reinforced by means of verbal feedback on their work. Because of this emphasis on problem solving, coupled with teacher control of these activities by means of class teaching, it seems apt to describe this group of teachers as engaging in *class directed enquiry*.

Style 3

This cluster consists of 12.1 per cent of the teachers and was in many ways the most interesting. The amount of group interaction was, on average, three times as high as for the rest of the sample. The decrease in time given over to individual attention allowed the teacher to engage in considerably more teacher directed interaction (questioning and stating) than, for example, teachers in Style 1. The main emphasis, however, was on making statements of fact rather than the presentation of ideas. This was coupled with a high level of verbal feedback and gesturing. Presumably, and the observer's descriptions tend to confirm this, these teachers preferred to structure the work of the group carefully before allowing them to engage in discussion among themselves. Hence there was an emphasis on giving information (S1) and, once the group began to interact, on returning to re-join the discussion and provide verbal feedback on the pupils' ideas and solutions to problems. Set against the general low level of cognitive questioning these teachers did nevertheless engage in above average amounts of open questioning. This suggests that they allowed the groups of pupils to come up with alternative answers to problems and did not always insist on their being the one correct answer. Such teachers appear to come closest in adopting the grouping strategy suggested by Plowden for coping with large sized classes. Although there was evidence for some less directed enquiry since these teachers also tended to ask more open questions the main emphasis must be placed on the information aspects of their teaching. Consequently this group might be thought of as *group instructors*.

Style 4

Fifty per cent of the sample came within this cluster. It appears to be a mixture of the other three since in the audience category, for example, these teachers had the second highest levels of individual, group and class interaction, even given that some of these differences are slight. They did ask the highest number of questions relating to task supervision (Q4), made more statements of critical control (S8) and heard more pupils read than did teachers in other styles but these features were not associated exclusively with one particular remaining cluster. Style 2, the *class directed enquirers*, also engaged in task supervision questions and reading while Style 1 teachers, the *individual monitors*, showed a similar need for an element of critical control.

Although overall there was considerable variation in the amount of higher order cognitive interactions between styles, when this was broken down between class and individual attention, then it appears that there is something about class teaching which is particularly conducive to such activity. For example, the *individual monitors* who have the lowest amount overall of this type of interaction nevertheless contrived to engage in 16.7 per cent of it when in conversation with the whole class. For the *group instructors* (Style 3) the corresponding figure is 19.5 per cent. Thus the use of certain types of tactics seems closely related to different organizational strategies and the impressionistic accounts for this group of teachers confirm that they all in one way or another make changes in their organization during the year. Some made *infrequent* changes shifting from a class to a more individualized approach as the year progressed. Others set up activity areas and the pupils *rotated* from one table to the next at regular intervals. The third sub-group carried out *frequent* changes which in many cases seemed unplanned, often in reaction to some undesired pupil behaviour. Thus one teacher, Miss S., tended to move swiftly to class activities at any time when the general level of 'busyness' dropped and the volume of noise rose to any marked degree. This additional evidence lends support to the description of the teachers in cluster 4 as *style changers* where the emphasis on certain sets of tactics varies according to the preferred pattern of organization at any time.

Notes

1 ASHTON, P. *et al.* (1975) *The Aims of Primary Education: A Study of Teachers' Opinions*, London, Macmillan Education.
2 TABA, H. and ELZEY, F. (1964) 'Teaching strategies and thought processes', *Teachers College Record*, 65, pp. 524–34.
3 GALTON, M., SIMON, B. and CROLL, P. (1980) *Inside the Primary Classroom*, London, Routledge and Kegan Paul.
4 STRASSER, B. (1967) 'A conceptual model of instruction', *Journal of Teacher Education*, 18, pp. 63–74.

Dilemmas of Schooling and Formal/Informal Teaching

(From Berlak, A. and H., 1981, *Dilemmas of Schooling: Teaching and Social Change*, London, Methuen, pp. 198–201.)

As a result of trying to make sense of the teaching they observed in a variety of English primary schools, the authors of the passage below have developed a set of concepts which they believe capture many of the important dilemmas facing teachers as they interact with children. 'The dilemmas are intended to formulate the range of tensions "in" teachers, "in" the situation and "in" society, over the nature of control teachers exert over children in school.' Sixteen dilemmas are distinguished and given short-hand titles (see the list below; for elaboration readers are referred to the text from which the extract is drawn.) To illustrate, 'teacher v. child control (operations)' captures the pull between the teacher exercising detailed control over what the children are doing in various curricular areas and towards allowing children to exercise their own control, e.g., deciding how to conduct their own enquiry or what method to use to solve a mathematical problem. Different teachers resolve this particular dilemma in different ways.

The extract describes how the distinction 'formal-informal' distinguishes in a *general* way between two sets of teachers observed by the authors but does not do justice to the variations within any one set or to the similarities across the sets. The authors believe that the range of differences in teaching approach can be more accurately characterized using the dilemma language.

The terms of the dilemma language
Control set:

1 'Whole' child v. child as student — (realms)
2 Teacher v. child control — (time)
3 Teacher v. child control — (operations)
4 Teacher v. child control — (standards)

Curriculum set:

5 Personal knowledge v. public knowledge
6 Knowledge as content v. knowledge as process
7 Knowledge as given v. knowledge as problematical
8 Learning is holistic v. learning is molecular
9 Intrinsic v. extrinsic motivation
10 Each child unique v. children have shared characteristics
11 Learning is individual v. learning is social
12 Child as person v. child as client

Social set:

13 Childhood continuous v childhood unique (childhood)
14 Equal allocation of resources v. differential allocation (allocation)

15 Equal justice under law v. ad hoc application of rules (deviance)
16 Common culture v. sub-group consciousness.

The terms 'informal' and 'formal' and others used as synonyms — progressive, open traditional — have been value-laden words in the so-called Great Debate in England and the increasingly bitter public controversy over 'back to the basics' and 'accountability' on the other side of the Atlantic. Proponents of informal education often associate it with freedom, child-centeredness, priority on creative expression, rejection of traditional distinctions between school subjects, and continue to argue that informal methods make a positive contribution to the solution of many of our pressing educational and societal problems. Conservative detractors, increasingly vocal, portray such methods as a source of the problems, as contributing in significant measure to a loosening, if not a total abandonment, of standards in basic subjects, placing the emphasis on psychological well-being to the detriment of intellectual development, pandering to immediate interests of children rather than developing in them respect for tradition and authority. Leftist critics sometimes take another tack; they portray progressive methods as perhaps well-intentioned, but just one more liberal-social democratic delusion that contributes to the maintenance of the status quo.

Despite their ambiguities, the labels formal/informal as commonly used in the schools we visited, do in some general way distinguish two sets of teachers, between Mr Sprinter, all the infant teachers at Port, Castlegate and the majority of infant schools we visited, the Heathbrook Junior and Port 'team' teachers, on the one hand, and the teachers at Highrock, and Mr Edgar, on the other. Teachers considered 'informal' by the teachers and heads we met do as a group organize learning in ways that are patently different from those considered 'formal'. However, it is only in dealing with the extremes that this division does not present insurmountable problems. The gamut of differences in approaches among teachers can be more accurately distinguished using the dilemma language. There is clearly a wide *range* of patterns that teachers and heads commonly associated with informal, and a range they associated with formal. In relative terms, what were called informal methods in the schools we studied may be characterized as patterns of resolution where there is greater teacher control over more realms of the child's development, generally tighter teacher control of time in the basics, but more child control over origin and duration in the non-basics. Informal teachers also exerted far tighter control over operations and standards in the basics than was evident in the more formal settings. A number of these claims contradict many commonly held notions about the differences in the two types of teaching. With respect to transmission of knowledge, there was, in informal classes, less separation of personal from public knowledge, greater reliance on holistic learning, more emphasis on intrinsic motivation and on each child unique modes of resolutions. There was, in general, a stronger child as person orientation. With respect to the societal dilemmas, there were more frequent childhood unique modes in 3R and non-3R activities in informal settings. And what have been called transformational resolutions were more frequently exhibited in these settings as well.

On the other hand, it is essential to recognize that the differences between the two styles are in many cases merely differences in emphasis on particular dilemmas. For example, all teachers used extrinsic motivation but it tended to be a more exceptional mode (except for a few children) in informal classrooms. The emphases on molecular learning and children having shared characteristics were implicit in all teachers' behaviors, but heavier, particularly in the basics, in more formal settings. Differences between formal and informal teachers regarding patterns of allocation, and sanctions are difficult to characterize simply. Our information is limited but it appears that there is a tendency in informal classrooms for a greater number of children to receive a somewhat more equal share, perhaps with the very 'clever' receiving somewhat less and the slightly 'backwards' more. However, there appear to be no sharp differences between informal and formal teachers' patterns of resolution to the common culture, *ad hoc* application, knowledge as problematical and learning is social v. learning is individual dilemmas, although the few places where we observed a heavy emphasis on learning is social were in informal settings. . . .

Our intent in this summary is merely to show in what way the language can be used to talk about how classrooms are similar to and different from one another. We want to stress that we are not claiming that the patterns we found in the settings we studied are necessarily linked to the common distinction, formal v. informal. A thorough study of the relationship between these variations and the attributions of formality-informality that we have speculated upon would require, among other things, more systematic, longer term observation, the gathering of data using the dilemmas to sharpen and focus observations, and a group of teachers that includes a higher proportion considered formal than we had in our study.

Whatever may be the merit of using the common terms formal and informal, they do, as we have shown, bypass and obscure many distinctions among teachers. There is nothing new in this point. The problems associated with describing schooling in terms of bipolar or tripartite categories, such as democratic-authoritarian, direct-indirect, or more recently, traditional, informal and mixed, has been noted repeatedly over the years. Division of the world into progressive v. traditional (Left v. Right) has long been a useful handle for those with political axes to grind and this is unlikely to change. However, the wide differences between the resolutions of Mr Sprinter, Mr Scott, Mrs Lawton, Mrs Martin and Mrs Newhouse should alert us to distortions that are created by categorizing teachers into two or three or half a dozen mutually exclusive types.

Teaching Styles and Children's Progress

(From Bennett, N. *et al.*, 1976, *Teaching Styles and Pupil Progress*, London, Open Books, pp. 79, 152–3, 154, 155, 155–6, 162.)

Of all the research into primary education conducted in the seventies, the best-known was Bennett's *Teaching Styles and Pupil Progress*. It had considerable political and educational significance as well as technical interest, though later analysis threw very considerable doubt on its findings (p. 29). The research attempted to establish the effects of different teaching styles on children's attainments and attitudes; its methodology and conclusions were fiercely contested but it contributed significantly to the climate of questioning and concern directed at primary schooling in the mid- to late-seventies. Its design and findings are summarized below; the teaching styles referred to are detailed on p. 11 of this source book.

To answer the question 'Do teaching styles result in differential pupil progress?' requires a research design which allows for a follow up of samples of pupils over an extended period of time during which they experience differing teaching approaches. By testing at the beginning and end of this period, progress can be assessed and differential effects, if any, established.

A quasi-experimental design was adopted. The first stage involved the selection of thirty-seven teachers to represent seven of the twelve types isolated in the teacher typology. These seven were chosen since they represented the whole range, and could be collapsed into three general styles, informal, mixed and formal. Types 1 and 2 represented informal styles, 3, 4 and 7 represented mixed styles, and 11 and 12 formal styles. . . .

Twelve teachers were initially chosen to represent each style, six each from types 1, 2, 11 and 12, and four each from types 3, 4 and 7, but an additional teacher was added to the informal sample because of the small size of one informal classroom. . . . The pupils who entered the classroom of these teachers in September 1973 were tested on a wide range of attainment and personality tests on entry, and again the following June. From these data, analyses were computed to ascertain the effect of teaching style across the group of pupils as a whole, on pupils of different sex, on pupils of differing achievement level and on pupils of differing personality type.

The results form a coherent pattern. The effect of teaching style is statistically and educationally significant in all attainment areas tested. In reading, pupils of formal and mixed teachers progress more than those of informal teachers, the difference being equivalent to some three to five months' difference in performance. In mathematics formal pupils are superior to both mixed and informal pupils, the difference in progress being some four to five months. In English formal pupils again out-perform both mixed and informal pupils....

Marked sex differences rarely appear, but differences among pupils of similar initial achievement, but taught by different methods, are often quite marked. In all three attainment areas boys with low achievement on entry to formal classrooms under-achieved, i.e. did not progress at the rate expected. This was not true of girls of a similar achievement level, who often over-achieved. At the other end of the scale pupils who had entered formal classrooms with a high level of achievement showed much greater progress than pupils of a similar achievement level in informal classrooms. Formal pupils were also superior to their counterparts in mixed classes in mathematics....

In order to encompass a wider range of pupil attainment, samples of imaginative and descriptive stories were also analysed. These analyses allowed an assessment of the equivocal link between creative writing and informal teaching, and also of the frequently heard criticism that informal teaching tends to depress skills in grammar, punctuation and spelling....

The evidence suggests that formal and mixed pupils are better at punctuation, and no worse at creative or imaginative writing, than pupils in informal classes. The link between the quality of creative output informality is not supported whereas that between formality and punctuation skills is. Creativity and formal grammar often seem to be incompatible objectives in the minds of many educationalists, but from this evidence formal and mixed teachers appear to be achieving both....

There is current concern about the effect of open plan schools on certain types of pupil and this concern is echoed in relation to informal teaching. The review of evidence pertaining to this problem clearly pointed to the fact that anxious, insecure children prefer, and perform better in, more structured environments. There was also some evidence that extroverted children cope more easily with less structured situations, and that motivation improves.

The findings on anxiety and motivation were supported in this study, and both showed a similar pattern. Degree of change was as expected in formal classrooms, less than expected in mixed and more than expected in informal classes. Motivation, in the form of attitudes to school and school work, does seem to improve under informal teaching, but at the expense of anxiety which also increases. This increase in anxiety can be interpreted in a number of ways, but perhaps the explanation of greatest theoretical validity is that a more nebulous structure, more often found in informal settings, is not conducive to the needs of many children.

In summary, formal teaching fulfils its aims in the academic area without detriment to the social and emotional development of pupils, whereas informal teaching only partially fulfils its aims in the latter area as well as engendering comparatively poorer outcomes in academic development.

The central factor emerging from this study is that degree of teacher direction is necessary, and that this direction needs to be carefully planned, and the learning experiences provided need to be clearly sequenced and structured.

Teaching Styles and Pupil Progress: A Re-analysis

(From Aitken, M. *et al.*, 1981, 'Teaching styles and pupil progress: A re-analysis', *British Journal of Educational Psychology*, 51, 2, p. 184.)

Five years on from the publication of *Teaching Styles and Pupil Progress* (*TS* in the passage below), the results of a sophisticated re-analysis of the original data were published. As a comparison with the previous extract demonstrates, these results were substantially different from the original ones. They were received with hardly a comment from practitioners or policy-makers. It is interesting to speculate why.

The teaching style differences in achievement which were found in *TS* are modified in the re-analysis. . . .

The only significant teaching style differences are in English, where the formal style has the highest mean, mixed the lowest, and informal is in the middle. In mathematics, the formal and informal styles are close, and substantially above the mixed style. In reading informal has the highest mean, mixed the lowest, and formal is in the middle. Though the differences may appear small, the four-point difference between formal and mixed in reading corresponds to a 6 to 8 months difference in reading age. It is of interest that the mixed style which was distinguished in the cluster analysis by a relatively high frequency of disciplinary problems, and by the lowest use of formal testing, gives consistently the worst results in the achievement model.

Teaching Styles and Children's Progress: Results from ORACLE

(From Galton, M. and Simon, B. (Eds) 1980, *Progress and Performance in the Primary Classroom*, London, Routledge and Kegan Paul, pp. 70–1, 71–2, 194, 199.)

The most sophisticated British attempt to date to assess the differential effects of teaching approaches on primary school children's attainment was undertaken by the ORACLE team from Leicester University. They attempted to relate teaching styles to pupils' attainment in basic skills (measured on modified Richmond Tests) and in so-called 'study skills'. Because of the problematic nature of these 'study skills' and doubts on the results obtained when these were related to teaching styles, the extract below concentrates on the relationship between styles and children's attainment in basic skills. The results reported were derived from tests of mathematics, reading and language skills administered to over 120 pupils (aged 8+ to 10+) at the beginning and end of the academic year 1976–77. The teaching styles referred to are described as Styles 1, 2, 3 and 4 (the last divided into three sub-types) on p. 16 of this source book. The extract concludes by indicating the common threads in interaction patterns linking the most successful teachers using the more successful styles. Readers might consider how useful this summary is, either to teacher-trainers or to classteachers, attempting to improve their own practice.

Pupil Progress: Summarizing the Results

Table 4.4 presents a summary of all the major findings with respect to the basic skills.... Two features of this table are particularly striking. First, unlike previous studies, based largely on self-reporting questionnaires, *no over-all best style emerges for all three tests*. While the *class enquirers* were most successful in mathematics and language skills, it is the pupils of the *infrequent changers* who make the greatest gains in reading. However, in language skills the *class enquirers* enjoyed no over-all superiority from either the *group instructors* or the *infrequent changers*. In mathematics the progress of pupils taught by *infrequent changers* did not differ significantly from that achieved by the group taught by the *class enquirers*.

The finding that, as far as the basic skills were concerned, there was no 'best buy' would seem important in the continuing debate about teacher effectiveness. Past research has usually been concerned to establish the over-all superiority of one particular teaching method over the remainder, but here there appear to be three different styles, allied to different proportions of class, individual and group work, which are available to teachers interested in improving pupil performance in the basic skills.

The least successful style would seem to be that of the *rotating changers*,

Table 4.4   Summary of results for teaching style and achievement in basic skills

1	2	3	4	5
Test area	Most successful style	Not significantly different from most successful style	Significant at 5 per cent from most successful style	Significant at 1 per cent from most successful style
Mathematics	*Class enquirers*	*Infrequent changers*	*Group instructors*	*Rotating changers Individual monitors Habitual changers*
Language skills	*Class enquirers*	*Group instructors Infrequent changers*	*Habitual changers*	*Individual monitors Rotating changers*
Reading	*Infrequent changers*		*Individual monitors Class enquirers Group instructors*	*Habitual changers Rotating changers*

who have considerable problems in improving the level of their pupils achievement in basic skills. . . .

In both this group of pupils and those of the *habitual changers* and the *individual monitors*, who were also less successful than either the *class enquirers*, *infrequent changers* or *group instructors*, the number of pupils who were involved in high levels of distraction was appreciably greater than would be expected from the over-all proportion in the sample. For the *rotating changers*, in particular, there were also fewer pupils who maintained a high level of work activity. It would seem, therefore, that both in terms of test results and also in terms of pupil behaviour there are particular problems associated with this style of teaching. . . .

The question arises as to the nature of the interactions between teachers and pupils which contribute to the latter's success. Each style has its own set pattern in the use of certain categories. However, it may be that over and above this there are certain behaviours which are characteristic of *all* successful teachers from within the three groups. To examine this issue, the most successful teachers from the *group instructors, class enquirers* and *infrequent changers* (in terms of overall pupil progress in basic skills) were extracted from the sample, and the profile of their use of the categories on the Teacher Record examined. . . .

With so few teachers it is not possible to make valid statistical comparisons, but it is interesting to look for categories where all the successful teachers are either above or below the average value for the whole sample. . . .

In summary, the successful teachers all engage in above-average levels of interaction with the pupils. They appear to devote considerable effort to ensuring that the routine activities proceed smoothly; they engage in high levels of task statements and questions, and provide regular feedback. At the same time, they also encourage the children to work by themselves towards solutions to problems. The majority make above-average use of higher-order interactions, including statements of ideas and more open-ended types of questioning. They also manage to avoid the need to provide children continually with instructions on how to carry out the set tasks. This comes about either because they prefer pupils to find out for themselves or because their initial instructions are so clear that there is little need to follow up by further exchanges. These teachers, while using different organizational strategies, and emphasizing certain other specific characteristics of their particular style, nevertheless have in common that they interact with the pupils more frequently than teachers using the less successful styles. Increased levels in the above kinds of teacher and pupil contact appear to be an important determinant of pupils' progress.

Formal or Informal Teaching: Which is More Effective?

(From Gray, J. and Satterley, D., 1981, 'Formal or informal: A re-assessment of the British evidence', *British Journal of Educational Psychology*, 51, 2, pp. 190–3.)

The passage below attempts to make sense of the controversial British research on the effectiveness of 'formal' and 'informal' methods of teaching. Three main British studies are examined, including Aitken *et al.*'s re-analysis of *Teaching Styles and Pupil Progress* (TSPP) and the authors' own re-analysis of that piece of research (reported elsewhere in the article from which the extract is drawn). Four other studies are also drawn upon. Most of these research studies are featured in this source book. Gray and Satterley's conclusions are summarized in their last two paragraphs. Compared with 'informal' approaches 'formal' approaches appear to be 'modestly' advantageous for language skills and mathematics but not for reading. However, the authors' final sentence deals a blow to those who believe in the meaningfulness and usefulness of the dichotomy underlying the reported research: 'teaching style, defined in terms of the "formal/informal" dichotomy is not a central concept in the study of teacher effectiveness.'

The findings from the TSPP re-analyses may now be integrated with those from several other British studies relating to the debate about 'formal' and 'informal' methods. For the purposes of this review we confined ourselves to studies based on British primary schools. We also placed greater weight in our interpretation of the evidence on studies employing a pre/post-test research design where teachers and/or teaching styles were the major focus of interest.

Three studies emerged as being most directly related to these purposes (Bennett, 1976; Gray, 1979; and Galton and Simon, 1980). The details of Bennett's study will already be familiar, but those of the other two studies may not be. It is also important to bear in mind that none of the studies we considered operationalised identical definitions of teaching styles; indeed a detailed analysis suggests that they related to each other only in the broadest sense.

Galton and Simon's study was based on 58 teachers of 8-to 10-year-olds in three local authorities. Six teaching styles were identified but using the iterative relocation method now rejected by Aitkin *et al.* as unsuitable for this purpose. The progress of children was monitored in a number of curriculum areas. None of the six teaching styles corresponded exactly to the formal-informal characteristics identified in TSPP (either in their original or re-analysed form). Indeed, the researchers were at pains to stress that their conception of teaching styles differed from this particular dichotomy in a number of important respects. They were aware, however, of the interest in making such comparisons and therefore assisted their readers in identifying which of their styles resembled the formal and informal ones of other studies. They suggest that their 'class enquirers' displayed most 'formal' characteristics and that their 'individual monitors' were, in contrast, more 'informal' (Galton *et al.*, 1980). There are a number of features of their research design and analysis, however, which complicate the interpretation of the results and whose influence on the overall pattern of results remains essentially unknown (Gray, 1980); for the purposes of the present review these will be ignored.

Gray (1979) based his study on the teaching of reading by teachers of top infant children (6+ to 7+) in two outer London boroughs. Classes were studied during the first year of the project and tested for reading progress. The research design was then repeated again for the next cohort of children with teachers surviving from the first year of the study. The final analyses were based on 41 teachers and their classes. Teachers were observed on several occasions and a description of their classroom activities in terms of a number of dimensions was 'negotiated' with them. The 'informal' and 'quite informal' categories in this study were based, in contrast to the other studies, on teachers' own understandings of these terms.

The study was deliberately designed to incorporate certain features that would make the interpretation of differences between classes somewhat less problematic than in previous studies. Retrospectively, however, it is clear that it achieved these improvements at some expense; in particular, it focused exclusively on reading as this was the only area of the curriculum in which top infant teachers were believed to share largely common objectives. These and other issues are explored at greater length elsewhere (Gray, 1979).

We present summary evidence from these three studies in Table 1. For each study we indicate the number of classes, the age-range of the children, the area(s) of basic skills tested and whether the results favoured a more formal approach when compared with a more informal one. In this last respect we indicate both the trend of the results and whether they were statistically significant. We shall consider, first, whether the trend of results favours more formal approaches, subject by subject, and then, subsequently, their statistical significance.

For reading, two of the results show a trend in favour of more formal approaches: Gray and Satterly (here) and Gray (1979, year 2). Both are, however counter-balanced by other findings. There was no trend in Aitkin's re-analysis in favour of more formal approaches (indeed, as Figure 1 shows the pattern was reversed with informal somewhat better than formal) nor in Gray's (year 1) or Galton and Simon's (1980) studies. For English, the trend in favour of more formal approaches in the Bennett re-analyses is supported by the finding from the Galton study. Maths also presents a similar story. Both the Galton study and the Gray and Satterly re-analysis suggest the

Table 1   Summary results for basic skills from three British studies of teaching styles

Study and source	No. of classes and age-range	Area of basic skills	Do results favour a more formal approach?	
			Trend	Statistical significance
Bennett (1976)	36	Reading	no	no
Aitkin re-analysis	(10+ − 11+)	English	yes	no
		Maths	no	no
Gray & Satterly re-analysis		Reading	yes	no
		English	yes	no
		Maths	yes	no
Galton and Simon (1980)	58	Reading	no	no
	(8+ − 10+)	Language (English)	yes	no
		Maths	yes	no
Gray (1979)	41	Reading (year 1)	no	no
	(6+ − 7+)	Reading (year 2)	yes	no

Notes: . . . Statistical significance has been defined in the Galton and Simon and Gray studies
. . . employing the conventional 5 per cent level.

results favour more formal approaches. [It can be suggested] that the Aitkin and Bennett re-analysis also marginally favours a more formal approach, although the reported size of the difference is very small. On balance, then, there would appear to be some evidence (albeit weak) that more formal approaches are more effective in raising scores in mathematics as well.

None of the differences between formal and informal approaches, however, attains statistical significance at the 5 per cent level, although some of them begin to approach it. The relationship between sample size and the power of a statistical test is well known. It could be argued that some of the differences of the size shown in Table 1 *would* become statistically significant if the samples upon which they were based had been larger. Of course with very large samples even trivial differences can achieve statistical significance. As we have argued previously, studies of teacher effectiveness really require larger numbers of teachers to be sampled (Satterly and Gray, 1976, p. 12). None of the differences in Table 1 is, in fact, as large as three points (approximately four to six months difference in progress) on a typical standardised test; if they had been, then we are confident that they would also have been statistically significant. In fact most of the differences between formal and informal approaches averaged around half this size. Even if such differences were statistically significant we would be reluctant to describe them as educationally significant, given both the problems of possibly unexamined but confounding variables and the difficulties of persuading teachers who had already developed one style to adopt another.

Against this view, it must be observed that, when the trend of results is examined, seven out of 11 of the comparisons in Table 1 favour a more formal approach and only one of the 11 a more informal one. A number of researchers have commented that conventional standards for statistical significance place a heavy burden of proof on the researcher and that potentially interesting findings are, as a result, in danger of being dismissed (Carver, 1978).

We examined a number of other British studies with a view to determining whether they provided confirmatory or contradictory evidence for these conclusions. All but one of these studies have also been reviewed by Anthony (1979) so readers may find it helpful to have a second opinion on them.

The most important of the four studies is probably that by Barker-Lunn (1970). As part of her research on streaming in junior schools she examined the effects of two teacher types (traditional and progressive) in non-streamed schools. She presented her evidence for each teacher type broken down by social class and ability level (see Barker-Lunn, 1970, Tables 5.6 a–c). For English the differences were modest and inconsistent. For maths the trend of the results favoured the more traditional type of teacher but the extent of the differences was, again, relatively small, rarely exceeding two standardised points.

The study by Cane and Smithers (1971) of the teaching of reading around 1960 in 12 infant schools serving disadvantaged areas claims that 'more teacher-directed' (i.e. more formal) schools were more successful in securing reading progress. This study has, however, been re-analysed and found to have a number of serious weaknesses (Gray, 1975). The claims for statistical significance depended heavily on the results from one school. When this school was dropped from the analysis the statistical significance of the results (based on the individual pupil as the unit of analysis) was very substantially reduced. The trend of the results still favoured the 'teacher-directed' schools, however, but closer inspection of the variables contributing to the construction of the 'teacher-directed' categories suggests that there were considerable problems in labelling them as such. More than half the variables employed to construct the categories seemed to have little to do with 'teacher-direction' at all. They included such variables as: 'teacher experience, "reception class experience", "age-range of class", use of sentence method' and 'number of teachers in school'. We conclude that the study offers no reliable evidence to contradict the view already established with respect to reading.

Anthony (1979) refers to a study by Kemp (1955) as offering support to the progressive case. However, since the study was a cross-sectional one and the correlations between measures of attainment and progressiveness were never greater than 0.16, we concur with Kemp's own assessment of the relationship rather than Anthony's. Kemp remarks: 'There is no evidence in this investigation that progressiveness is harmful in its effects on attainment, nor that it is particularly helpful' (p. 75).

The study by Gardner (1966) offers some very limited evidence that more informal approaches may be more suitable for English and reading and more formal ones for arithmetic. We share Anthony's doubts, however, about the extent to which the findings from this study may be generalised, since the schools in the sample were deliberately chosen to be 'good of their type'.

Finally, a recent report by HM Inspectorate provides some limited details of the cross-sectional evidence collected in their survey of primary schools. They report that: 'In classes where a didactic approach was mainly used, better NFER scores were achieved for reading and mathematics than in those classes using mainly exploratory approaches' (DES, 1978, p. 95). Unfortunately, they provide no evidence of how large the differences were nor whether the classes exposed to the two teaching styles were matched in most other respects. This finding is, therefore, of dubious utility in the present context.

In sum, we do not believe that any of this additional evidence conflicts with our earlier conclusions, which were that 'formal' teaching styles were probably unrelated to progress in reading and only modestly related to progress in English and maths. The apparent superiority of more 'formal' approaches over 'informal' ones in these latter areas needs to be tempered by the knowledge that the gains were *not* statistically significant in conventional terms and that they were small. We doubt, however, whether they occurred by chance: the pattern of results seems more consistent than one dictated by chance events.

These comments return us to the question we have addressed before, both here and elsewhere. When is a finding educationally as well as statistically significant? Given the somewhat rough-and-ready nature of quasi-experimental research designs and the problems of controlling adequately for additional and external factors, we incline to the conclusion that teaching style, defined in terms of the 'formal/informal' dichotomy is not a central concept in the study of teacher effectiveness.

References

ACLAND, H. (1976) 'Stability of teacher effectiveness: A replication', *J. Educ. Res.*, 69, pp. 289–92.

AITKIN, M.A. and BENNETT, S.N. (1980) 'A theoretical and practical investigation into the analysis of change in classroom-based research', Final Report to SSRC on grant HR5710, Centre for Applied Statistics and Department of Educational Research, University of Lancaster.

AITKIN, M.A., BENNETT, S.N. and HESKETH, J.(1981) 'Teaching styles and pupil progress: A re-analysis', *Br. J. Educ. Psychol.*, 51, pp. 170–86.

ANTHONY, W. (1979) 'Progressive learning theories: The evidence', in BERNBAUM, G. (Ed.) *Schooling in Decline*, London, Macmillan.

BARKER-LUNN, J.C. (1970) *Streaming in the Primary School: A Longitudinal Study of Children in Streamed and Non-Streamed Junior Schools*, Slough, NFER.

BENNETT, S.N. with JORDAN, J., LONG, G. and WADE, B. (1976) *Teaching Styles and Pupil Progress*, London, Open Books.

BROPHY, J.E. and EVERTSON, C.M. (1976) *Learning from Teaching: A Developmental Perspective*, Boston, Allyn and Bacon.

CANE, B. and SMITHERS, J. (1971) *The Roots of Reading*, Slough, NFER.

CARVER, R.P. (1978) 'The case against statistical significance testing', *Harv. Educ. Rev.*, 48, pp. 378–99.

CRONBACH, L.J. (1976) *Research on Classrooms and Schools: Formulations of Questions, Design and Analysis*, Stanford Evaluation Consortium, Stanford University.

DEPARTMENT OF EDUCATION AND SCIENCE (1978) *Primary Education in England: A Survey by HM Inspectors of Schools*, London, HMSO.

GALTON, M. and SIMON, B. (Eds) (1980) *Progressive and Performance in the Primary Classroom*, London, Routledge and Kegan Paul.

GALTON, M., SIMON, B. and CROLL, P. (1980) *Inside the Primary Classroom*, London, Routledge and Kegan Paul.

GARDNER, D.E.M. (1966) *Experiment and Tradition in Primary Schools*, London, Methuen.

GRAY, J. (1975) 'The roots of reading: A critical re-analysis', *Research in Educ.*, 14, pp. 33–47.

GRAY, J. (1979) 'Reading progress in English infant schools: Some problems emerging from a study of teacher effectiveness', *Br. Educ. Res. J.*, 5, pp. 141–57.

GRAY, J. (1980) 'How good were the tests?' *The Times Educational Supplement*, 6 November.

GRAY, J. and SATTERLY, D. (1976) 'A chapter of errors: Teaching styles and pupil progress in retrospect', *Educ. Res.*, 19, pp. 45–56.

GRAY, J. and SATTERLY, D. (1978) 'Time to learn', *Educ. Res.*, 2, pp. 137–42.

KEMP, L.C.D. (1955) 'Environmental and other characteristics determining attainment in primary schools', *Br. J. Educ. Psychol.*, 25, pp. 67–77.

SATTERLY, D. and GRAY, J. (1976) 'Two statistical problems in classroom research', School of Education, University of Bristol.

SEARLE, S.R. (1971) *Linear Models*, New York, Wiley.

STENHOUSE, L. (1980) 'The study of samples and the study of cases', *Br. Educ. Res. J.*, 6, pp. 1–6.

Inside Primary Classrooms: A View from ORACLE

(From Simon, B., 1980, 'Inside the primary classroom', *Forum*, 22, 3, pp. 68–9.)

The passage below neatly summarizes the main findings of one of the major aspects of the ORACLE research programme: the nature of teacher-pupil and pupil-pupil interaction in classes containing children of junior age. Along with the national primary survey the research did much to dispel myths about primary education, at least as represented in the fifty-eight classes of the research study. The final paragraph provides a brief pen-picture of primary classrooms which some readers have found comforting and others disturbing. More observational studies of primary classrooms are needed, especially of those containing children of infant age and those where 'good practice' (however defined) is believed to be found.

Since the ORACLE research programme was conceived and designed, in the early 1970s, primary education became a highly charged political issue as a result of *Black Paper* criticisms (from 1969) of 'permissive' or 'progressive' teaching techniques and approaches, the mass media exposure accorded to the Tyndale teachers who espoused an extreme version of so called 'progressive teaching', equivalent mass media exposure accorded to Neville Bennett's small-scale research project published as *Teaching Styles and Pupil Progress* (1976), culminating in Jim Callaghan's Ruskin College speech in October 1976 which warned against the use of modern methods in the primary school. An image was, it seemed, almost deliberately being built up of the primary schools dominated by way out anarchic teachers where the pupils did what they liked when they liked, and where the virtues of hard work and structured learning had no place. In the first *Black Paper* Timothy Raison was quoted as attributing the student unrest of 1968 and 1969 to the 'revolution in the primary school'.

In this situation the findings of the ORACLE research, based on close classroom observation in the academic year 1976 to 1977 are of some interest. Generally speaking they show that, for the ORACLE sample at least, the public image of the primary school created by the mass media is or was very wide of the mark. This comes out clearly from two of the main findings, and, such is their importance, it is worth devoting space to each.

First, the 'typical' pupil in the ORACLE sample was found to be 'fully involved and co-operating on his task' (that is, working) for well over half the time in the normal teaching/learning sessions. But in addition he was 'fully involved and co-operating on routine activities' (that is, activities related to his task) for another 12 per cent of the time while he spent nearly 5 per cent of his time 'waiting for teacher' to ask a question, have his work looked over, etc. This means that for three quarters of normal lesson time the 'typical' (or average) pupil was, in one way or another, engaged on the task in hand. This represents a high work rate; few adults, I suspect, reach this level. Admittedly, facts like these tell us nothing about the *quality* of the pupils' work but they do indicate that concentration or involvement on 'approved' tasks is high in the classrooms observed.

Information of this kind was obtained by observers who coded pupils' activities every twenty-five seconds on an observation schedule developed in earlier research projects. The observer focused on individual children in a pre-arranged order. At each coding the curricular area in which the pupil was engaged was noted. This made it possible to reconstruct the curriculum in the main classroom sessions for the 'typical' pupil in the study. And this brings us to the second of our two main findings.

Far from any neglect of the 'basic skills', as was generally averred, it was found that these form major components of the curriculum now as in the past. Roughly one third of the 'typical' pupils' time in the ORACLE classrooms was spent on skills relating to literacy, one third to numeracy, while the remaining third was spent on 'general studies', including topic and project work in the field of history, geography and environmental studies, and on science (only four per cent of the time) and arts and crafts. In other words we found, with the HMI survey, a heavy concentration of the basic skills. This raises wider question which we cannot go into here, but at least it appears to give the lie to ignorant pronouncements about the unstructured and permissive dominance of the primary school curriculum.

The study has also revealed some rather disturbing or, better, thought provoking facts about the interaction process in junior classrooms. Although some class and group teaching took place, the dominant modes of interaction between teachers and pupils were individualized on a one-to-one basis. In classes with an average size of thirty, as was found to be the case, this means that, while the teacher engages in interaction with pupils very actively for most of the lesson time, each individual pupil receives very little of the teacher's time. The 'typical' pupil, it was found, interacts individually with the teacher for only 2.3 per cent of lesson time; as a member of a group he interacts with the teacher for even less time (1.5 per cent). Most of his interaction with the teacher the pupil experiences takes place when the teacher is addressing the class as a whole — as a member of the teacher's audience, amounting to 12.0 per cent of lesson time. Thus, although the whole thrust of the Plowden Committee's prescriptions is towards the individualization of the teaching-learning process, in practice pupils work entirely on their own for the vast majority of lesson time, experiencing only very short, limited, individual interactions with the teacher.

The evidence raises a key issue relating to the use of grouping and group work in primary classrooms. Although pupils are normally seated in groups, while other forms of grouping also exist (e.g. curriculum groups in mathematics or language), in practice it seems most pupils are normally engaged on their own individual tasks. Co-operative group work, where pupils co-operate together to solve a problem, construct a model, etc., was found to be very rare. Many pupils never experience it at all.

The other feature worth referring to here is linked to this. The teachers' interactions with pupils, her questions and statements, appear to be primarily didactic. There is little of the probing type of questioning which encourages enquiry and discovery learning, or which stimulates thought and imagination; most are questions of fact or concerned with supervising the child's work — that is, making sure that the pupil has a clear grasp of his materials and knows how to set about completing his task. Generally the same seems true of teachers' statements; thought-provoking, stimulating or enquiry-based types of statement are rare. Most are concerned with telling the child what to do. Surprisingly it was found that teachers maximized thought provoking (or 'higher order') questions and statements when they were teaching the class as a whole. In the individual one-to-one situation interaction was primarily didactic. This clearly calls into question the traditionally accepted dichotomy between 'traditional' and 'progressive' teaching. Those teachers who engaged in more class teaching maximized enquiry based questioning and statements; those who maximized individualization were primarily didactic in their interactions (telling).

The teacher who individualizes the classroom seems to face an impossible, or at least a very difficult situation. She necessarily must engage in a succession of short interactions with individual children in turn; ensuring that they know what to do and are able to complete their work successfully. In this situation, with classes at their present size, it seems that she simply does not have time to engage in prolonged one-to-one interactions with individual pupils of a thought-provoking or enquiry stimulating nature. In the whole class teaching situation, where she can concentrate her mind and those of her pupils on a specific issue or topic, such questioning, of course, becomes possible and entirely practical. Thus it is in this situation that such teaching is maximized. The potentialities of co-operative group work and teaching, it appears, are not yet being exploited in the ORACLE classrooms, although some teachers did so. It seems that this is an area where further research and development, in the form of assistance to teachers as to its organization, might be very rewarding. Above all a radical reduction in class size to an average of, say, about twenty pupils or less (as is the case now, for instance, in Sweden and Denmark) would open quite new possibilities in terms of raising the level and the quality of individualized interaction in the classroom.

The material concerning teachers was gained by the observers using a teacher observation schedule, which paralleled that used with the pupils. Analysis of the data derived from the Teacher Record (as it was called) made it possible to group teachers in terms of the way they organized, and interacted with, their pupils. There emerged four distinct teacher 'styles' having different characteristics reflected in the names the research team gave them. Briefly these are (i) *individual monitors*, who maximized individualization within the classroom — these tended to be young and female, (ii) *class enquirers* who maximized class teaching, though on average using it for only 30 per cent of the time; these tended to be older teachers and male, (iii) *group instructors* who maximized the use of grouping, but whose interaction with their groups was primarily didactic, and (iv) a complex group called *style changers* who were further sub-divided into three groupings.

Each of these four main groupings of teachers were differentiated from each other not only by their audience — the way they organized their classes — but also by their use of the different interaction categories on the Teacher Record. There were, in other words, real differences in their interaction patterns, as well as differences in the way they organized their classes ...

In sum, ORACLE found the classrooms investigated to be orderly and well managed, the pupils highly involved in their work which itself focused largely on the basic skills of numeracy and literacy. It has established the existence of a variety of teaching 'styles' and forms of organization in the (largely) unstreamed classroom. It found a high level of individualization (the primary mode across *all* styles) and a relatively low cognitive interaction level between teachers and pupils. Its data throws doubt on the usefulness, or viability, of differentiating teachers on the progressive/traditional dichotomy — the ORACLE teachers fell into neither of these two simple categories. The materials gained support the view of the primary school classroom as a complex organism and of teaching as involving a wide variety and high degree of skill. Above all the evidence points to the need, if the Plowden prescripts as to the teacher's role are to be implemented, for a massive and radical reduction in the size of primary classes.

Informal Primary Education: Teachers' Accounts

(From Nias, D.J., 1988, in Blyth, W., *Informal Primary Education Today*: *Essays and Studies*, Lewes, Falmer Press, pp. 142–6.)

The small scale research underpinning Jennifer Nias's article elicited accounts and descriptions from six primary teachers of what it means to teach informally. In being based on practitioners' own perspectives, this research differs from previous studies cited in this volume, which are based upon researchers' analyses and classifications. The extract summarizes the main features of informal teaching identified by the teachers. The author relates the analysis to historical thought underlying child-centred philosophy, and asks how the nature of informal teaching matches views of the nature of knowledge.

It is commonplace that teachers seldom see one another in action, and discuss their classroom methods and the assumptions underlying them even less frequently. Yet the accounts given by these six experienced teachers have much in common despite their different education, training and career history, and the varying contexts in which they were teaching. There might be several reasons for this, for example, a conscious or unconscious desire to supply me with responses of which they thought I would approve; shared socialization into a common professional culture; similar influences during training which, though in different institutions, took place for five out of the six between the mid-1960s and mid-1970s.

It is also possible, however, that they had a common view of education, forged from their own experience of working with children in situations which did not require them to instruct, direct or dominate. Their accounts suggest that as experienced practitioners they were guided by educational principles relating to learning, teaching and the context in which both take place which were the same irrespective of the school and the pupils in which and with whom they were working. These principles themselves may be rooted in a set of beliefs about the nature of knowledge and how it is acquired, but since I asked the teachers to describe their practice, not to examine the philosophical origins of it, without further information my analysis must be speculative. Not withstanding, at the heart of their descriptions seem to lie two related beliefs — that knowledge is actively constructed by each learner rather that being passively received or stored and that it is therefore in two senses individual, being both personal and unique. It follows from these beliefs that the function of the teacher is to encourage each learner to engage actively with the material to be learned. This in turn requires that learners have the will to become and remain involved in constructing their own knowledge — that they are, in short, motivated to learn. So, much teaching becomes a matter of arranging the optimal conditions under which each learner can, in the often-quoted words of the Plowden Report, become 'the agent of his own learning'. The teachers' work is likely to include directing learners to material which will engage their attention and be within their capacity, helping them to set themselves appropriate goals, assisting them to talk purposefully about and monitor their progress towards these ends and organizing the context, direction, pace and scope of their endeavours. In such a situation the organization of time, space, resources and attention must be flexible, learners should be free to seek help, guidance and stimulation from many sources. Moreover, since in schools one teacher has the task of simultaneously helping many pupils to construct their own learning, it is imperative that the latter learn to help one another as well as themselves; in the crowded, dense conditions of the classroom, learning must be co-operative as well as autonomous.

Whether or not this summary expresses the epistemological beliefs of these teachers, they certainly wanted their pupils to assume responsibility for and take control of their own learning. To these ends they tried to ensure that classroom activities were perceived by their pupils as having meaning, purpose and value (whether or not the impetus came initially from the learner or the teacher). In particular, they therefore sought to involve them in direct experiences, from which they could draw and to which they could impart their own meanings, and in practical activities, by means of which they could act upon, interpret, transform and make sense of their experiences. In these senses, as Rowland (1984) persuasively argues, they encouraged their children's classroom learning to resemble their play.

However the resemblance does not stop there. Like play, the learning in these classrooms was both individualistic and collaborative. Self-directed and self-controlled learning is, by definition, egocentric; it serves personal ends and is achieved by the expenditure of individual effort and resources. While accepting and to some extent encouraging these characteristics of individualized learning, these teachers also encouraged interaction. They arranged for children to work with partners and in groups and to have access to other adults. Wherever possible they also participated in the children's activities themselves, as co-learners, by presenting alternative viewpoints and new ideas and as critics of the emerging end products. Implicit in these arrangements is the idea that the development of autonomous learning depends upon discussion; the self can best develop through challenge from and with the support of others.

There is a further similarity between self-directed classroom learning and children's play; neither are constrained by adults' ways of organizing knowledge. These teachers encouraged their pupils to draw upon all the curriculum areas with which they came in contact. Their learning ranged widely, guided by their felt need for specific information and skills and not by their teachers' desire that they should attain specific learning outcomes. Yet, because they were learning in a collaborative context, they were open to suggestions and intervention from their teachers who permeated the curriculum with opportunities to learn, practise and apply both the basic skills of numeracy and literacy and more complex cognitive skills such as classification, comparison, conjecture and the making and testing of generalizations. In short, what the children learnt was the outcome of interaction and negotiation between their own interests and the guidance of their teachers.

Negotiations of this kind could only go on, however, in an atmosphere of mutual trust. Teachers wanted to know their pupils very well and to have a relaxed, informal relationship with them not only because it created a pleasant working atmosphere for all of them, but also because it was through that relationship that they could, as it were, enter into their pupils' play and influence their learning. In other words, teaching went on by means of, rather than simply as a consequence of, the open communication which existed between teachers and pupils. Their relationship enabled learning to be negotiated rather than imposed, but was at the same time the tool by which this was accomplished.

Now it is not easy for teachers to sanction, let alone encourage, playlike activities in their classrooms. They are expected to discipline the children in their care and are accountable for their learning. Moreover, an essential part of 'being' a teacher is to feel in control of the classroom (Nias, 1988). Yet, paradoxically, it was confidence in that control that enabled these teachers to behave as they did; it is only those who are secure in their power that can afford to give it away. So, 'good relationships' with pupils served a second purpose. By helping teachers to relax and 'be themselves' they facilitated the transfer of control over learning to pupils themselves. To put it another way, for teachers to feel 'in control' may be a necessary condition for the development of autonomous learning among children. It is small wonder, then, that inexperienced or insecure teachers find it hard 'not to teach formally'.

Moreover, there is ample evidence from recent reports of Her Majesty's Inspectorate that even experienced teachers at present need encouragement to use in the classroom the natural capacities for learning which children display in their play. As the 9–13 Middle School Survey (HMI, 1983) points out, pupils in these schools were given more opportunities in extra-curricular activities than they were in any other aspect of school life to learn and display social responsibility, cooperation, independence, initiative, decision-making, choice. Yet 'the quality of their responses to (such) opportunities indicated that schools could profitably extend their range' (4.6). We need seriously to consider why teachers evidently find it easier, or consider it more appropriate, to cultivate important qualities such as these in their pupils' 'play' but not in their 'work'.

Moreover, the view of learning and teaching which emerges from these accounts is not new. It has been current in educational thinking, in Europe and North America, for at least 200 years, expressed as it is in the work and writings of educationalists such as Rousseau, Pestalozzi, Froebel, Montessori, the McMillan sisters. Dewey, Isaacs and Neill. It has found frequent expression in private schools, from the more widely-known such as Abbotsholme and Bedales to a multitude of suburban kindergartens. It has appeared and reappeared in state education, its practice documented by teachers such as Holmes (1952) and Tustin (1950) and advocated both by educational writers (for example, Caldwell Cook, 1917; Catty, 1949) and by official reports, in particular, the Hadow Report (CCBE, 1931), and the Plowden Report (CACE, 1967). More recently, it has run as one thread through all the recent surveys of primary and middle schools by Her Majesty's Inspectorate and through the Report of the Education, Science and Arts Committee (1986), notwithstanding the fact that they are set in the context of accountability, assessment and cuts in resources. It supports the notion that classrooms can be places in which pupils are actively engaged in constructing their own learning and solving their own problems, guided and assisted by teachers with whom they enjoy a relaxed but mutually respectful relationship, exploring many aspects of human experience without losing hold of 'the basic skills'. In this sense it is not radical.

References

Cace (Central Advisory Council for Education) (England) (1967) *Children and their Primary Schools* (the Plowden Report) 2 vols., London, HMSO.

Caldwell Cook, H. (1917) *The Play Way: An Essay in Educational Method*, London, Heinemann.

Catty, N. (1949) *Learning and Teaching in the Junior School*, 1st edn., London, Methuen.

Ccbe (Consultative Committee of the Board of Education) (1931) *The Primary School* (the Hadow Report), London, HMSO.

Education, Science and Arts Committee of the House of Commons (1986) *Achievement in Primary Schools*, London, HMSO.

Hmi (1983) *9–13 Middle Schools: An Illustrative Survey*, London, HMSO.

Holmes, R.G. (1952) *The Idiot Teacher*, London, Faber and Faber.

Nias, J. (1988) *On Becoming and Being a Teacher*, London, Methuen.

Rowland, S. (1984) *The Enquiring Classroom*, Lewes, Falmer Press.

Tustin, F. (1950) *A Group of Juniors*, London, Heinemann.

Teaching Modes

(From Rowland, S., 1984, *The Enquiring Classroom*, Lewes, Falmer Press, pp. 3–5.)

Over the period of a year, Stephen Rowland gathered and recorded data on children's learning in an upper junior classroom. He combined the roles of teacher and researcher as he worked alongside the class teacher in a participative way. In his book he analyzes the children's work and experiences and develops a wide range of theoretical insights into learning and development in the context of daily classroom life.

This extract deals with different teaching modes, the transmission and the interpretative. His research explored the way in which, through the interpretative mode, children are able to exercise a controlling influence over their own learning, developing competence as mature, autonomous learners.

At the risk of oversimplifying a highly complex and philosophical matter, there appear to be two broadly different approaches to teaching which I shall call the transmission mode and the interpretative mode. According to the transmission mode of teaching, the teacher is seen as having, or having access to, certain knowledge and skills and as having the responsibility of transmitting these to the learner. Teaching proceeds according to objectives which, in principle at least, are predetermined by the teacher for any particular teaching period. The effectiveness of the teaching and learning can then be judged by the extent to which these objectives are met, that is, the desired knowledge and skills have been successfully transmitted. Characteristically, this mode of teaching concerns itself not so much with the processes by which children learn, but with the products of that learning, and indeed only those products which relate directly to the predetermined teaching objectives. With its emphasis upon the predetermined products of teaching, this form of learning is, on the face of it, testable. It is an approach to teaching and learning which fits well with an educational system which is concerned to sort and grade children through various levels of public examination, [however] the transmission mode of teaching offers the classroom enquirer little access into how that process takes place. If our prime concern, in evaluating our teaching, is to examine the extent to which our predetermined objectives have been met, then there is a severe danger that we shall fail to see how the children understand, especially where their understanding is not in line with those objectives. On so many occasions during this present study, I was taken aback by the way in which a child had understood a situation totally differently from how I would have expected. In such instances the child's understanding, and my own insight into it, could only be developed given a relative freedom from too tight a set of teaching objectives.

The approach to teaching which played an increasing, though not exclusive, part in my own classroom practice prior to this study, and is, I would argue, an important element in any teacher's classroom enquiry into the nature and processes of children's learning, is an interpretative mode. While objectives play an important part in how the teacher provides resources and offers experience, skills and knowledge to the children, the act of teaching is not seen as being determined or evaluated only in terms of those objectives. According to this mode, the process of teaching and learning is two-way. It involves not only the child's attempt to interpret and assimilate the knowledge and skills offered by the teacher, but also the teacher's attempt to understand the child's growing understandings of the world. This concern to understand the children is not merely an attempt to evaluate whether or not a teaching objective has been successful (as in the 'examination'), but is a fundamental aspect of the interaction that takes place between teacher and learner as they learn together. The meaning of the knowledge, skills and experience involved in any teaching/learning act is not defined by the teacher alone, but is open to a process of reinterpretation as the children attempt to relate the experience afforded them to their existing knowledge. It is through such processes of reinterpretation, as teachers and learners strive to understand each other, that we gain some access and insight into the children's understanding. It is in this way also that we can evaluate the effects of our teaching.

This interpretative mode of teaching places considerable emphasis upon the autonomy of the children. The choices they make and the ways they interpret the resources of the classrooom are significant indicators to us of their understanding. To allow insufficient exercise of choice, or to inhibit the idiosyncracy of their interpretation, may not only close off possible avenues of their learning, but will also close our access to that learning. For this reason it was important, in this present enquiry, that I should be able to work with the children in a way which respected their autonomy.

From my experience of working on my own in a classroom, I had begun to realize that whenever I looked really closely at what the children were doing, the choices they were making and the forms of expression they were using, then a picture began to build up of a child who was, in some sense, more 'rational' than I had previously recognized. It seemed that, the closer I looked, not only the more I saw, but the more intelligent was what I saw. I had read so much educational writing that stressed the limitations of children's skill, knowledge and experience. What increasingly impressed me was that given these limitations, an interpretative mode of teaching reveals children to be making appropriate sense of their world.

Of course, with a class of thirty or so children one cannot always be relating to individuals or groups of children in a sufficiently close manner to gain this kind of optimistic insight. Nevertheless, it was those occasions when I was able to reflect sufficiently to provide some understanding of why the children worked in the way they did, that motivated me as a teacher. A few such insights into their learning were worth more than a battery of objective measures of their performance.

Handling Classroom Complexity

(From Desforges, C. and Cockburn, A., 1987, *Understanding the Mathematics Teacher*, Lewes, Falmer Press.)

This research, conducted with seven experienced teachers, took a careful and sympathetic look at the teaching and learning of mathematics in first schools. It set out to understand why, despite current thinking on mathematics education, and a plethora of material aides, classroom practice still does not match the aspirations of the 'mathematics education establishment'.

The study has added considerably to our knowledge of classroom processes, as experienced by teachers and children, and to our understanding of the constraints impinging on teachers' classroom behaviour and decision-making. This extract illustrates clearly the challenge of complex information-processing facing teachers throughout each and every working day. It also offers valuable insights into classroom change, and of the many pressures which, for teachers, work counter to the realization of curriculum ideas.

Once the mathematics action started there was a quantum leap in the reported intensity of the information processing in the form of problems to be solved and dilemmas to be resolved. For example, Mrs G. was discussing the demonstration sheet shown in figure 13.

She turned her attention to Michelle who had her hand up.

Mrs G.: Michelle, what number should I put in the first box? (Michelle looks horrified.)
Mrs G.: Ah panic! Don't you want to do it? Come and try.

At this point Mrs G. recalled thinking,

She panicked when I asked her. She is very keen to do things but she did not want to be wrong. When I saw her face I thought, 'Now shall I suggest she doesn't do it?' But then I thought it would be a good moment to try and move her on a bit. So I decided I wanted her to see it through. Because even if she wasn't very sure of it it would be a good teaching point for her and she would learn better by that rather than somebody else helping her do it.

The other teachers frequently expressed concern about their pupils' confidence and emphasized the problems involved in trying to strike a balance between developing children's independence and maintaining their confidence. Mrs F., for example, noted how she carefully gauged how long each child might be given to answer a question, 'You can't say, "after two and a half minutes I will interfere." In two and a half minutes, Elizabeth would be hysterical whereas someone else might say, "I'm still thinking." It depends on the individual child.'

Figure 13   Place value demonstration sheet

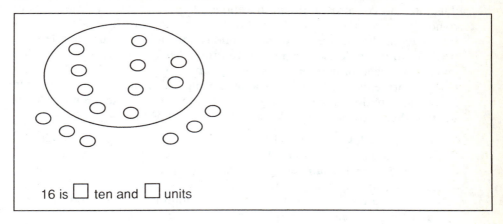

16 is ☐ ten and ☐ units

In one particular case in which 7-year-old Roscoe appeared unsure about how to tackle a task, Mrs F. commented,

> He's very unsure. He's looking for reassurance. I try to keep a blank face. It's very hard and it's very hard for the child as well because there they are, staring up at this po-faced person who is not giving anything away. It's very difficult because your instinct is, particularly with a child like Roscoe who hasn't got a lot of confidence, is to interfere and to help. But interfering is not going to help him. You can only help him by solving his problem and the way to do that is to let him work it through. It's difficult. It's ever so difficult.

Mrs B. was faced with two different dilemmas early on in her lesson on addition. After explaining the procedure for three minutes she was aware that two members of the group still did not know what to do. Instead of prolonging the oral part of the lesson, she decided that the children should set to work individually.

> I did not want to keep the rest of the group waiting and although I know that two of them did not fully understand, I thought it better to go on to the written work rather than risk boring them to tears.

A few minutes later, Mrs B. was aware that both Thomas and Andrew wanted her help,

> I was sensing that Thomas was coming up to a crucial point where he was going to understand. I knew that Andrew was also so — 'oh dear, what should I do?' But I think Thomas was in more urgent need of help at that particular second in time. So I decided that Thomas had to be dealt with and Andrew would just have to wait.

These incidents are taken from a stream of events and reflections. They illustrate the concerns and considerations of the teachers but they do not remotely convey the teachers' sense of being bombarded from all sides with information, distractions, and interruptions and of feeling under relentless pressure to make decisions and resolve problems. The following paragraphs give some image of one teacher's perceptions of this challenge. The extract below represents one minute of a session in which the teacher had been following a routine procedure to get children to demonstrate 'number stories for ten' that is to break ten down into two component parts.

Mrs D.:　Make a ten stick of cubes that are all the same colour. (Children do so.) Right. Check that you've got ten. Now we are going to make number stories that add up to ten. Now show me with your cubes a number story that adds up to ten.

(The children break up their sticks and mutters of 'one add nine' and 'two add eight' can be heard. Ross breaks his into two fives, looks round, re-builds his ten and breaks it into one and nine.)

Mrs D.:　No Ross. You were right. I just said, 'show me a number story'.

(Ross reproduces two sticks of five.)

Mrs D.:　Now. What have you got Ross?

Ross:　Five add five.

Mrs D.:　Five add five is ...?

Ross:　Ten.

Mrs D.:　Right. Ten. Hazel what have you got?

Hazel:　One add nine.

Mrs D.:　One add nine makes ...?

Hazel:　Ten.

Mrs D.:　Ten. Right. What have you got Kai?

Kai:　Three add six equals ten.

(Kai is holding up a stick of six and a stick of four.)

Mrs D.:　Three add six equals ten. Noooo ... Have another look.

Kai:　Four add six.

Mrs D.:　Four add six makes ten.

Robert:　Two add seven.

Mrs D:　Two add seven makes ten? You count again. What do you think they are Darren S.?

Darren S.:　Two add eight.

Mrs D.:　Two add eight. What have you got Darren L.?

Darren L.:　Three add eight.

Mrs D.:　(Waving away Freddie from another group.) No. Not three add eight. What have you got Richard?

Richard:　One add nine.

Before examining the teacher's comments on her decisions during this extract it is worth noting that she had thirty-five children in a very small room. She was working with one of three groups. Having organized their work she had to decide which children to call on. Her decisions were influenced in part by her knowledge of the children which had been acquired over the year and in part by the momentary changes in the events which unfolded before her. Mrs D.'s comments on the action were as follows:

> I saw Ross do something unusual in making five add five. As soon as someone said 'one add nine', he (Ross) started to put his back. I was also trying to see what everyone else had done and who was looking at whose. Louise, Hazel and Lindsay are never too sure. I saw Hazel had it right so I called on her to give her a bit of confidence. I saw Kai had it right. I am having terrible battles with him because he won't write things down — he won't finish, especially if he thinks you are watching him. I was not surprised when he said it wrong even though he had it right. Robert was the same. He had three and seven and said 'two add seven'. He and Kai both knew the larger number but probably guessed the smaller number instead of counting it. They might expect to know two and three and four without counting. The work is totally inappropriate for Darren L. He should not be in this group but I have to keep an eye on him. There was no point in going on about his error at that stage. I waved Freddie away without a second thought — he knows the rules. Richard is a bit like Darren L. I am not sure he should be in this group but I saw he had it right and that he was not paying attention, so I got him to announce. He is a puzzle. He knows loads of number bonds but cannot count consistently up to ten. He says he likes adding up but does not like counting. He is difficult to talk to because I cannot follow what he says.

In this one brief instant of teaching a routine task the teacher found herself sustaining the general pace and direction of her lesson, pushing for completion, monitoring individual responses and comprehension, choosing one child to boost confidence another to check understanding and yet another to attract attention. All the while she found it necessary to interpret their particular responses in the light of her knowledge of their typical behaviours. The wrong answer of one child was judged worth correcting immediately whilst that of another was judged better left to another occasion. These complex interactions are shown in diagrammatic form in figure 14.

Whilst the diagram is complex — and doubtless less complex than the mental processes it is intended to represent — Mrs D. found all this relatively normal. Her account is typical of those given by teachers as they conduct what they consider to be routine lessons. The demand for decisions is perceived to be incessant — and exhausting. It is small wonder that each of the teachers reported that they occasionally went into 'automatic pilot' and

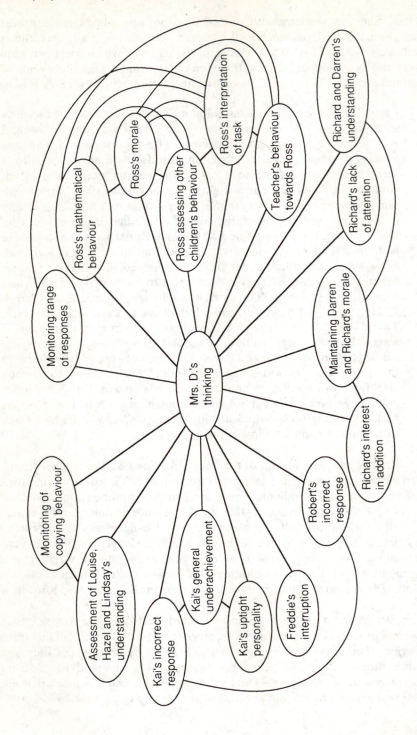

Figure 14 Some of the factors (and the interrelationships between them) Mrs D. considered during a minute of her teaching

held a period of routine questioning in order to, 'have a bit of a rest for a second' or, 'to give my brain a breather'.

Granting the speed and complexity of the issues the teachers nonetheless reported relatively few instances in routine sessions when they had, in their terms, to make 'major decisions'. As soon as they stepped into more exploratory work however, they reported facing yet more challenging problems. This is illustrated in the following account. Mrs G. set out to introduce her third year infants to the names of three dimensional shapes. She had the children sitting in a circle on the carpet. They had established that a globe was sphere shaped. A globe had been passed round. Its spherical properties had been pointed out and felt.

Mrs G.: Sphere. That's right. Now can anyone else tell me anything that's a sphere? Adam? (who has his hand up)
Adam: Square.

At this point Mrs G. recalled, 'I was ever so surprised he said that. I nearly fell off the chair. He is so keen and so shy. I thought, 'how on earth am I going to cope with this without putting him down, without smashing the bit of confidence he has got? It really was about the most inappropriate thing he could have said.'

She decided to ignore his answer and to get Adam to feel the globe and describe it as a sphere. She then turned her attention to another child. Seconds later, in giving a further example of an everyday object that is a sphere, Ben offered 'Half the world.' Mrs G. noted

I thought, oh dear! I cannot get into all that now. If he had said it later when we had got the main idea established I could have developed it using plasticene. As it was, lots of the children were just beginning to get the idea and I thought it would be too confusing. I suspected he (Ben) had the idea and would have benefitted from some extension but I decided to pass over his suggestion for the sake of the rest of them.

There followed a ten second period of acceptable responses for sphere shaped objects and then Samantha suggested, 'a circle'. Mrs G. thought,

Help! this is going to be a lot more difficult than I thought. How am I going to explain the difference between a circle and a sphere?

In an attempt to do this she asked Samantha to put her hands all around the globe and then asked her to compare that with a circle (a hula hoop on the floor). As the child did so it occurred to Mrs G. that Samantha would be able to feel the depth of the hoop and she thought,

We were getting deeper and deeper into it. What could I use? I haven't got the time to cut a circle out of paper. I'll have to make do with the hula hoop and hope she sees the difference. If I cut out a circle the point might be lost and the group might lose interest.

Throughout the next minute the children gave examples of spheres, all of which involved the idea of a ball; a cricket ball, a golf ball, a football and a bouncing ball were all offered. It looked as if things were back on an even keel when Gary suggested. 'a head'. Mrs G. experienced her fourth dilemma in under two minutes.

At first I was pleased. That was a nice idea. It was quick to relate it to spheres. Then I thought that a head is not a perfect sphere. It was really difficult to balance up because I did not want them to get wrong ideas at the beginning — they are really capable of that. At the same time I did not want to bog them down with pernickety bits and pieces. It was hard to sort of weigh that out. I was really struggling.

In this brief span, Mrs G. had perceived that she had to resolve a number of difficult problems involving conflicts of concern for mathematical concepts, children's personalities and interests, individual and group needs, the management of materials and for timing. Once the teacher engages in relatively free discussion with the children, pupils' responses become unpredictable and the teachers perceive themselves as having to make the best of what they get. Levels of uncertainty, ambiguity and risk are perceived to rise drastically and so much so that a few moments in 'automatic pilot' become increasingly attractive.

2 Children and Learning

Children's Behaviour in Junior School Classrooms

(From Boydell, D., 1975, 'Pupil behaviour in junior classrooms', *British Journal of Educational Psychology*, 45, 2, pp. 128–9.)

Prior to the full-scale ORACLE research project (pp. 25–7 and 34–7) Deanne Boydell drew up and piloted both the Pupil Record and the Teacher Record, later used in the main study. The passage below summarizes the findings of one of her exploratory studies of informally arranged classrooms based on the use of the Pupil Record. It indicates the level of involvement of children in their work and their ability to work without supervision, but in drawing attention to the facts that children's interactions were mainly with pupils of the same sex and that many recorded interactions were short, it throws doubt on the effectiveness of group work as envisaged in the Plowden Report. Its tentative conclusions were later confirmed by the large-scale study.

The results of this exploratory study show that despite the relatively high amount of time children were interacting with other children, away from their base place and mobile, they were involved with their work or waiting to see the teacher for almost three-quarters of each lesson. In view of the relatively low amount of adult contact of any kind these findings support the common belief that children have a considerable ability to engage in independent or group work with a minimum of supervision.

However, the findings relating to pupil-pupil interaction suggest that it might be more difficult than is generally supposed to set up the group work conditions envisaged in the Plowden Report (1967) so that apathetic children 'may be infected by the enthusiasm of a group' and able children benefit from 'the cut and counterthrust of conversation . . .' (para. 757).

In the first place the observed sex bias militates against group discussions involving boys and girls, thereby reducing the chances for children to 'learn to get along together, to help one another and realise their own strengths and weaknesses, as well as those of others' (para. 757). In the second place only half the interaction was concerned with the children's own work and it is debatable whether this incidence of involved activity is compatible with a view of group functioning in which children 'get the chance of discussing, and so understanding more clearly, what their problem is' (para. 758). Finally, most of the recorded interaction had been initiated in the previous 25 seconds. This suggests that sustained conversations in which children explain and develop their ideas and arguments may be relatively uncommon and this casts some doubt on the extent to which children are gaining from 'opportunities to teach as well as to learn' (para. 757).

Observation studies, such as the one reported here, enable checks to be made on commonly voiced assertions about the way children behave in different types of classroom. It is clear from this evidence that informal classrooms do not necessarily involve as much time wasting as their critics might imagine, nor as much sustained, work-orientated interaction as their advocates sometimes suppose.

Reference

CENTRAL ADVISORY COUNCIL FOR EDUCATION (England) (1967) *Children and Their Primary Schools* (The Plowden Report), London, HMSO.

Classroom Tasks

(From Bennett, N. *et al.*, 1984, *The Quality of Pupil Learning Experiences*, London, Lawrence Erlbaum Associates, pp. 213–8.)

This passage summarizes the findings of a research project into the quality of the learning environments provided by sixteen teachers in infant schools and departments. It focuses particularly on the nature of classroom tasks — their planning and presentation, their curriculum content, the intellectual demands they make on children and their appropriateness or match to children's attainments. The research represents a welcome concentration on the fine-grained examination of the curriculum as actually transacted in infant classrooms.

The focus of this study has been on task processes in classes of 6 and 7-year-old children whose teachers were rated as better than average by the advisory service in the education authorities concerned. Working closely with these teachers showed clearly that they were dedicated and conscientious people. Few with experience of working with infant teachers would doubt this description. The questions posed in this study relate to how such dedication is harnessed in attempts to provide appropriate learning experiences for their pupils.

In appraising the quality of learning experiences the demands on the children of the tasks set were first ascertained. Although there were often marked differences in the classrooms studied, tasks demanding practice of existing knowledge, concepts or skills predominated. This was particularly apparent in language work where over three quarters of all tasks set demanded practice. A typical task was a request from the teacher for the class to write a story, usually accompanied by exhortations on neatness and appropriate grammar. Here the demand was for the practice of well-understood routines and rarely did such tasks impart or demand the acquisition of new knowledge. This staple diet of little new knowledge and large amounts of practice was rarely varied to include tasks which required either the discovery or construction of new or different ways of perceiving problems, or the application of existing knowledge and skills to new contexts.

The teachers studied held strongly to the philosophy of individualization and it was therefore expected that differential demands would be intended for children of differing levels of attainment. High and low attaining children certainly received different curriculum content but they experienced similar patterns of task demand. Thus similar ratios of incremental to practice tasks were planned for both groups of children. This pattern was further confounded by the fact that teachers found it much more difficult to transform an intended incremental into an actual incremental task for high attainers. In reality therefore high attaining children received less new knowledge and more practice than their low attaining peers. This is the opposite pattern to what might have been expected with the probable consequences of delays in progress for high attainers and lack of opportunity for consolidation for low attainers (cf. Brophy and Evertson, 1976).

The main reasons for teachers failing to implement intended demands were twofold; poor or misdiagnosis, and failures in task design. Many mismatches in demand occurred because the teacher did not ascertain that the child was already perfectly familiar with the task content. Poor or non-diagnosis thus underlay the fact that many incremental tasks actually made practice demands. Task design problems were also relatively frequent. In such cases the requirements for the performance of the task did not match the teacher's intention.

Little improvement in patterns of task demand happened as a result of transferring to a junior class or school. Here the pattern changed markedly as the term progressed. Revision tasks predictably predominated in the early weeks as the teachers ascertained the base from which to start. Thereafter incremental and practice tasks were the most prevalent.

Here too there were marked differences in the classrooms studied but in general there were more incremental and few practice tasks in this term than in the infant classes. This pattern was more apparent in junior than primary schools and particularly so in the language area. This would indicate a quickening pace in knowledge acquisition. However this general pattern hid the rather surprising trend that the number of incremental tasks decreased, and practice tasks increased, as the term progressed. Thus children were rapidly introduced to new concepts and skills early in the term with little opportunity for consolidation, whereas later in the term knowledge acquisition fell away to be replaced by more and more practice.

Teachers' task intentions during this term were similar to those found in infant schools. They planned large amounts of practice and revision for high attainers and a high input of new knowledge with little opportunity to practice for low attainers, with the same predictable consequences.

High attainers also experienced, as they had in the infant classes, tasks which did not make the intended demand. Thus they received 80 per cent more practice tasks than intended, indicating little extension of concept acquisition, whereas low attainers experienced equal amounts of incremental and practice tasks which left little opportunity for consolidation. In number work the pattern was even more notable. Here low attainers received three times more incremental than practice tasks. The same problems of mis- or non-diagnosis and task design underlay the mismatching of intention and actual demand.

The quality of a pupil's learning experience is also related to the match between the intellectual demand of tasks and the pupil's attainments. In both number and language work at infant level teachers were able to provide a match on approximately 40 per cent of tasks. About a third were too difficult for the child and a little over a quarter were too easy. This general pattern masks marked differences in the classrooms studied. There was also an indication that teachers in the infant schools were somewhat better at matching than those in infant departments of primary schools. It was also very clear that the quality of matching varied in relation to the children's intellectual standing in the classroom. High attainers were underestimated on over 40 per cent of tasks assigned to them, a pattern similar to that reported by HMI (1978). But an equally clear pattern of overestimation was found for low attainers. Of their assigned tasks 44 per cent were overestimated in both language and number work.

Matching was worse in the first term of junior schooling where the proportion of matched tasks in number work fell to 30 per cent. The incidence of mismatching was particularly severe for high attainers since three-quarters of the tasks they received were underestimates. Low attainers again suffered from overestimation, a trend which was more marked in junior schools than junior departments. It was also interesting to find that the quality of matching declined as the term progressed. In the last observation period for example most of the incremental tasks were overestimates and practice tasks underestimates.

Teachers were adept at recognizing a task that was proving too difficult but were totally blind to tasks whose demands were too easy. The reasons for this are at least twofold. Firstly the teachers' typical management style required them to be seated at the front of the class, and as a result supervision was limited to quick observational sweeps of the classroom. The usual image was of a class working cheerfully and industriously. This, indeed, is the second reason for a teachers' lack of recognition of too-easy tasks. Children always worked in this way irrespective of appropriateness of the task set. From the teachers' point of view, children were busy, and busy work equated with appropriate demands.

Thus in the short term, inappropriate work appeared to have little direct emotional or motivational consequences for children of this age. Although cognitive problems, which manifested themselves in unproductive or confusing learning experiences, were all too clearly apparent in the post task interviews, this cognitive confusion was masked from the teachers by the children's cheerfulness and industry. The teachers avoided the immediate consequences of such confusion by rewarding individual endeavour, and by restricting their considerations of children's work to the product, not the process of such work, a facet taken up later.

Intended classroom learning is embedded in the content of the tasks teachers provide for children. A detailed analysis of the structure of curriculum content was therefore carried out for number and language.

In number, all teachers used some kind of sequenced scheme. Children worked through these schemes 'at their own rate,' although the teachers perceptions of 'rate' in this context appeared to refer to rate of mechanical progress through the scheme rather than rate of understanding. The content of the task, often in the form of work cards, was thus individualized, even though task demand was not. Little teaching was undertaken. Children were usually told to carry on from where they had last left off.

In contrast no sequential schemes appeared to be used in language. Most tasks were generated from the teacher's source of ideas. Most tasks were designed to develop writing skills, the typical approach being to introduce the topic as a class lesson involving discussion prior to its specification as a common class task. There was therefore no differentiation of task demand for children of differing levels of attainment. And as was stated earlier the great majority of such tasks required only the practice of established concepts and skills for high attainers. Writing was thus characterized by a lack of sequence and a lack of development.

It is also of interest to note that there was a clear differentiation in the tasks presented between reading and writing skills. Writing tasks were for the development of writing skills, and reading skills were to be enhanced by phonics and comprehension exercises. As such there was no integrated language approach.

Although different in source, presentation, demand and sequence, number and language tasks had in common a teacher stress on procedural rather than cognitive aims. They were interested in the production and presentation of work rather than in the identification or discussion of cognitive processes.

Although an accurate general picture, enormous differences in content provision were observed between classes, and within the classes studied.

In mathematics some classes covered almost twice as many areas as others. Further, the 'work at your own rate' philosophy precluded many low attainers from experiencing a wide range of content met by their more academically advanced peers even in the same classroom. Only half of the low attainers experienced division and money problems for example. The fineness of the sequence of development within any specific area, e.g. subtraction, also varied widely. In some classes the content was covered in a series of giant, sometimes quite mystifying leaps, whereas in others the same operations were developed in finely graded stages.

The width of the curriculum also varied greatly. In some classes a very narrow range of content was covered yet in the same period of time other teachers managed a much wider range with apparent success. These wide differences in provision appear to result from the selection of the particular mathematics scheme used. But within-class differences stem more from the teachers' decisions regarding individualization of instruction. 'Covering the basics' thus has a bewildering variety of meanings, but as yet there is no evidence of what implications these may have for subsequent mathematical understanding. What is clear however is that generic phrases such as 'the basics,' 'the four rules of number' or 'own rate' are almost meaningless in practice.

A wide variety of provision was equally evident in language work. But here it was the common and predictable features of writing experiences which attract attention. Teachers had uniform and restricted aims which, in three quarters of tasks observed, were to practice writing with particular attention paid to quantity and grammar, especially full stops and capital letters. Teacher evaluation focused on quantity, neatness and grammar irrespective of how the task was specified, or the attainment level of the child.

The children did little to focus the teachers' attention on to their bland and uniform diet. As well as the ubiquitous cheerfulness and industry they were totally clear about how to please their teachers irrespective of their overt demands. Thus, for example, the exhortation to 'write me an exciting story' was clearly interpreted as a request for a given number of lines of neat writing with due attention to full stops and capital letters, and in this interpretation they were correct.

Despite this diet however some progress was made in writing. When this was assessed after 6 months the children wrote, on average, more words, generated more ideas and used more connectives. They also wrote stories which were judged to be better on quality and organization. On the other hand there was little or no development of those aspects which teachers stressed the most. More than half the children failed to use full stops appropriately and correct usage of capital letters remained almost static. The overt encouragement by teachers for exciting stories appeared to have no impact since no change in imaginative content was recorded over the 6 months period.

The failure of children to deploy correct grammatical usage when not under the direct supervision of teachers could result from lack of appropriate teaching or it could be that such exhortations were premature. Only future studies will tell.

It was shown earlier that poor, or misdiagnosis, underlay many failures to transform an intended into an actual task demand. Another crucial role for diagnosis is in delineating children's cognitive confusions prior to the provision of adequate explanations. The evidence shows that here too diagnosis is a central problem. The teachers did not diagnose. They reacted to the product of a child's task performance rather than to the processes or strategies deployed in attaining the product. Thus procedural matters, such as taking the child through the rules of carrying numbers or providing spellings, predominated, rather than diagnosis of the nature of the child's cognitive misconceptions. This was usually undertaken at the teachers' desk in an atmosphere of 'crisis' management as teachers' attempted to attend to the queues whilst simultaneously supervising the class visually. Their evident frustration was an obvious consequence, and, given their chosen managerial style, unavoidable. Often the only individual teaching that children received was at the teacher's desk, but teaching within the above context hardly seems designed to enhance individualized learning, although it must be recognized that classes of thirty children impose severe constraints on teachers time and attention.

Nevertheless teachers cannot afford to disregard children's misconceptions. This maxim, together with the all too obvious problems teachers had with diagnosis, led to the development of an in-service course from which it was hoped to gain a better understanding of this from another group of experienced teachers. The ultimate aim was to provide practical advice for teachers which took into account normal classroom constraints.

Through the use of actual case studies and transcripts, followed by training in the use of diagnostic interviewing in their own classroom, teachers came to understand and accept the utility and necessity of diagnosis. Over time they learned to derive tentative hypotheses or hunches about the nature of the children's misconceptions. But they simply could not sustain an analysis of the child's responses. They fell back to direct teaching, stressing procedure rather than understanding.

A number of reasons accounted for this failure. The interviews were conducted within the framework of the typical crisis management style, i.e. that teachers are the providers of instant solutions to a constant stream of problems. As such the interviews got in the way of management. The second reason was that teachers could not stop teaching. There was a constant urge to rush into direct teaching at the first sign of error, before the misconception had been properly diagnosed. The third reason was that conducting a good diagnostic interview requires considerable skill. Teachers are not trained in such skills and find it difficult to acquire them. No doubt accumulated experience is hard to discard. And finally to conduct an effective interview requires an understanding of the processes to be attained, and experience in the manner in which children can and, typically, do, misinterpret processes.

Focusing on classroom tasks, and the influences of teachers, pupils and classroom context on their quality and performance, has brought into sharp relief a number of concerns, some serious, relating to the demands and appropriateness of tasks; to decisions regarding curriculum content; to the adequacy of teacher diagnosis and explanation; and to classroom management strategies. Most of these receive scant attention in the research literature (cf. Rosenshine, 1983) but are central factors in achieving and maintaining the quality of pupil learning experiences.

What has emerged in general terms is an increased understanding of the formidable problems teachers face as they strive to implement the laudable philosophy of individualizing instruction, and the equally formidable array of skills that are required to carry this out effectively. The objective here however is not to criticize teachers for not being perfect but to provide a clear specification of the apparent problems with a view to improvement.

References

BROPHY, J. and EVERTSON, C. (1976) *Learning from Teaching*, Allyn and Bacon.
DES (1978) *Primary Education in England: A Survey by HM Inspectors of Schools*, London, HMSO.
ROSENSHINE, B. (1983) 'Teaching functions in instructional programs', *The Elementary School Journal*, 83, 4, pp. 335–52.

Classroom Tasks: A Response

(From Pollard, A., 1985, *The Social World of the Primary School*, London, Holt, pp. 5–7.)

No professional would deny the importance of the concept of 'match' in the classroom if children are to have challenging experiences that contribute to their continued learning. Pollard suggests that the practice of 'match' for the teacher is far from simple and easy, given the complex demands of a large class of children. This extract also suggests that researchers need a more adequate and comprehensive understanding of classroom processes as a basis for valid interpretations of their findings.

For many years now the contribution of psychology to our understanding of teaching and learning processes has been very great. Studies of cognition and studies of child development have been particularly valuable and influential. While in no way decrying such work, I believe its practical utility has often been reduced by the failure of researchers to test and locate their studies in a socially meaningful analysis of the classroom situations in which teaching and learning are expected to take place. I think, therefore, that if it is possible to develop a greater understanding of the social world of primary schools it could be helpful with regard to these basic issues.

Let me take as an example the question of the 'match' between a child's knowledge and understanding and the task which a teacher might set for him or her. This is an important current issue because one of the most significant trends of recent years in primary education has been the gradual emergence of new views about how children learn and how they should be taught. The dominance of Piaget's developmental child psychology (Piaget, 1959) and of the Plowden Report's prescriptions (Central Advisory Council for Education, 1967), often crudely summarised as 'learning through experience', has been challenged. This challenge has grown since the mid-1970s, with some HMI support (Department of Education and Science, 1978), and it emphasises the appropriateness, consistency and structure of the curriculum which is provided for a child. Of course the importance of children's experience is not ignored, but it is argued that the level of 'cognitive demand' in work tasks is particularly important and that it should be very carefully matched to the child's existing level of knowledge or skill. The example which has been chosen is thus a critical one.

There seems to me to be two aspects of this issue which are particularly salient. The first concerns what it is that has to be matched and the second concerns how matching is to be achieved in classrooms.

Regarding what has to be matched, the simple answer is in terms of the appropriateness of cognitive demand — a factor which is obviously crucial.

A second factor though, is motivation, and it is to this that social, subjective and qualitative issues are important. Motivation in a classroom is not simply to do with 'stimulating the children's interests', for such a strategy is totally decontextualised. It is also about establishing a social atmosphere in which children will want to work and in which they know their efforts will be valued and judged fairly. In addition, it concerns setting tasks and providing activities which relate positively to children's social relationships, their expectations and their cultural understandings about work tasks. If this is not done the work set is likely to be regarded as 'unfair' and the children's motivation will be reduced. A task should thus be socially as well as cognitively appropriate. Both types of matching are necessary if children are to apply themselves fully to learning, and each is insufficient on its own.

The second salient issue regarding matching concerns how it is to be achieved in classrooms on a day-to-day basis. In this regard the valuable study by Bennett *et al.* (1984) is very interesting. Bennett and his colleagues worked with 16 teachers of 96 six- to seven-year-old children in primary and infant schools. The degree of cognitive match in the work that the teachers set was assessed for number tasks and for language tasks. In number, 43 per cent of the tasks were found to be matched, with 28 per cent being too difficult and 26 per cent too easy. In language only 40 per cent were matched: 29 per cent were too difficult and 26 per cent were too easy. The proportion of correctly matched work was thus low. As Bennett and his colleagues commented, '. . . although there were marked differences in the classrooms studied, tasks demanding practice of existing knowledge, concepts or skills predominated' (Bennett *et al.*, 1984, p. 213). Evidently a great deal of routine work was done despite the fact that the teachers were 'clearly conscientious and dedicated'. More specifically, Bennett *et al.* focused on two major problems which the teachers encountered: providing an accurate diagnosis of the child's understanding and designing appropriate tasks.

This is a sympathetic and supportive study which recognises the pressure on teachers in crowded classrooms, the need to respond to individual children when required and the need to manage crises as they occur. However, when it comes to proposing classroom solutions it is disappointing because it reveals only a limited appreciation of the subjective concerns and motivations of teachers and children which could account for the observed results. For instance, Bennett *et al.* suggest that teachers seemed 'totally blind' to tasks with demands which were too easy (Bennett *et al.*, 1984, p. 215) and attribute this to a tendency to equate task appropriateness with children seeming 'busy' when viewed from the front of the class. . . . Many more issues are likely to have been involved. Teachers and children adapt to their classroom life together and their social strategies often mesh to produce sets of stable, routine practices which are understood and used to 'cope' with the situation. In my opinion, with class sizes of between 25 and 30 children the social understanding that a teacher 'should be' and 'does feel' fairly content if the children remain 'busy' is often a regrettable but necessary reality.

My point is that teaching and learning are processes which have social, interactive and pragmatic dimensions. The issues are not simply cognitive or organisational but involve the perspectives and practical concerns of teachers and children as they work together. An understanding of common patterns in the subjective perceptions of teachers and children is thus a necessary complement to other types of insight about teaching and learning in classrooms.

References

PIAGET, J. (1959) *The Language and Thought of the Child*, London, Routledge and Kegan Paul.

CENTRAL ADVISORY COUNCIL OF EDUCATION (England) (1967) *Children and Their Primary Schools* (The Plowden Report) London, HMSO.

DEPARTMENT OF EDUCATION AND SCIENCE (1978) *Primary Education in England*, London, HMSO.

BENNETT, M., DESFORGES, C., COCKBURN, A. and WILKINSON, B. (1984) *The Quality of Pupil Learning Experiences*, London, Lawrence Erlbaum

Curriculum Provision: Priorities and Consistencies

(From Alexander, R.J., 1984, *Primary Teaching*, Holt, pp. 54–9.)

From the concepts of 'teaching style' and 'match', researchers moved on to look at 'time spent' in relation to tasks and curriculum areas. This concept became a focus of concern both for researchers and HMI in the seventies and eighties.

Whilst comparing and contrasting some significant studies in this extract, Robin Alexander questions the assumptions underlying the curriculum classifications upon which the studies are based. He questions, for example, the lack of attention given to areas such as drama, dance, personal and social development in analysis of children's learning. In addition, he points to the problem of applying subject-based research categories to a time analysis of primary curriculum which might be essentially holistic or integrated in nature.

These kinds of studies have, nevertheless, begun to offer more tangible evidence of how time is spent in classrooms. They have laid to rest many of the myths about neglect of the basics which challenged primary education in the 1970s. In their wake, the studies have also brought evidence of a narrower curriculum than that envisaged by Plowden or that advocated by HMI in their *Curriculum Matters* papers.

The most obvious indicator of curriculum priority is the amount of time spent by the child in each area. However, while in secondary schools such calculations are straight forward, and a timetable analysis will suffice (see Wilcox and Eustace, 1981), in primary schools time allocations are more difficult to ascertain. There are four reasons for this. First, the class-teacher system enables teachers to be highly flexible from one day or week to the next whereas a published secondary timetable is necessarily rigid and pre-dictable: thus the typical week, let alone the typical day, may be hard to define. Second, variation in curriculum emphasis: one child might be having extra remedial reading while others at the same time are undertaking a topic. Third, the organisational practice of having different activities going on simultaneously makes the recording of time allocations very difficult. Fourth, there is the ideological disinclination of many primary teachers to define their teaching in terms of others' curriculum labels.

These difficulties seem to be reflected most prominently in the analysis by Bassey (1978) of infant pupils' activities. Precise figures are given for the 'general activities' of 'class talk', 'play time', 'administration' and so on, but not for the conventional curriculum areas of mathematics, language and the rest. In contrast the figures from his junior teachers were unambiguous:

Curriculum area	Average number of hours per week for pupil	Percentage
Language	7	30.4
Mathematics	5	21.7
Thematic studies	4	17.4
Physical education	3	13.0
Art and craft	2	8.7
Music	1	4.3

(Bassey 1978, p. 28)

In other words, in crude numerical terms, the 'basics' of language and mathematics take up something over half the child's time, and everyday observations readily confirm in particular the practice of giving children one hour of mathematics every day of the week, usually in the morning (when the child, supposedly, is 'fresh': when he is tired he can undertake art, music, science and the other 'non-basic' activities).

A similar temporal emphasis on the 'basics' is shown in the ORACLE study. Different figures emerged from the pupil and teacher records: Galton, Simon and Croll (1980) point out that they can only be expected to coincide when classteaching (i.e. the pedagogical technique, not the primary organisational device of class teaching) is the norm. This discrepancy is particularly marked in creative writing and what they term 'general studies' (religious education, history, geography, social studies, science) because much of the work is topic/project based. Their figures for the 'real' or actual curriculum were as follows:

	ORACLE percentage
Language	35.7
Mathematics	30.0
Art and craft	10.2
General studies/thematic studies	24.3

It would be misleading to juxtapose the ORACLE and Bassey figures as they stand, because the former relate only to observed activities in the classroom, so that once PE and music are included the percentages of each of the four areas above are reduced. However, though a fine calculation on the basis of the authors' data is impossible, if one adds to the ORACLE figures the Bassey allocations for PE and music and recalculates the ORACLE percentages, the figures become remarkably similar.

Thus, as Galton, Simon and Croll remark after comparing figures from ORACLE, Bassey and the Bullock Report (DES, 1975), 'teachers seem to be both consistent and accurate in their estimates of time spent on the broader curricular areas' (Galton, Simon and Croll, 1980, p. 186).

However, this picture of consensus and consistency is rudely disturbed by the figures which emerged from the HMI primary survey. As Richards (1982) points out, in rough or 'coarse-grained' terms the national curriculum picture, and the educational priorities it represents, is clear, but at the more significant level of analysis of the curriculum as experienced by individual children, there is wide variation. HMI identified 36 items (DES, 1978a, pp. 77–9) found to occur individually in at least 80 per cent of the survey classes:

Language: listening and talking

- (a) children were taught to
  - (i) follow instructions
  - (ii) follow the plot of a story
  - (iii) comprehend the main ideas in information given to them
- (b) children talked informally to one another during the course of the working day
- (c) discussion took place between children and teachers when new vocabulary was introduced

Language: reading and writing

- (a) in 7 and 9 year old classes children practised reading from a main reading scheme and from supplementary readers
- (b) in 9 and 11 year old classes children read fiction and non-fiction which was not related to other work they were doing in the classroom
- (c) in 11 year old classes children made use of information books related to work in other areas of the curriculum
- (d) at each age children were encouraged to select books of their own choice
- (e) children were given handwriting practice
- (f) children undertook descriptive and narrative writing
- (g) in 9 and 11 year old classes children did written work on pre-scribed topics related to other parts of the curriculum

Mathematics
Work was done to enable children to learn:

- (a) to use language appropriate to the properties of number, size, shape and position
- (b) to recognise relationships in geometrical shapes, numbers, ordered arrangements and everyday things
- (c) to appreciate place value and recognise simpler number patterns
- (d) to carry out suitable calculations involving +, −, × and ÷ with whole numbers
- (e) to understand money and the value of simple purchases
- (f) to use numbers in counting, describing and estimating

(g)   in 7 year old classes children undertook practical activities involving addition, subtraction, multiplication and division

In 11 year old classes children were taught to:

(h)   estimate and use measurements of length, weight, area, volume
(i)   work with the four rules of number including two places of decimals
(j)   calculate using decimals
(k)   use fractions, including the idea of equivalence, and apply them to everyday things
(l)   use various forms of visual presentation including three dimensional and diagrammatic forms

Aesthetic and physical education
The programme of work included:

(a)   singing
(b)   listening to music
(c)   two or three dimensional work showing evidence of observation of pattern *or* colour *or* texture *or* form
(d)   in 7 year old classes, practice of skills in gymnastics *or* games *or* swimming
(e)   in 9 and 11 year old classes, gymnastic skills
(f)   in 9 and 11 year old classes, practice of skills in playing games
(g)   in 11 year old classes, swimming lessons

Social abilities and moral learning
Work was arranged to promote the following:

(a)   reliability and responsible attitudes
(b)   consideration for other people; e.g. good manners, concern, friendship
(c)   respect for surroundings and the care of materials and objects in the classroom and school
(d)   participation as a member of a group or team, learning to follow rules and obey instructions
(e)   involvement in the development of religious ideas and moral values during the school assembly
(f)   in 9 and 11 year old classes, awareness of historical change and causal factors in relation to the way people lived or behaved in the past
(g)   in 9 and 11 year old classes, work relating to at least one of the following aspects of geography; population, agriculture, industry, transport, or resources within or outside the locality

(DES 1978a, pp. 77–79. Reproduced with the permission of the Controller of HMSO.)

HMI then showed that the 'coverage of items varied from class to class and showed no overall consistency' (p. 74). Some items, such as reading practice and mathematical computation, took place in all classes observed. On the other hand, science did not appear at all on the list reproduced above because it was not undertaken in even the minimum 80 per cent of classes. Similarly, 'some work of a geographical nature' was undertaken in only 60 per cent of the 7 year old classes (though in 90 per cent of the 9 to 11 year old classes) and 'some attention to the study of the past' in 60 per cent of the 7 year old classes, 90 per cent of the 9 year old classes and almost all 11 year old classes.

When grouped into the four main curriculum categories of 'mathematics', 'language', 'aesthetic and physical education' and 'social abilities' (a curiously misleading label for this unregarded rump of the primary curriculum), the percentages reveal a disturbing lack of consistency nationally.

Percentage of classes undertaking all widely taught items in each subject

	7 year olds	9 year olds	11 year olds
Mathematics	65	76	58
Language	54	43	53
Aesthetic and physical education	73	63	58
Social abilities	65	46	61

(DES, 1978a, p. 85)

Percentage of classes undertaking all widely taught items for combinations of two or more subjects

	7 year olds	9 year olds	11 year olds
Items for language and mathematics combined	42	37	39
Items for language, mathematics, aesthetic and physical education combined	35	28	28
Items for language, mathematics and social abilites combined	33	24	32
All items combined	29	19	24

(DES, 1978a, p. 86)

The HMI figures suggest that 'consistency' is a concept in need of careful qualification where the character of primary children's curriculum experience is concerned. On the positive side, following the claims and rumours generated in the post-Plowden years, HMI were able to state in the survey press release (with some relief, no doubt), that:

> High priority is given to teaching children in primary schools to read, write and to calculate, and there is no evidence to support the suggestion that teachers neglect the basic skills. (DES, 1978c, p. 1)

Beyond the 'basics', however, the picture is much more variable: no observational or experimental science in 80 per cent of the classes observed; superficiality and lack of direct observation in art; craft making a smaller contribution to the work than is desirable; a lack of response to the challenge of a multi-cultural/multi-faith society in religious education; fragmentation, superficiality, repetition and lack of progression in history and geography.

The subsequent first school survey (DES, 1982a) provided a similar analysis: initial teaching of reading soundly undertaken, but with a subsequent neglect of extended reading skills; written activities competent, but of limited range (insufficient descriptive and expressive writing); spoken language attended to, but listening skills neglected; mathematical computation given priority, but little application to contexts where the skills might be applied; a lack of development in religious education; very little attention to 'the wider circumstances in which they (the children) live', to their situation in time and place; a lack of progression in understanding and skill development in science, though a more positive picture than in the 1978 survey; a neglect of three-dimensional and observational work in art and a failure to realise the 'educational value of art and craft work'; music given little or no role in 20 per cent of the schools and conceived in a limited way elsewhere (in contrast to the 1978 survey which showed specialist teachers promoting it more competently in 7 to 11 year old classes); lack of progression and challenge in physical development.

It must be remembered that HMI's own investigative framework can hardly be accused of being over-ambitious or unrealistic. As we have seen, the observation schedules reflected what HMI saw rather than what they hoped to see. In a sense then, despite the evident failure of some classes and schools to approach even such institutionally derived norms, HMI's own framework is a limited one educationally: there is little attention in it to the issues concerning personal and social development that I discussed above, little detailed consideration of drama, dance, health education or other curriculum areas which feature in substantial numbers of primary schools, and, in particular, no suggestion whatsoever that existing conceptions of the curriculum for pre-adolescent children and existing curriculum priorities might need to be questioned. In this respect the HMI surveys, particularly the 1978 survey (which is more systematically presented and conceptually less open-ended than its successor) carry the same dangers as a vehicle for professional and curricular development as the Schools Council 'aims' survey of Ashton, Kneen, Davies and Holley (1975). Being grounded in the practices and opinions of serving teachers they have an attractive 'realism' and legitimacy, and feature prominently in initial and in-service discussions of the purposes and character of primary education. But embedded in the aims of the study are some highly questionable assumptions about children's development and learning, the nature of knowledge and the relationship of the child and the educational process to their cultural and societal contexts.

Similarly, whatever the extent of criticism of current practices in the HMI surveys, the existing overall curricular frameworks and priorities remain unexamined. Using such documents in the context of a holistic curriculum appraisal can simply confirm just those values, assumptions, prejudices and misconceptions which most clearly need to be challenged.

References

ASHTON, P.M.E., KNEEN, P., DAVIES, F. and HOLLEY, B.J. (1975) *The Aims of Primary Education: A Study of Teachers' Opinions*, London, Macmillan.

BASSEY, M. (1978) *Nine Hundred Primary School Teachers*, Slough, NFER.

DEPARTMENT OF EDUCATION AND SCIENCE (1975) *A Language for Life* (Bullock Report), London, HMSO.

DEPARTMENT OF EDUCATION AND SCIENCE (1978a) *Primary Education in England: A Survey by HM Inspectors of Schools*, London, HMSO.

DEPARTMENT OF EDUCATION AND SCIENCE (1978c) Press notice, 26 September.

DEPARTMENT OF EDUCATION AND SCIENCE (1982a) *Education 5–9: An Illustrative Survey of 80 First Schools in England*, London, HMSO.

GALTON, M., SIMON, B. and CROLL, P. (1980) *Inside the Primary Classroom*, London, Routledge and Kegan Paul.

RICHARDS, C. (1982) 'Curriculum consistency', in Richards, C. (Ed.) *New Directions in Primary Education*, Lewes, Falmer Press.

WILCOX, B. and EUSTACE, P.J. (1981) *Tooling Up for Curriculum Review*, Slough, NFER.

Opportunity to Learn

(From Bennett, N., 1987, 'The search for the effective teacher', in Delamont, S. (Ed.) *The Primary School Teacher*, Lewes, Falmer Press, pp. 51–6.)

The notions of 'time on task' and 'opportunity to learn' have generated numerous classroom studies in recent years. In these, researchers have attempted to identify correlations between 'achievement' and the time pupils spend on classroom tasks. In the following extract, Neville Bennett examines some of the complexity that lies behind such apparently simple correlations. Quantifying the time a child spends on a learning task says nothing of the quality of the task itself, nor the degree of engagement the learner is able to achieve. If a child cannot understand a task and interact purposefully with it, then no amount of time on it will achieve mastery. There are many other variables at work in determining whether or not children learn in classrooms, though 'curriculum allocation', 'time on task' and 'opportunity to learn' should not be discounted in analyses of learner achievement.

Opportunity to Learn

The basic assumption of the opportunity to learn model is that there is no direct relationship between teacher behaviours and pupil achievement since all effects of teaching on learning are mediated by pupil activities i.e. pupil learning activities are central to their learning. In particular, the amount of time a pupil spends actively engaged on a particular topic is seen as the most important determinant of achievement on that topic. In this model, the pupil therefore becomes the central focus with the teacher seen as the manager of the attention and time of pupils in relation to the educational ends of the classroom. In other words, the teacher is conceived as the manager of the scarce resources of attention and time.

The opportunity to learn model has spawned a good deal of research since the mid-1970s and is summarized here around the model shown in Figure 1 (Bennett, 1978 and 1982).

The focus is on pupil achievement and the factors delineated by empirical studies which relate to that. The broadest definition of opportunity to learn is the amount of interaction children have with school i.e. the extent to which they are exposed to schooling. Quantity of schooling is measured in terms of the total amount of time the school is open for its stated purpose and is defined by the length of school day and school year. Length of school day has, for example, been found to vary as much as six hours per week in Britain even in the same geographical locality. The pupils' exposure to schooling can also vary in relation to the amount of time that they are absent, and to the policy of their school regarding the amount of homework

Figure 1   Summary model of research on opportunity to learn

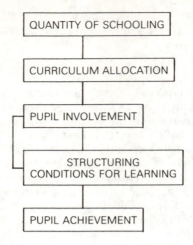

given. Homework is here conceived as extending the quantity of schooling. There are indications that length of school day, absence, and homework all relate to pupil achievement.

The time available for schooling is allocated to various curriculum activities, and in Britain, where there is no central or local control of curriculum, the curriculum emphasis or balance varies markedly from school to school and from class to class in the same school. In our national enquiry into open plan schools, for example, we spent a whole week in a national sample of schools observing exactly what educational and curriculum experiences children were being provided (Bennett *et al.*, 1980). Figure 2 shows the difference in curriculum allocation across this national sample. This shows, for example, that the average amount of time spent on mathematics in junior classes was four-and-a-quarter hours, but that this varied from two-and-a-half hours in some classrooms to over seven hours in others. Similarly, the average amount of time devoted to language was seven-and-a-half hours, but in some classrooms it was as low as four hours and in others as high as twelve hours. A similar picture has been presented by other research (for example, Bassey, 1977), and together this research indicates that children receive quite different educational diets dependent on the school they happen to go to, and, as in other areas of human functioning, diet appears to relate to growth. The evidence would indicate that different curriculum balances result in different patterns of knowledge acquisition (Berliner and Rosenshine, 1976; Fisher *et al.*, 1978).

Curriculum allocation can be conceived as the opportunity that teachers provide for pupils to study particular curriculum content. Pupil involvement or engagement can be conceived on the other hand as the use that pupils make of that opportunity provided by the teacher. Many studies have

Figure 2   Curriculum Allocation

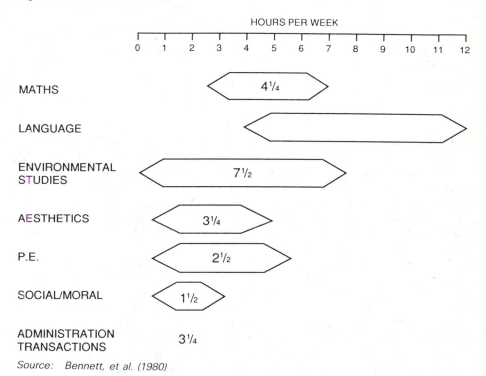

HOURS PER WEEK

MATHS — 4¼

LANGUAGE

ENVIRONMENTAL STUDIES — 7½

AESTHETICS — 3¼

P.E. — 2½

SOCIAL/MORAL — 1½

ADMINISTRATION TRANSACTIONS — 3¼

Source: Bennett, et al. (1980)

provided descriptions of the extent of pupil involvement, or time on task, across all school ages, and although the working definitions of pupil involve-ment are not always completely compatible, there appears to be a law of two-thirds emerging. On average, pupils appear to be involved in their work about two-thirds of the time, but this varies markedly from class to class, and from pupil to pupil in the same class.

In our study of open plan schools, we found marked discrepancies in the average amount of pupil involvement from class to class and school to school. In some classes, average involvement was nearly 90 per cent whereas in others it was less than 50 per cent. These differences have important implications since curriculum allocation and pupil involvement interact. Table 2 illustrates this in mathematics.

Pupils in class 3 were allocated least time for mathematics — 138 minutes or just over two-and-a-quarter hours per week. This contrasts with the amount of time allocated by the teacher in classes 1 and 2, where it amounted to six-and-a-quarter and six-and-two-thirds hours respectively. However when pupil involvement is taken into account the actual working time on mathematics reduces to less than one-and-a-half hours per week for

Table 2   Comparison of classes 1, 2 and 3 on allocation and involvement (%)

Class	Time allocated		Involvement	
	Percentage	Minutes	Percentage	Minutes
Class 1	25.0	375.0	58.4	219.0
Class 2	26.5	397.8	89.9	357.6
Class 3	9.2	138.0	62.6	86.4

pupils in class 3 or about seventeen minutes per day. The similarity of allocated time in classes 1 and 2 turn into a considerable discrepancy on actual working time since pupils in class 2 achieve a 90 per cent involvement rate against less than 60 per cent in class 1. Thus the former achieve an actual working time of nearly six hours a week as against just over three-and-a-half hours per week in class 1. Pupils in class 2 were thus involved in mathematics for over seventy minutes per day compared to seventeen minutes per day for pupils in class 3.

Research relating pupil involvement to achievement has generally reported positive relationships but of widely differing strength. In general, however, the data would seem to lend support to William James argument of 1902 that, 'whether the attention comes by grace of genius or by dint of will the more one does attend to a topic, the more mastery of it one has'.

The amount that pupils are involved with their tasks is not however a complete explanation of achievement. Time has been likened to an empty box (Gage, 1978) which requires filling with suitable content. There is, for example, no point whatsoever having pupils highly involved on tasks which are incomprehensible or in some other ways not worthwhile. The element in the model entitled 'Structuring conditions for learning' reflects this. The cluster of variables which have been of concern here include the presentation of the task; the sequence, level and pacing of content; the matching of tasks to children; teachers' levels of expectations of their pupils, and types of feedback from teacher to child. Nevertheless it has to be said that researchers working within the opportunity to learn paradigm have rarely extended the scope of their studies beyond pupil involvement.

The results of studies in this paradigm have been used to develop experimental intervention programmes with the purpose of improving pupil achievement and/or classroom management (Emmer *et al.*, 1981; Gage and Coladarci, 1980; Good and Grouws, 1979), and for the development of prescriptive models of teaching such as the direct instructional model. The rationale for this model was based on the research evidence which suggested that the following instructional variables are usually associated with content covered, academically engaged minutes and achievement gain.

1   Teachers maintaining a strong academic focus with encouragement for the academic progress of each student.

2 Teacher rather than student selection of activities.
3 Grouping of students into small and large groups for instruction.
4 Using factual questions and controlled practice in teacher-led groups. (Berliner and Rosenshine, 1976)

In other words, teachers should run a structured, orderly teacher directed classroom with an academic focus and with frequent monitoring and supervision of the pupils whilst maintaining a warm and encouraging climate.

A very similar picture has been painted by the most recent, and most extensive, study of junior schooling in this country (ILEA, 1986). The teaching from which the highest pupil achievement is gained was characterized as follows: a structured setting where the work is chosen by the teacher, where one subject is taught at a time, during which the time spent communicating with the whole class is important, stressing intellectually challenging questions and high expectations. The class presents as a work-centred environment in which more teacher time is spent discussing the content of work with pupils, where a high level of pupil industry is apparent, where pupils clearly enjoy their work, and where there are low noise levels and little pupil movement. The teachers keep adequate records of pupils' achievement and involve parents in the education of their children. Overall, the teachers manage to create and maintain a positive classroom climate.

Nevertheless, the ILEA study, like other studies in the opportunity to learn approach, neglected the curriculum tasks and activities on which pupils were engaged. Time is thus a necessary, but not sufficient, condition for learning. Therefore exhortations to increase curriculum allocation or to improve levels of pupil involvement or industry are of no avail if the quality of the tasks set is poor or not related to pupils' intellectual capabilities. The activities of the learner on assigned classroom tasks may be seen as crucial mediators in converting teacher behaviours into learning behaviours, but so far there has been little description, analysis or explanation of how classroom tasks are assigned or worked under normal classroom conditions and constraints, despite the fact that most intended school learning is embedded in the tasks teachers assign to pupils.

References

Bassey, M. (1977) *Nine Hundred Primary School Teachers*, Nottingham, Nottingham Primary Schools Research Project, Trent Polytechnic.
Bennett, S.N. (1978) 'Recent research on teaching: A dream, a belief and a model', *British Journal of Educational Psychology*, 48, pp. 127–47.
Bennett, S.N. (1982) 'Time to teach: Teaching learning processes in primary schools', *Aspects of Education*, 27, pp. 52–70.
Bennett, S.N., Andreae, J., Hegarty, P. and Wade, B. (1980) *Open Plan Schools: Teaching, Curriculum and Design*, Slough, NFER.

BERLINER, D.C. and ROSENSHINE, B. (1976) *The Acquisition of Knowledge in the Classroom*, Technical Report IV-I, Beginning Teacher Evaluation Study, San Francisco, CA, Far West Lab.

EMMER, E.T., SANDFORD, J.P., EVERTSON, C.M., CLEMENTS, B.S. and MARTIN, J. (1981) *The Classroom Management Improvement Study: An experiment in elementary school classrooms*, Austin, TX, Research and Development Centre for Teacher Education, University of Texas.

FISHER, C.W., FILBY, N.N., MARLIAVE, R., CAHEN, L.S., DISHAW, M.M., MOORE, J.E. and Berliner, D.C. (1978) *Teaching Behaviours, Academic Learning Time, and Student Achievement*, Final Report, Phase IIIB, B.T.E.S. San Francisco, CA, Far West Lab.

GAGE, N.L. (1978) *The Scientific Basis of the Art of Teaching*, Columbia, NY, Teachers College Press.

GAGE, N.L. and COLADARCI, T. (1980) 'Replication of an experiment with a research based in-service teacher education programme', Program on Teaching Effectiveness, School of Education, Stanford University.

GOOD, J. and GROUWS, D.A. (1979) 'The Missouri Mathematics effectiveness project: An experimental study of fourth grade classroom', *Journal of Educational Psychology*, 71, pp. 355–62.

ILEA (1986) *The Junior School Project*, London, ILEA Research and Statistics Branch.

Time and Structure for Children to Write

(From Calkins, L.M., 1983, *Lessons from a Child*, London, Heinemann, pp. 30–2.)

This research study by Lucy Calkins is in marked contrast to the large scale statistical studies, in which a wide range of variables are examined, and attempts made to find correlations. This is a case study of an individual child, Susie, and some of her classmates. The researcher followed Susie's writing progress, as the class teacher changed her teaching approach by introducing 'writing workshops' into her literacy curriculum. Lucy Calkins worked with the class teacher, Pat Howard, supporting her in the curriculum change, and monitoring classroom developments. Pat Howard's experience is cited elsewhere in this volume (p. 145).

In this extract we see how a different view of 'writing', and a consequent re-structuring of time for writing, fosters a greater depth and quality in the children's experiences.

This case study approach to research, with the attendent narrative style of presenting the findings, gives the reader graphic insights into classroom and learning processes. It also illuminates the point made by Neville Bennett in an earlier extract (p. 85) that discussion of 'time for learning opportunities' needs to be accompanied by analysis of quality of learning.

When the year began, writing was squeezed into fifteen-minute time slots. The entire school day was like that: a collage of little bits. Ten minutes for spelling, fifteen minutes for a quiz. Ten minutes for a penmanship ditto. Twenty minutes for page 36 in the social studies text. Graves likened the schedule to driving in city traffic: the children shifted from first to second gear, but never got into high gear for there were no broad stretches of time. [...]

Writing well, as we were to learn, requires a different pace than we are used to in our schools. The initial fifteen-minute writing slot was stretched into twenty minutes, then thirty, forty. By the middle of October, Mrs Howard's children spent three or four hours a week in writing workshop and then, to get even more time, they sometimes elected to write during recess.

The chipmunk's funeral had been the first time Susie and Diane asked to bring pencils and paper onto the playground during recess. Soon they didn't bother to ask. Diane and Susie wrote the script for a puppet show during three consecutive recesses, and then spent hours of time at home making the puppet. When Susie wrote a story for her sister's birthday present, that, too, was written during recess. 'You need to have all the time you want for a piece of writing', Susie once told a visitor to her classroom. 'Otherwise you're afraid to look back, afraid to see that it's not what you wanted, that it's not all you could do'.

Time was all the more valuable if it was regular, scheduled time, for then the children could plan for writing. They could think about their writing at home, as Amy did in devising the lead to her fox report. 'I was lying in my bed, just thinking and thinking. I heard my sister come home. She went into her room and closed the door', she said, adding, 'A beam of light shone through the crack in her door, and when my cat Sidney looked up, it made her squint'. Amy continued, 'So I thought of how to start my report and I held it in my head 'till I got to school'.

Debbie also rehearsed for writing when she was at home. 'Sometimes if I'm stuck on what to write about, if I know writing will be the next day, I get my Mom to help me, When I was a little girl I used to sing all these songs and here I am, in chorus. So my Mom last night starts singing the songs and it refreshes my memory and I'm ready for writing time'.

As the schedule for Mrs Howard's classroom became predictable, the children began writing as if there was a tomorrow. 'I'll just write it fast', Susie would say, 'and tomorrow I'll read it over'. By late October, Mrs. Howard's children were writing every Monday, Wednesday and Friday from 9:10 to 10:30. Soon, not only the schedule for writing but also the agenda within each writing workshop, was predictable. Writing always began with a ten-minute mini-lesson, followed by a fifty-minute workshop for writing and conferences, followed by some method of sharing work-in-process. When other teachers heard about this consistent routine, they were surprised. 'Isn't it boring to do the same thing each day?' 'Don't you need to change things, to motivate the kids?'

I sympathized with their questions and so did Pat. We'd each entered the school year believing creative writing required a creative classroom structure; earlier in the year and in preceding years, Pat's writing sessions had been a kaleidoscope of new approaches and agendas.

Things had begun to change when Pat wanted time to observe and work with individual youngsters. 'I don't want to spend my time choreographing', she said. She'd already built consistent structures into reading time so she could work with individuals — now she did the same during writing.

Eventually we realized this structure was not only helpful to Pat, it was also helpful to the children. 'Creative' classroom structures do not give children freedom, as we might suppose, any more than do 'creative bedtime hours'. When classroom environments are always changing, always haphazard, this not only puts teachers into the position of choreographing, it also puts children into the position of waiting for their teachers' changing agendas.

Mrs Howard found that it was important not only to have a predicatable timetable for writing, but also to have consistent expectations — or, more bluntly, rules. Marion Howe, a writing process teacher from New York who has learned from Mrs Howard's work, recently explained the ironic importance of having a few, simple rules.

Because I insist all children are involved in the writing process during writing time, I can give children the freedom to move naturally and independently between rehearsal, drafting, revision and editing. Because I insist that when one piece is finished, another is begun, I do not have to set class deadlines. Because children know all final work must be edited, they can edit when they are ready. Because I insist children do not disturb others with their peer conferences and because I've taught them how to have productive conferences, the kids can talk together with whomever, whenever they need help.

It is significant to realize the most creative environments in our society are not the ever-changing ones. The artist's studio, the researcher's laboratory, and the scholar's library are each deliberately kept simple so as to support the complexities of the work-in-progress. They are deliberately kept predictable, so the unpredictable can happen. Similarly, Mrs. Howard and I became convinced that the juxtaposition of a complex, changing craft such as writing and a simple consistent environment freed the children to make choices as they wrote.

Children with Special Educational Needs

(From Croll, P. and Moses, D., 1985, *One in Five: The Assessment and Incidence of Special Educational Needs*, London, Routledge and Kegan Paul, pp. 132–4.)

This research by Diana Moses and Paul Croll confirmed the estimations in the Warnock Report, that between one in five and one in six children have special educational needs. It also revealed that the teachers, in general, believed integration into mainstream classes to be the best form of provision for these children. Integration, however, is not without its difficulties for mainstream teachers who emerged, with credit, in the study for facing difficult tasks under less than favourable circumstances. Inadequate knowledge and understanding of appropriate assessment procedures was one major source of concern. In addition, the learning and behavioural styles of the children presented challenges to the teachers' classroom organization, as is shown in this particular extract which focuses on the children's classroom experience.

Summary: The Classroom Experience of Pupils with Special Educational Needs

[Our] analysis [here is based upon research which] compare(s) the classroom experience of two overlapping groups of pupils identified by their teachers as having special educational needs, namely, children with learning difficulties and children with behaviour problems, with a sample of control pupils. The overall classroom context in terms of the framework of class organisation and curriculum content was very similar for the different groups of pupils. In terms of the framework provided by the teacher, the children with special needs were part of the ordinary class. An exception to this is found in the relatively lower amount of time the children with special needs spent in the context of group instruction with the teacher and work involving co-operation with other pupils, but these activities form only a small part of the average child's classroom experiences.

In terms of their behaviour and interactions in class, however, a number of differences emerged between the two groups of special needs children and the rest of the pupils in the class. The first of these is that both groups of special needs children spent a good deal less time than the other pupils engaged in work and other approved activities and, conversely, more time distracted from approved tasks. This difference is greatest in the case of work directly on a curriculum task. The children in the two special needs groups had higher levels of aggressive behaviour than control pupils, although overall levels of such behaviour were low, and also spent a great deal more of their time than control pupils fidgeting. They were not, however, more likely to move around the classroom.

Teachers spend more time on an individual basis with the children with special needs than with other pupils although this is necessarily only a small part of the child's classroom experience. Levels of interaction with other pupils on the part of children with special needs is very similar to that of the control sample, although it is rather less likely to be concerned with work and other approved activities. However, interaction with other pupils even as a distraction from work is only a little higher among the two groups of special needs pupils. Where they differ considerably from the control pupils is in distraction from work which does not involve interaction with other pupils. This solitary distraction from work is about double that of the control pupils.

[Our] results ... confirm Moses's hypothesis that there is a distinctive set of behavioural characteristics among children with learning difficulties, a 'slow learner behaviour pattern'. This involves lower levels of engagement in work, particularly work directly on a curriculum task, high levels of fidgeting and much more time than other children spent on their own, distracted from their work. Teachers spend considerably more time with these children on an individual basis than they do with other pupils but, like the rest of the class, the children with learning difficulties have most experience of interaction with the teacher as part of a class audience. The children with behaviour problems share most of the characteristics of children with learning difficulties (and half of them are also in the learning difficulties group). Differences include teachers being rather less likely to work with them as members of a small group and a higher level of distraction from work in interaction with other pupils than is found among the children with learning difficulties.

Some of these results suggest, by implication, the difficulties that teachers may have with children who have learning difficulties and behaviour problems, particularly in finding ways of engaging them in their work. This should be put in context, however. Although their children do less work than most pupils they are still directly engaged on curriculum tasks for, on average, about half of their time in class and spend about seven-tenths of their time on some sort of approved activity. They are fidgeting but not constantly moving about the class, and aggressive behaviour, although higher than among the controls, is still very low. Interaction with other children in the class is the same as that of the control pupils, and the children with learning difficulties are not above average in engaging in distracting interaction with others. They do, though, take up more of the teacher's time than other pupils, and their levels of solitary distraction from their work suggest that this extra attention cannot be sufficient to engage them in their work to the extent achieved by most children.

Society in the Classroom

(From Pollard, A., 1985, *The Social World of the Primary School*, London, Holt, pp. 107–10.)

Under scrutiny, schools reveal particular forms of social structure, organization and values which have a consequence for the ways in which children see themselves, and the ways in which they learn and achieve. There are particular implications for equal opportunities. In studying the social world of the primary school, Andrew Pollard drew on his teaching and research experience in a range of infant, junior, primary and middle schools. Teachers, he suggests, consciously or inadvertently, perpetuate the values and structure of society at large within the microcosm of the classroom. This extract draws on research data to show ways in which that might be happening. It suggests that the primary classroom may be a fertile and effective training ground for the outside world of work and industry.

The way in which social and cultural values and beliefs influence schooling processes is both a very difficult area and too significant to ignore. I offer a very simple account of it here, first by considering some commonly held ideas about our economic system and then by introducing the concept of hegemony to illustrate how such ideas both spread to and can be generated from the micro situation of the classroom.

Our present economic system is perhaps best described as a form of 'state capitalism' in which large public industries, multinational corporations and financial institutions predominate. They are supported by the various agencies of the welfare state, of which education is one. Underpinning the economic system in a fundamental way are two necessities: high levels of consumption and high levels of production. The importance of these factors is constantly stressed in both public and private spheres, for instance through advertising and 'conspicuous consumption' in the case of the former and through acceptance of the work ethic and the need for industrial efficiency in the case of the latter. I would argue that this concern for consumption and production can be seen as elements of a hegemony — the dominant set of ideas which support the existing social and economic system and which permeate the thinking of the people living within it (Gramsci, 1978). Thus even a system which is grossly divided and has an unequal distribution of wealth, such as British society, is legitimized and accepted because the ideas upon which it is based have become taken for granted as 'common sense' and are even regenerated in everyday practice.

This particular power of the hegemony lies in the fact that an immediate action by an individual in response to a particular situation is likely to draw on commonsense thinking which, though it 'works' in the short term, also has the long-term effect of reproducing the values on which the system as a whole is based, and to which, ironically, the initial action was responding. There is thus a continuous dialectical movement between the macro and micro levels in which the social and economic structure and individuals in interaction together generate and regenerate the hegemony. Examples of this phenomenon are readily available in schools.

For instance, in my study at Moorside I collected examples of many forms of teachers' talk — instructions, comments, questions, etc. In the general area of school-work I identified examples which seemed to relate to productivity and efficiency. For example:

Effort	'You're not trying at all.'
	'That's very poor.'
	'Don't be so careless.'
	'Let's make a really big effort today.'
Perseverance	'Try once more.'
	'Concentrate.'
	'Hard luck, you'll have to do it again.'
	'Try a bit longer.'
	'No, you've not quite finished yet.'
Neatness	'Make it look good.'
	'Do it carefully.'
	'That's a nice, neat page.'
	'God, you look a mess.'
	'OK, tidy up now.'
	'Yeah, that's nice.'
	'Print it neatly'.
	'Leave the classroom straight.'
	'Your writing's a mess.'
Regularity	'Is that your best work?'
	'I don't think you're trying today.'
	'I know you can do better than that.'
	'Which side of the bed did you get out of?'
Speed	'Hurry up!'
	'Get a move on.'
	'Who's going to finish first?'
	'Has anyone finished yet?'
	'Be quick.'

There is nothing unusual about these concerns. They would be found in most of our schools and many people would applaud the fact that such values are encouraged. In my view, though, they also form part of the dominant hegemony; they can be traced to the 'Protestant ethic' first documented by Weber (1976), are regularly articulated by governments and industry at a national level, and are also regarded as the main means of 'getting on' by millions of people. Concerns such as these form a major part of the dominant values of our society, and teachers working in schools within that society tend to reinforce them. However, it is crucial to note the significance of these concerns for teachers at the practical level of their day-to-day work. In this regard values such as these are directly linked to teachers' immediate concern with *instruction* as an interest which enables them to cope with their working conditions. 'Keeping their noses down' is common sense for teachers in many classroom situations, but it also reinforces the hegemony.

A second set of social values also existed at Moorside, grouped around issues of behaviour and social relationships. For instance:

Self-control	'Stop being silly.'
	'Don't be a baby.'
	'Don't shout out.'
	'Don't just rush.'
Obedience	'Do what I tell you.'
	'Behave yourself.'
	'Did you hear what I said?'
	'Any more acting daft and there'll be trouble.'
Politeness	'Good morning, children.'
	'What do you say?'
	'Please?'
	'That's not a very nice thing to say, is it?'
Quietness	'Stop talking.'
	'OK, quieten down.'
	'Shut up.'
	'Silence now.'
Respect for authority	'Hands up if you want something.'
	'I said so.'
	'Don't argue with me.'
	'Ask me first.'
	'Don't be cheeky.'
	'Stand aside when I come through.'
	'Listen to me when I'm talking.'
	'"Yes *sir*" is what you say.'
Truth	'Let's have it straight now.'
	'I don't believe a word of it.'
	'Are you lying to me?'
	'That's a good story, isn't it?' (said doubtfully)

Again we see here the emphasis of attributes which could be said to meet industrial needs in terms of preparing a productive and compliant workforce. However, the grouping stems more immediately from teachers' practical concern with sustaining *order and discipline*. Several of the social values identified — politeness, respect for authority, quietness — derived from teacher·strategies designed to pre-empt trouble, while others — obedience, self-control, truth — emerged primarily during attempts to recoup situations.

At the same time there is evidence of concerns in schools which reinforce the expectation of mass private consumption. A simple but direct example is the common ritual in infant schools of cataloguing birthday presents in assembly before the child receives his or her 'claps'. More significant, though, is the routine stress on individualism and competitiveness. For instance:

Achievement	'Have you got that right?'
	'Well done; that was good.'
	'Good, that's right.'
	'No, that's wrong.'
	'You've got them all right. Excellent.'
Individualism	'Don't copy.'
	'Don't help each other.'
	'Do it yourself.'
	'Do your own work.'
	'Stop cheating.'
Hierarchy	'Who got ten out of ten?'
	'Who got most?'
	'That's not so good as Neil's.'
	'How many did you get?'
Self-reliance	'Well, look it up.'
	'Go and find out.'
	'You *can* do it.'
	'Everyone should be able to do it on their own now.'

Once again these values are both commonly accepted as being important in society outside schools and seen to have a degree of commonsense justification within them. Competition has always been an excellent means of achieving simultaneous productivity and control in a classroom, as elsewhere, and encouraging self-reliance often results in some immediate pressure being taken off the teacher. Interestingly, recent observational studies have shown that, even when teachers organise their classes for group work, the children in fact work as individuals for most of the time (Galton, Simon and Croll, 1980). Control, noise levels, diagnosis and assessment may well be eased by this, but it is also significant that it promotes the individualism and the competition which underpin mass consumption.

References

GRAMSCI, A. (1978) *Selections From Political Writings*, Volumes 1 and 2, London, Lawrence and Wishart.

WEBER, M. (1976) *The Protestant Ethic and the Spirit of Capitalism*, London, George Allen and Unwin.

GALTON, M., SIMON, B. and CROLL, P. (1980) *Inside the Primary Classroom*, London, Routledge and Kegan Paul.

Making Sense of School

(From Jackson, M., 1987, 'Making sense of school', in Pollard, A. (Ed.) *Children and Their Primary Schools*, Lewes, Falmer Press, pp. 81–5.)

Margaret Jackson's research is concerned to investigate ways in which children starting school become familiar with the rules and routines of daily classroom life. In the process, she comments on the differences between teachers' expectations, as they socialize children into work and classroom routines, and the strategies which children themselves evolve in order to make sense of their new world in their own way. Mismatch between these two raises a question about whether children's individual and unique learning strategies are in danger of being extinguished early on in school life if they do not conform to the existing social order which the teacher has established.

One way of analyzing data . . . is to consider the process of making sense of school as a process of developing social competence. Children need to become aware of the expectations and demands of the school situation so that their own learning will become appropriate to the constraints of the situation in the classroom. Evidence from the data which I collected showed that some of the children were not aware of the classroom expectations. These children were not regarded by the teacher as being successful because the product of their learning process did not match the product which was expected.

We can consider the children's developing social competence in three main areas:

   (i)   in procedural and organizational routines;
   (ii) in interpersonal relations;
  (iii) in learning 'how to be taught'.

Procedural and Organizational Routines

The organization of the classroom environment, both in management of time and materials, is an important part of life in a reception class. Hamilton's account (1977) of first days in school show how, during this time, much of the teacher's concern is with procedure. These procedural routines are an integral part of the transition from being an individual at home to being one of a large group at school. A young child's capacity to grasp the organizational procedures of the classroom has an influence on the learning process. As Cook-Gumperz (1986) says,

> . . . familiarity with the subtleties of classroom social organization is
> a pre-condition for gaining access to learning opportunities. (p. 60)

The following incident showed how one child missed learning opportunities because of her unfamiliarity with the procedural routines of the classroom.

Donna

The whole class was told to get out writing books, pencils and namecards, sit at a table and practise writing their names. In her record of work the teacher said that this was to serve both as practice in letter formation and also as a help in learning how to write their names. Donna spent a long time looking for a pencil, sharpening it and then finding a space in which to sit. When she was finally settled she did not start writing but began comparing her name-card with that of her neighbour. She counted the letters, pointed out those which were the same, got up and found both names on the drawers and named each letter. After five minutes the teacher came and told Donna off for not getting on with her work.

In this short time Donna showed a great deal of knowledge about written language: she could identify letters and showed good visual discrimination in matching; she showed awareness of different combinations of letters to form words; she knew that the names on the drawers signified to whom each drawer belonged. She did not actually practise any letter formation but paid great attention to each letter and how the particular combination of letters made up her name. In fact, Donna displayed considerable metalinguistic knowledge.

One cannot criticize the teacher for feeling that Donna had not 'done her work'. Although there was nothing concrete to show for it, Donna had probably gone a long way to achieving the teacher's original aims. With a class of over thirty children it is difficult for a teacher to be aware of all the learning that is going on and it is easy to see why she felt that Donna was 'wasting her time'.

In this small incident Donna made sense of the activity by making it her own and becoming actively involved in her own learning. She used her current knowledge based on past experience as a basis for her present learning; she made, tested and reformulated hypotheses; she used language functionally within a social context. Language plays a central role in the child's coming to terms with the environment. Before starting school a child has already achieved considerable understanding of languge as a system. Experience of language has been used to construct a system of rules and the overgeneralization of these rules that frequently occurs in the spoken language of young children reflects the strategies they use to construct and modify their own 'grammar'. Learning language, however, is more than learning a system and as they learn the rules of form children also learn rules of use; they learn how to use language as a resource for communicating with other people within a variety of contexts. Donna was using her knowledge of written language as a resource for her own learning. In fact, Donna's knowledge was greater than that which was required for the given activity. She used that knowledge to make the activity her own, to bring meaning to the task, to make learning the personal and active process she had known it to be in the past.

However, in the classroom, the ultimate power rests with the teacher. Thus a child has to conform to the organizational norms of the classroom to exploit the full learning potential of the situation. Donna did not do this and despite her sophisticated manipulation of the text she was perceived by the teacher as not fulfilling the demands of the required task and as causing a disruption within the classroom. It seems then, that for a child, active learning and relevant use of past experience and knowledge are not enough in the classroom. Conformation to expected behaviour patterns is what is also required by busy teachers.

Interpersonal Relations

A classroom can be seen as a social community and the relationships which are formed in the community have influence on the learning which takes place. A model of collaborative learning requires children to use language for negotiation, questioning, identifying issues, planning actions and establishing learning relationships and making sense of school demands a social competence within this interpersonal context. It involves forming understandings, not only of the physical but also of the social environment. Children are required to collaborate with each other and with adults and to recognize and respond to different roles in different situations. The range of social relationships with an adult is just one illustration of the complexity of social understanding required. Being in the school assembly, working in a small group with the teacher and sharing an activity on an individual basis are all very different social contexts and require different responses. The child whose past experience does not include using language in these ways or for whom the school experience is so strange could find this difficult. Tina, in the following incident, made sense of the physical context of the classroom environment before she felt able to enter into the social context.

Detailed observation was made of Tina during two full days. The first of these was after she had been in school for exactly one week and the strongest impression of this first day's observation was of the isolation she experienced. She watched and listened to all that was going on but resisted any attempt to make her join in, either by the teacher or another child. Tina spent a long time in the home corner and when the other child playing there tried to include Tina in a game, Tina just silently walked away. She walked round and round the home corner, exploring and trying out all the things in it. When the teacher came and talked to Tina about what she was doing, there was again no response and as soon as the teacher left Tina started to do something else. It seemed that at that stage Tina just wanted to absorb and watch all that was going on in the classroom for herself. Extracts from the field notes describing just two minutes, show Tina's intense investigation of the physical environment:

> *11.19:* Tina goes back to the phone. She puts the receiver which was dangling down, back on the phone. Sits down on the end of the bed. Stands up again immediately. Walks back to till. Picks up and looks at it from all sides. Tries to look inside. Takes money out of till drawer and puts it back in. Picks up money from floor and from box of spare money and puts in till drawer.
>
> *11.20:* Walks along, opening all cupboards, looks in each one then closes door. Looks inside saucepans on stove. Closes till.
>
> *11.20:* Walks to edge of home corner and looks around classrooms. Goes to bed, sits down, stands up. Walks to number table, watches children working. Walks round edge of classrooms.

The second day's observation of Tina took place two months later and again she spent considerable time in the home corner. It is interesting to make comparisons between the two occasions. On the second day Tina was playing with the other child, engaging in dramatic play and talking about what she was doing. She provided an almost continuous running commentary on her activites, sometimes addressed to me, sometimes to the other child and sometimes to herself. Generally she was labelling objects and actions but sometimes she provided an interpretation of what was going on. She also discussed and planned with the other child what they were going to do. The field notes show Tina's increased verbalization:

> *9.34:* Tries to put up ironing board — puts it up upside down. Turns it round the right way. 'I don't know where the iron is now.'
> Sits on the high chair. 'I'm the baby, I'm sitting in the high chair.'
>
> *9.35:* Takes plate and spoon out of cupboard — sits back. 'I'm a baby.' Sucks a skittle.
> Tells another boy to sit on the bed but he refuses. 'I'm having a bottle.'

Tina, during these first two months in school, had made sense of the situation to the extent that she was now able to contribute to and attempt to control the social context of the play. At the early stages of Tina's school life the teacher identified Tina as likely to have problems because she felt that

Tina was not playing an active enough role in classroom activities for effective learning to take place. It could well be that the expectations of the teacher were too great. Tina's sense-making strategies may not have fitted in with the school expectations but they enabled her to come to terms with the vast array of new experiences. She began by exploring, observing and investigating and later she used her newly-acquired knowledge to express herself and the issues that were currently important to her. Just before Tina started school her mother had had a new baby but it was not until Tina felt familiar and confident with the new classroom environment that she felt able to use her new understanding to explore the new situation at home. She needed to make sense of school before she could relate it to the rest of her life and use it for active learning. For Tina that process involved observation and assimilation before participation.

Learning in the reception class is very much about collaboration with others and a lot of interaction with others is expected and encouraged ... It seems that until young children are able to use language as a resource for negotiation with others and as a means for establishing collaborative learning relationships, the pattern of learning in the classroom remains inaccessible.

Learning 'How to be Taught'

Children come to school as active learners. They have probably had experience of investigating their own environment and learning through real and important problem-solving. Frequently they have had the sole attention of a concerned adult who has been learning alongside the child. Learning has been 'embedded' in concrete situations of everyday life.

In school children are required to conform to the pattern of learning of their classroom and this may not be the same as their previous active learning. Donna adapted the prescribed classroom activity, creating her own problem-solving situation and collaborating with another child. However, in doing this, she was rejecting the specific demands of the teacher and it is rare that children are given the power to do this in the classroom. An important part of 'making sense of school' is learning to confine active learning to the constraints of the situation.

School learning rarely expects children to be completely passive and frequently there are clear patterns of participation. Tina did not follow these patterns and 'made sense of school' in her own way. [She was] classified by [her] teacher as likely to have problems because [her] sense-making processes [were] not as expected.

I would thus argue that social competence in learning 'how to be taught' requires discernment of and compliance with the accepted learning patterns of the classroom.

References

COOK-GAMPERZ, J. (1986) *The Social Construction of Literacy Studies in International Sociolinguistics*, Cambridge, Cambridge University Press.

HAMILTON, D. (1977) *In Search of Structure: A Case Study of a New Scottish Open Plan Primary School*, London, Hodder and Stoughton.

Starting School

(From Barrett, G., 1986, *Starting School: An Evaluation of the Experience*, Centre for Applied Research in Education, University of East Anglia, pp. 2, 4.)

The main insights offered by the research into starting school, commissioned by Assistant Masters and Mistresses Association, are summarized here by the author. The research drew upon the views and experiences of children, teachers, parents and headteachers, and aimed to identify significant issues and practices which might help teachers to initiate reception children more successfully into school learning. As the summary of the reseach shows, the demands on children starting school are many and complex. Links between home and school can be far from coherent for the child, and views of parents and teachers can be markedly different. In addition, teachers are not always appropriately trained, nor adequately resourced to offer the best kind of support and opportunity to children in these crucial early stages. The research has added to our understanding of the multidimensional nature of the problem facing families and schools, as they seek to secure the best provision for our youngest school children.

The main conclusions of the research may be summarised as follows:

1   *Children need to learn, know and use 'survival skills' in order to function confidently in a classroom.* These include very basic things like knowing:

— who they are and what they can do;
— that 'experience' has some meaning for them;
— that they have a right to their own interests and knowledge;
— what school is for — and what it is in physical terms;
— how to be with, consider and communicate to other adults and children when necessary;
— who teachers and other school adults are and what they are for;
— how to help themselves as in taking coats off, going to the lavatory or being able to organise themselves in a chosen activity;
— how to cope with and overcome 'not knowing' things and the feelings this arouses.

Not knowing any of these, but particularly the first and last, leads to children feeling uncertain, out of control and apparently confused. At the extreme their responses were difficult to cope with in large classes but frequently (initially at least) related to confusion rather than 'bad' behaviour. Knowing the above depended on experience, expectations and opportunity to learn and practise them.

2   *Teachers' ideas of 'development' learned in training do not help them understand what reception children know and how they respond to school.*

... we have so many pre-conceived ideas about what a child ought to be able to do when they come into school and very rarely do we actually admit to school — I've never admitted to school — a normal child, a child who is totally ready for school (in every way) and yet invariably we are aiming our teaching at the normal reception child.

3 *Teachers need to be able to respond to individual children as need is identified because the relevant curricular experiences and survival skills of children vary greatly.* For instance some children have not learned to move confidently in large spaces with large numbers of people, but may already be able to read, another child may not know what a book looks like but can confidently find their way around the classroom and school and talk to people.

4 *The staff-pupil ratio in infant classes is inadequate — particularly in the Summer term if Summer born children are admitted as rising fives into existing classes.* Teachers whose schools had three intakes during the year were unanimous in spelling out the disadvantages for these children — and the extreme stress on themselves in trying to maintain a calm, relaxed, caring and learning environment for all the children.

5 *Ideas about 'work' and 'play' in classrooms need to be clarified to ensure that parents, teachers and children can communicate with understanding about curricular activities.* For example some teachers referred to 'work' as 3 Rs activities but many children used the term in relation to any form of 'hard' learning regardless of activity if there was an adult expectation attached to it. Many teachers valued and used structured play activities as important means of effective learning for children but felt some parents only saw 'work' at desks as important which in the long run may be less effective educationally.

6 *Teachers, parents and other professionals felt a need for more links between themselves and children's home and school learning.*

... they have learned to do a lot of things before they come to school without any systematic programme, just at their parents' elbow but we give the impression that once you step through school there are certain things that you don't do as parents and so a lot of natural support that children have been given has actually been taken away because of the schools' attitude ... so I do honestly think that we've got to re-think our ideas.

Gender and the Classroom

(From French, J.C., 1986, 'Gender in the classroom', *New Society*, 7 March.)

The next two extracts deal with the difficult, but crucial issue of gender differences in the classroom. Both authors conducted classroom research which highlighted significant differences in the classroom behaviour of boys and girls, and consequent differences in the way teachers responded to the sexes. Research of this kind implicitly raises similar kinds of concerns to those raised by Andrew Pollard's extract (p. 92). To what extent do social structures and patterns of responses laid down in the microcosm of the classroom affect children's long term self-images and achievements? How can our awareness of differences and inequalities be used to change classrooms? To what extent can teachers overcome, in the classroom, the influences bearing on them and their pupils from outside? These are important concerns for all who have a hand in shaping children's classroom experiences and consequent development. Research studies of this kind are constantly needed to add to our knowledge of these issues, and to our understanding of how they might best be handled.

Gender and the Classroom

A recent American study reported in Findings (29 November, 1985) observed that female pupils receive considerably less attention from teachers than males. This finding will come as no surprise to British readers — research carried out on this side of the Atlantic has also long indicated that teachers devote more of their time and energy to boys, and tend to focus lessons around their interests.

But to explain these tendencies by reference only to what *teachers* do is, as the American study points out, to do less than justice to a complex phenomenon. It may lead us to assume that all would be well if only teachers could be persuaded to amend their sexist attitudes. Unhappily, as those involved in anti-sexist initiatives discover, solutions are not so ready to hand. There is also the problem of the pupils.

Teachers have long observed that girls and boys behave differently. Girls are reported to be conscientious, compliant and docile; boys to be boisterous, demanding and restless. Although these descriptions are in need of some refinement, they are not totally without foundation. And change is dependent on recognising their reality for teachers as well as challenging sexism in the profession and seeking improvements in the economic position of women.

Over the past twelve months, I have co-directed an investigation of girls and boys in the infant classroom. It was based on video recordings of the children in their first term, in the middle, and towards the end of their infant schooling. The videos made somewhat depressing viewing. Even in the reception class, there are numerous differences in behaviour which, probably unconsciously, affect the ways in which teachers respond to the two sexes.

It is common practice in British infant schools for the teacher to gather the class together as a group each day to talk about some matter of topical interest. These occasions provide both an intellectual and a physical focus for the classroom researcher. On the one hand, there is much to be learnt from observing children in groups. On the other, the fact that the class is gathered together dispels the recurrent fear that the important and interesting things are happening behind one's back and away from the camera!

The usual procedure is for the teacher to position herself on a chair at the front, while the children group themselves, disciple style, at her feet. A close look at the resulting configuration shows, however, a tendency for boys to place themselves on the periphery of the group, sometimes kneeling up or stretching their legs out and leaning back on their hands. If space is at a premium, they perch on nearby chairs and tables. By contrast, the majority of girls congregate, cross-legged, at the front or in the middle of the group.

The result is that a number of boys are highly visible. The teacher, seated on a chair, above the level of the children, finds her natural line of gaze falling on the margins of the group, that is on the boys. She literally overlooks the girls in the body of the class. Pupils chosen to speak in the lesson are then more often found to be those positioned at the boundaries rather than the centre — and thus to be boys.

Some boys are also noticeably mobile and active. Shuffling in their seats, their gaze frequently straying from the teacher, they pose an ever-present threat to the order and unity of the lesson. Reminders, Joyce Grenfell style, to 'sit', 'leave Daniel alone' or 'pay attention' are frequently addressed to boys and seldom to girls. Questions too are often posed to those whose attention appears to be wandering. 'Now who can tell me what day it is today?' asks one infant teacher. Several hands are raised, but she spots Darren staring out of the window. And so it is: 'Darren Thompson, can you tell us what day it is today?'

Coupled with this physical prominence is a tendency for boys to be more active and demanding of interaction. Calling out and correcting the teacher, are predominantly male activities.

With the exception of one or two girls in our study (out of appoximately 30 lessons observed) the girls were, in comparative terms, model pupils. Although interested and eager to participate; they tended to comply with the classroom rules of handraising; and they waited for permission to speak. Their very observance of these rules made them unproblematic from the point of view of class discipline and, consequently, meant that the teacher devoted less time to them.

So, although the teachers *may* have held sexist attitudes which in-fluenced the ways in which they treated their pupils, the behaviour of pupils also exerted an influence. Within the context of a busy classroom, it is difficult not to give more attention to boisterous children with limited powers of concentration, and easy to leave the conscientious and compliant to their own devices. This is in no way to blame the pupils for what happens, but to draw attention to the fact that lessons are not a one-sided affair — teachers respond to input from their pupils.

The situation is exacerbated as pupils grow older and become more aware of their capacity to manipulate situations and people. In some top junior classes which I observed as part of an earlier study, groups of perhaps four or five boys had established themselves as the dominant pupils. They were described to me by teachers as 'real characters'. As well as calling out witty or topical comments on the lesson and what other children had to say, they had developed a keen sense of 'news value'.

Interaction in the classroom requires that, in order to involve and keep the attention of as many of the class as possible, teachers cannot allow any one child to talk for too long. Quickfire question-and-answer sequences interspersed with longer expositions by the teacher are thus the order of the day. Teachers ask questions which call for a word or phrase in reply, and most pupils respond with short, to the point, answers.

The Way the Boys Take Over

The so-called 'characters' came up with such unusual and newsworthy answers that the teacher was frequently prompted to investigate further. This meant that these boys were effectively invited to tell a story or to voice an outlandish opinion in detail. One boy in particular used every possible opportunity to promote an image of himself as 'different'. While the rest of the class enjoyed the afternoon spent at the local sports centre, Tom did not. While most children got up between seven and eight in the morning, Tom got up at four-thirty. While other pupils had one or two pets, Tom had what amounted to a private zoo.

Whatever the majority view or position, Tom or one of his fellow characters could be relied upon to adopt an opposing stance. Thus there was the boy who, alone among peers, declared English to be an unimportant subject, and the one who boasted a dog which needed twelve walks a day or, more correctly, every 24 hours, since some of them were in the night. And at the end of the lesson, pupils such as these had always had far more speaking turns than anybody else, and had taken up a considerable propor-tion of the time available.

At the secondary level, too, small groups of boys monopolise the proceedings. In a series of secondary school science lessons which I recorded and analysed, enthusiastic boys had to be quashed and girls almost forced to participate. Inundated with offers by male pupils to draw diagrams on the board, or to demonstrate experiments to the class, the female teacher had either to nominate specific girls, or to notify them in advance of her intention to involve them: 'So Richard, Neil and Andrew are going to do the demonstration. Then I'm going to ask one or two of the girls, who don't usually volunteer to do the experiments, to comment.'

Perhaps more worryingly, questions which required the children to reason to provide solutions to problems or to infer the underlying relationship of disparate experiments, for example, were commonly answered by one of two or three bright, eager and confident boys. Their hands were frequently the only ones raised in response to questions such as 'So what can we conclude from this experiment?' or 'What does this tell us about changing the state of things?' The teacher rarely picked on non-volunteering members of the class in this sort of context.

Girls, of whatever ability, tended to volunteer or to be selected where the question involved the recall of information. Itemising the steps in the experimental method, already described by the teacher, or listing the apparatus, visible on the teacher's bench, were especially popular.

Taking the infant, junior and secondary levels as a whole, it is clear that although boys *do* get more attention from teachers, it is not simply *because* they are boys. Undoubtedly, there are teachers who, consciously or unconsciously, prefer boys, and consequently spend more time on them. Presumably, some teachers similarly prefer girls. But it is also the case that the pupils who feature most prominently in the classroom landscape, and whose activities demand a response from the teacher, are boys. It is this relationship of gender to a range of other factors that makes generalisation difficult and solutions hard to procure.

There are several issues to consider. First, it is unlikely that teachers will be able or willing to give less attention to restless or troublesome children. The practical constraints of getting through the lesson, keeping the attention of the class, and maintaining face, particularly at the secondary level, frequently take precedence over ideals held at the level of theory. An unfortunate consequence of this is that the type of pupil whose self-esteem and standing is enhanced by showing off in class may be given subtle encouragement, through the attention it attracts, to continue doing so. Patterns of behaviours are thus established and perpetuated.

It is similarly difficult to give less attention to the sorts of bright and enthusiastic children described in connection with the secondary science lessons. Their inclination to engage teachers directly in conversation, to present problems or to volunteer opinions, calls, like troublemaking, for a response, from the teacher. The constraints of time mean, quite simply, that the more time spent with such pupils the less time there is for those who, though perhaps equally bright, are less forthcoming.

On the issue of the greater visibility of boys in the classroom, the outlook is perhaps more hopeful — children and teachers are moveable objects! In one of the few infant classes where girls participated on an (almost) equal basis, the teacher's policy was to wait for the children to settle themselves on the floor, and then to move her chair a little further back. In this way, she did not overlook anybody and those at the front or in the middle of the group were as likely to be noticed as those on the periphery.

The overall situation is not, however, promising. Teachers can be made aware of the issues. They can monitor their lessons and perhaps identify subgroups of dominant pupils. They can also confront the possibility of their own sexism. But change also requires fundamental shifts in the attitudes of pupils. Girls would need, from the start, to acquire qualities of self-confidence and assertion, and to be less willing to accept or even endorse the behaviour of their male counterparts. And, importantly, they would not have to be made to feel, by peers, parents or teachers, less feminine as a consequence.

Boys' notions of masculinity would likewise have to be challenged. The aura of arrogant self-confidence exuding from dominant boys would have to be dispelled. The troublemaker, the clown and the raconteur would have to be despised rather than admired. In short, we would require a full-scale assault on society's gender consciousness. Despite the gains made by the feminist movement, this is something of a forlorn hope. It is, increasingly, socially acceptable for females to adopt the so-called masculine virtues, but people still become very edgy at the thought of this process happening the other way round. And as the Manchester-based Girls into Science and Technology project workers found, the most determined action taken within the school cannot effectively counter the influence of peer group, magazines, television and family.

Gender and the Classroom

(From Clarricoates, K., 1987, 'Child culture at school: A clash between gendered worlds', in Pollard, A. (Ed.) *Children and Their Primary Schools*, Lewes, Falmer Press, pp. 192–3, 197–200.)

Disruption was invariably initiated by the boys, this disruption for a time halted further work advancement and the girls reacted by expressing resentment against the boys. They regarded the boys as 'silly', 'lazy' and 'thick'. One way of controlling the boys who were disrupting their chances of getting on with their work was to call upon the teacher to disapprove of the offending boys. Perhaps the teacher did not intercede but it had the required effect of curtailing the boys' action. The girls, in fact, reported that the boys seemed to want to 'get into trouble'.

So far, the picture that is drawn seems to be that of girls as archetypal 'good pupils'. However the 'conformist' interpretation of this behaviour has to be reanalyzed in the light of the young girls' needs for recognized competence and self-esteem, not merely as 'wishing to please the teachers'. The girls indulged in *non-conformist* behaviour far more than teachers realized i.e. they ate and shared sweets 'undercover' of their desk lids and secretly passed verbal and written messages to each other. They considered themselves 'clever' in not being found out. This sort of behaviour was neither meek and passive nor aggressive but in certain instances — when a teacher felt that some of the girls were subverting her/his authority — this did cause tension. However, because there is no behavioural typescript for deviant behaviour for girls (Davies, 1979) they were categorized as 'silly' by teachers who found their behaviour puzzling. The girls seemed to be less influenced by each other (which some sociologists may regard as proof of a lack of solidarity) than the boys, who tended to prove to each other that they were part of the 'in-group'. The girls did not automatically define female teachers as adversaries, and had many common understandings with them which may have been assisted by the sex of the teachers. Certainly, it is too easy to assume that academic striving and achieving are synonymous with 'conformity'...

In Dock Side, space and who dominated it was an important issue. One of the reasons for this was the lack of it, being a cramped, Victorian edifice. Within the classroom, despite limited space, there was some attempt to provide a 'play area'. Specific corners were marked out in each infants' class which varied according to the size of the room and the number of children present. It became apparent that it was mainly boys who tended to occupy this space with girls restricted to their desks and the surrounding area. I assumed that there would be some interchange with regard to the utilization of space but, as the days turned to weeks and months, the pattern remained consistent. The boys dominated the area, expecting first choice of toys and going to particular lengths to keep at bay either the girls or another group of boys. I must point out that the tactics used to repel other groups of boys or the girls were different in that though physical tactics were used to 'repel all borders', with girls there was also sexual ridicule combined. Girls did venture into the 'play area' when it was vacant or to retrieve an item of equipment. Lisa tended to be the only girl who appeared to have free access in this space and was on particularly 'good' speaking terms with the boys, along with her best friend Katy. I soon found out why. Lisa was prepared to threaten any contentious boy with violence, not only from herself but her 'big brother' who happened to be in the second year juniors and who was not squeamish about beating up little boys from the infants.

Long Meadow provided a strong physical contrast with Dock Side. It was the largest and most spacious of the four schools; sex-segregated toilets and corridors made available the exclusivity, by sex, of facilities. In both the infant and junior classes some of the teachers encouraged the extensive use of numerical and play equipment, seeing it as a problem solver, since it diminished the amount of disruption amongst the boys, who were able to dominate more space with their verbal and physical activity.

In Applegate and Lintonbray, as in Dock Side, space tended to be an issue strongly contested between the girls and boys. In the middle (7–9-year-olds) and senior (9–11-year-olds) classes of Lintonbray there was no space set aside for play areas, whilst in the infants (5–7-year-olds) class some attempt was made to provide space for play. There were the usual constructive toys and books occupying makeshift shelves in this space. The infants' teacher ensured that most of the children were involved in some form of activity or project and in this way there appeared to be 'equality' in the use of the play space between the boys and the girls. However, observations revealed something quite different which shows that analysis must include not only *who* occupies space but also *how* such space is occupied. Before the end of the school day the children in this particular class gather in the play space for their 'end-of-the-day' story. There was the usual rush for places and during the ensuing scuffle which accompanied such jostling for positions it became clear that the low-lying book-cases and who sat on them represented high status within the class. On a number of occasions when some girls attempted to occupy such places they were invariably pushed off with screams such as 'it's only for us boys'. The teacher did rebuke the boys for their harsh behaviour in certain circumstances — when a kick or a punch accompanied the 'scream' — but they were not for insisting on occupying such an 'exalted position' in the play space. She was to all intents and purposes, unaware of the aspects of power being acted out in this form of spatial dominance.

In Applegate such forms of dominance were also being acted out in the recreation spaces provided. This was particularly apparent in the middle juniors where there was a fair sized room adjoining the classroom for activities 'of a less serious nature'. Harsh physical behaviour from the boys towards the girls was frowned upon, in accordance with the ethos of the school, but this did not pre-empt certain forms of spatial dominance being enacted. Researchers have noted that ridicule is used as a means of control by male pupils in schools (Shaw, 1977; Spender and Sarah, 1980; Mahoney, 1985). On a particular occasion two girls were attempting to retrieve an abacus from one of the many cupboards within the room. Five boys, already ensconced in a project, resented their 'intrusion' and jeered at them: 'I suppose you'll need that seeing as you can't count', stated one. The other boys start to laugh. The girls retorted reminding one boy, Carl Haymers, that he'd only 'got nought out of ten for a recent mental arithmetic test'. The boys returned the remark with threats and the girls feeling outnumbered retreated from the room.

This is just an example from a long catalogue of 'masculine' behaviour which undermines girls' skills and confidence. Verbal practice which included jokes and even threats were constantly made as a way of gaining space from the girls, with no fear of disciplinary action. The issue is one of power, and until that is recognized no action to challenge such behaviour will be forthcoming.

Cross-group and intra-group rivalry was apparent in all the schools. Boys in particular made a great show of who was 'top dog' amongst themselves and also banded together in order to express their collective dominance as a group. In addition when an individual boy sought to dominate a girl in some respect, he called on others for support, and in certain cases even used the teacher.

It was 11.30 am and the second year infants class at Long Meadow had resigned themselves to their work books. A group compared each other's work amongst themselves. Paul stated: 'I've done more than you!' 'No you haven't', replied the indignant girl. Paul turned for support from Stephen and Neil 'I've done more than her, haven't I?' 'Yeah, you have, so there...' The girl shrugged and attempted to get on with her work.

But the boy, Paul, would not leave it there, but went on about it and had caused quite a good deal of disturbance around him. He shouted to the teacher 'Miss, Miss, I've done more than her, haven't I?' The harassed teacher wanted an end to the disturbance and agreed with him in the hope he would return to his work. 'See!' said Paul determined to have the last word.

Some of the boys appeared to have a constant fear of being beaten by the girls. A situation, which an unthinking teacher, exacerbated on a number of occasions. A male teacher informed a games class in Dock Side, who were clambering over items of sports apparatus, that the girls were 'beating' the boys in climbing up the rope. Almost immediately the boys went into paroxysms of activity in order to prove that they were 'better'; they attempted to outrun, outclimb, outdo each other and the girls. To them it was important not only to 'beat' their counterparts, it was also necessary that they should be seen doing so. The girls condemned boys for being rough and aggressive whilst the boys condemned girls for appearing to be the 'good pupils', since it is through the display of reverse qualities of what girls do that boys gain and reward status.

A further way in which the boys were able to dominate classroom life was in being able to gain the teacher's attention much more often. On many occasions when a girl made attempts to show her work to the teacher she was unable to gain her attention. Some degree of forcefulness was necessary to divert the teacher and some girls lacked the confidence to do this. However, one of the most often used means of dominance was teasing and joking. Certain jokes depend upon shared assumptions, which encompass the 'sexual prowess' of men, the idea that women are the objects of derision and the willingness of the audience to ratify these attributes by laughing. The use of sexual ridicule was used as a very effective weapon against the females:

> Whilst laying out old newspapers for a painting and craftwork session in a class of 8-year-olds, one of the boys came across the 'Page 3' section of *The Sun*. Giggling to three of this friends he held up the paper to a girl in the class and taunted her: 'This is what you'll look like when you grow up, Tracy'. The girl felt offended and turned to the teacher 'No I won't, will I Miss?'

The teacher looked on but not impassively, the ridicule had also affected her as indicated by her uneasy response: 'I try not to make anything of such incidents ... you know what children are like'. She then went on to confiscate the newspaper depicting the semi-nude woman from the boy who was still flaunting it at a number of the girls. This form of ridicule was used to lay claim to a specific space and also to confirm the 'physical inferiority' of women. This kind of sexism cuts across class (Wood, 1984):

> In the first year juniors of Applegate, Oliver was playing with clay in the project area. He proceeded to mock the female body by affixing clay points to his chest; 'Hey, this what you'll have when you get big', to the girl present. The other two boys with him joined in the laughter while Claire fled the area humiliated.

Upon hearing so much noise the teacher came to investigate. Claire stated that the boys were being 'naughty'; she could not express her confusion or the form of insult aimed at her (and *all* females) despite her articulacy but as Holly (1985) states girls do understand the nature of sexism and neither have they accepted its inevitability. Claire did not enter the project area alone, but always made sure she was with other girls during the rest of my participant observation in this class.

In ascertaining that boys negotiated space for themselves, it must not be forgotten that girls attempted to do likewise — although their methods differed. This was particularly apparent with regard to their relationship with the male teachers (amongst junior girls). Girls tended to congregate more at male teachers' desks and stay longer than the boys. They were often given the task of handing out classroom materials which gave them a temporary position of power, and one which they sometimes used to extend their influence further. With the support of the teacher a girl, Joanna, was able to refuse the demands of a particular boy who was asking for one of the books she was giving out:

> I'll give you a book when I come to your table.
> I want one now! demanded the boy.

The boy was made to return to his seat under the auspices of the teacher: 'Sit down Robert Johnson, the only person who should be out of their seat should be the one giving out books'. Joanna proceeded to give out the books to her friends first and made the boys wait 'til last. However, this particular kind of influence is double-edged, in that duties in question can be seen as mirroring the 'service' role that women play in the outside world.

References

DAVIES, L. (1979) 'Deadlier than the male? Girls conformity and deviance in schools', in BARTON, L. and MEIGHAN, S. (Eds) *Schools, Pupils and Deviance*, Nafferton.

HOLLY, L. (1985) 'Mary, Jane and Virginia Woolf: Ten-year-old girls talking', in WEINER, G. (Ed.) *Just a Bunch of Girls*, Open University Press.

MAHONEY, P. (1985) *Schools for Boys? Co-education Reassessed*, Hutchinson.

SHAW, J. (1977) 'Sexual divisions in the classroom'. Paper given at the Teaching Girls to be Women Conference, Essex, April.

SPENDER, D. and SARAH, E. (1980) *Learning to Lose*, Women's Press.

WOOD, J. (1984) 'Groping towards sexism: Boys' sex talk', in McROBBIE, A. and NAVA, M. (Eds) *Gender and Generation*, Macmillan.

The Intellectual Search of Young Children

(From Tizard, B. and Hughes, M., 1987, 'The intellectual search of young children', in Pollard, A. (Ed.) *Children and Their Primary Schools*, Lewes, Falmer Press, pp. 31–4.)

Carefully conducted research with pre-school children in their home setting has greatly added to our understanding of learning in the early years. Research on language development in the home shows that interaction between pre-school children and their parents is a powerful learning experience. It is one of the most important contexts in which children come to understand their world, and in which they become competent language users themselves, well before formal schooling.

This extract shows, in close detail, how a young child pursues understanding in this favoured one-to-one interactive language context. It also links in with themes raised in earlier extracts on children starting school, demonstrating the possibilities for sustained talk and problem-solving in the home in a way which reception classes can rarely offer.

Intellectual Search: Struggling with Several Complex Ideas

The learning potential of what we have called 'passages of intellectual search' is well illustrated in the following long episode, in which the child's confusion about the relationship between money, work and consumer goods was exposed, and to some extent clarified. The conversation started while Rosy and her mother were having lunch, and was triggered off by the appearance of the window-cleaner in the garden. Rosy's mother went off to the kitchen to get him some water, and called out to her neighbour, Pamela.

Child: What did Pamela say?
Mother: She's having to pay everybody else's bills for the window-cleaner, 'cause they're all out.
Child: Why they all out?
Mother: 'Cause they're working or something.
Child: Aren't they silly!
Mother: Well, you have to work to earn money, don't you?
Child: Yeah ... If they know what day the window-cleaner come they should stay here.
Mother: They should stay at home? Well, I don't know, they can't always ...

At this point the window-cleaner appeared at the dining-room window, and cleaned the window while Rosy and her mother carried on with lunch. The conversation switched to what they might have for pudding, and what they might do that afternoon. Rosy, however, was still thinking about the window-cleaner . . .

1	*Child:*	Mummy?
2	*Mother:*	Mmm.
3	*Child:*	Umm . . . she can't pay everybody's, er . . . all the bills to the window-cleaner, can she?
4	*Mother:*	No, she can't pay everybody's bills . . . she sometimes pays mine if I'm out.
5	*Child:*	'Cause it's fair.
6	*Mother:*	Mm, it is.
7	*Child:*	Umm, but where does she leave the money?
8	*Mother:*	She doesn't leave it anywhere, she hands it to the window-cleaner, after he's finished.
9	*Child:*	And then she gives it to us?
10	*Mother:*	No, no, she doesn't have to pay us.
11	*Child:*	Then the window-cleaner gives it to us?
12	*Mother:*	No, we give the window-cleaner money, he does work for us, and we have to give him money.
13	*Child:*	Why?
14	*Mother:*	Well, because he's been working for us cleaning our windows. He doesn't do it for nothing.
15	*Child:*	Why do you have money if you have . . . if people clean your windows?
16	*Mother:*	Well, the window-cleaner needs money, doesn't he?
17	*Child:*	Why?
18	*Mother:*	To buy clothes for his children and food for them to eat.
19	*Child:*	Well, sometimes window-cleaners don't have children.
20	*Mother:*	Quite often they do.
21	*Child:*	And something on his own to eat, and for curtains?
22	*Mother:*	And for paying his gas bills and electricity bill. And for paying for his petrol for his car. All sorts of things you have to pay for, you see. You have to earn money somehow, and he earns it by cleaning other people's windows, and big shop windows and things.
23	*Child:*	And then the person who got the money gives it to people . . .

It seems until turn 11 Rosy was under the impression that the window-cleaner pays the housewives, and not the other way round. In the course of the conversation the relationship between work, money and goods is slowly outlined for her, but it is still unclear from her last remark whether she has really grasped all that has been said. The conversation in fact continues later on, after Rosy has watched her mother actually hand over the money to the window-cleaner:

1 *Mother:* I expect the window-cleaner's going to have his lunch now.
2 *Child:* He would have all *that* much lunch [stretches arms out wide] because he's been working all the time.
3 *Mother:* Mm ... I expect he gets very hungry, doesn't he? I expect he goes to the pub and has some beer and sandwiches.
4 *Child:* He has to pay for that.
5 *Mother:* Yes, he does.
6 *Child:* Not always, though.
7 *Mother:* Mm, always.
8 *Child:* Why not?
9 *Mother:* They won't give him any beer and sandwiches if he doesn't have any money.

At this point Rosy clearly wonders why he cannot do without money to go to a pub:

10 *Child:* But why doesn't he use his own food?
11 *Mother:* Well, he might do, I don't know, perhaps he brings his own sandwiches, do you think?
12 *Child:* He go to a pub and he has his lunch some *and* he has it at his home.
13 *Mother:* Oh, he wouldn't do both, no.
14 *Child:* He would do all of those a few times. But he usually go to a pub.

Rosy's mother ends the conversation, with an example of 'planning ahead' child management, (see Tizard and Hughes, 1984, chapter 4)

15 *Mother:* Mm. Come on, sit up. Now I'm going to do the washing up, then I'll read you a story, and then I'm going to read the newspaper a bit.

Rosy's remarks in this third conversation (especially turn 6, 'Not always, though') suggest that she has only hazily grasped what she has been told, and her understanding of money transactions still seems shaky. This is not because she lacked the intellectual capacity, nor because her mother's explanations were too complex. Rather it seems likely that this conversation reveals something which is characteristic of the slow and gradual way in which a child's understanding of an abstract or complex topic is built up. It may take a considerable time, as well as several more conversations like the one above, before Rosy has grasped the complexities of the relationships involved, and she may have to return to the same topic again and again before she achieves full understanding.

It is interesting to consider why Rosy keeps asking questions on this topic. Clearly, her initial questions were asked out of curiosity aroused by the unusual event in the daily routine — the arrival of the window-cleaner and the subsequent conversation between her mother and the neighbour. But her later return to the topic suggests something beyond this initial curiosity. Indeed, it suggests that Rosy is at some level aware that she has not grasped the relationships involved, and that her questions are motivated by her desire to clarify her misconceptions. Why she should be aware of her own lack of understanding is not clear — she could perfectly well have stayed with the idea that the neighbour did receive money from the window-cleaner, and got on with her lunch. The fact that she did not suggests that she was at some level dissatisfied with her own grasp of the situation, perhaps because it didn't fit with other facts that she knew, and wanted it sorted out.

Confusion about the relationship between work, money and goods seemed to be less common among the working-class children. Perhaps because their fathers' work was more clearly related to money, rather than to the interest of the job, or because with a more limited income the arrival of the weekly pay packet was a more important event, the relationship between money and work was more often discussed in working-class families.

It should be clear by now that mothers often gave answers to the children's questions that were less than full, or that failed to meet the central point of the question. Advances in children's understanding seemed to depend as much on their own efforts to achieve greater clarity as on the quality of their mothers' initial explanations.

Reference

TIZARD, B. and HUGHES, M. (1984) *Young Children Learning*, London, Fontana.

Children's Control of Learning

(From Rowland, S., 1984, *The Enquiring Classroom*, Lewes, Falmer Press, pp. 150–2.)

Here Stehpen Rowland draws together some of the main insights emerging from his teaching and research experience with junior school children. His research offers us a vivid and detailed account of classroom learning processes from which he has developed theories about the nature of teaching and learning. One of his key concerns, which he explores here, relates to the way in which children come to exercise control over their own learning experiences in order to make sense of them. A second concern considers the 'holistic' nature of learning. In this, he looks at the ways in which children acquire skills, knowledge and understanding in response to real challenges which they are motivated to master, and which have relevance for them. Learning thus takes place in a meaningful context and is not separated, in a mechanistic way, from the situations for which it is intended. Stephen Rowland's work echoes many of the themes about the nature of learning arising in several of the extracts in this book, linking understanding of early learning to later development.

I have traced the theme of the learner's control in relation to the external human and material resources of the classroom. But we can also see learning as being the attempt to control the internal life of thought and imagination. In respect of this inward life, control consists in a sense of awareness. What our evidence suggested was that even at the age of 9 or 10, given the external conditions of control, children are able to demonstrate an awareness not only of the subject matter they investigate, but of the very form of their investigation. A level of abstract thinking was apparent in which they were able to stand back from the immediacy of their experience (be it a scientific enquiry, a practical task or a 'philosophical' debate). They appeared able to operate not only upon the materials with which they worked, but also upon these operations themselves. Such thinking fore-shadows what Piaget described as formal operations. It appeared to be important, for this level of thinking to be expressed, that the children make their *own* abstractions within a language context which is theirs. These are important elements of the children's control over their investigations.

I interpreted much of the children's scientific activity as closely parallel-ing that of the adult scientist, with hypotheses being framed, tested, refined and even, at times, deductive reasoning being employed. It appears that the young children's work, as scientists or philosophers, was limited not so much by any limits in their cognitive style as by the limitations of their knowledge and experience. The plausibility of viewing the children's activity as like that of the adult scientist depends upon our recognition that the children may be working at the frontiers of their understanding.

Writing is another process through which control is exercised, for by representing the world in written language the writer reflects upon it with a higher level of awareness. When children write about their experience, or their imaginings, they are not merely recording them. They make that experience or image objective to them — they stand back from its immediacy — so that it may be shaped or transformed by being written. In this respect, the children's writing contained this same element of operating upon their experience as did much of their practical and scientific investigations.

Children like to write about the unusual, whether imagined or real. What was striking in this kind of writing was that the process of writing appeared to be largely directed towards relating the unusual to more every-day experience. Children, like adults, enjoy fantasy, but fantasy, to be meaningful and significant, must have its roots in reality. Story writing seeks to provide this relationship, and so, through their imaginative writing, children are brought to newer understandings of reality. This was particularly evident in those stories in which the children were led, through the process of writing, to consider characterization and the 'eternal' problems of the human condition. This approach to the interpretation of children's writing, which seems justified in that it allowed sense to be made of their stories, leads one to view the child writer as confronting the same kinds of literary issues as confront the adult writer. It is also a process through which children operate upon, and gain a degree of control over, their imaginative powers, powers which are, arguably, at the heart of the intellect.

Through my attempts to interpret the children's classroom activity I have now sketched out two aspects of their control: first, its outward manifestation as an attempt to control their own learning activity in relation to the external material and human world; and second, its inward manifestation as an attempt and process by which they gain a degree of control over their intellectual and imaginative powers.

In my understanding of how growth takes place, these two aspects of control are brought together. Outwardly, skill is seen as arising and being developed in response to the requirements of the activity and its goals. Rather than being an aspect of development which requires practice in isolation before it can be used towards creative ends, it in fact emerges in response to those ends. Its development takes place within a context which provides not only motivation for its practice, but one which enables the child to see its purpose and develop an awareness of it.

This awareness of a skill, or rather, the awareness of a need for a skill, appears to be an essential condition for its emergence. An awareness that there is something we need to know, a skill we need to master or a convention we need to adopt is a starting point for further growth. It is the inward aspect of the need for control. Following the children's work, it appeared that this awareness grew as a result of their inventiveness. As the children invented ways of resolving their problems, so they became prepared — or reached a 'state of readiness' — for new knowledge. Thus inventiveness and the mastery of conventions are not opposing aspects of learning, but on the contrary, the one paves the way for the other. To suggest that a teacher emphasizes the development of skill rather than the development of creativity, or vice versa, is to fail to recognize this close relationship between them. Children cannot invent all that they need to know. But invention can bring them to an awareness of the form that newly required knowledge might take. It is as if it shapes a space in the child's understanding which is thus made ready to accommodate new learning.

A role for the teacher at these points of growth should be apparent. We have to watch out for cues from the children that this state of awareness has been reached. Through 'conversation' we attempt to promote it and to elicit cues. Such cues may be interpreted as an implicit request by the child for control to be temporarily delegated to the teacher (or indeed to another child, book or other instructional resource) for a sequence of instruction. It is important that this control be handed back to the child at an early stage, so that any new knowledge gained can be reinterpreted in terms of the child's activity and its purposes, her broader experience, and can be incorporated into her expanding repertoire of inventiveness. Only then will instruction confirm the validity of invention as being the source and motive for learning, rather than undermine the inventiveness which children are so eager to bring to the classroom in the early years of their schooling.

I have now drawn out the central strands of argument that emerged from interpretations of some of the children's work in Chris Harris's classroom. Many of these ideas had begun to take shape in my earlier classroom practice and were suggested by the accounts which Michael Armstrong gave of children's work, in my own classroom, in his book, *Closely Observed Children*. They thus represent not the product of a research project in isolation, but the present point in a continuing struggle to understand children by teaching them, which is given focus and direction by means of a sustained classroom enquiry.

Understanding Classroom Effectiveness

(From Mortimore, P. *et al.*, 1988, *School Matters*, London, Open Books, pp. 226–31.)

The Inner London Education Authority Junior School Project differed from some previous major studies of the primary school in that it focused on pupil progress as well as on attainment throughout the junior years. Others had attempted to correlate variables with attainment only. In this, the study has given a new perspective on 'school effectiveness'.

The findings suggest that, whilst home background and social class affect pupil achievement, schools and teachers also have crucial roles to play. Their effect is so significant that the best schools and teachers can reverse the social disadvantages which working-class children may bring to formal schooling. By the same token, a child's progress can be depressed by less favourable school circumstances.

The research identified school-wide factors that were influential in determining progress. These are reported elsewhere in these series (Volume 2). This extract discusses the factors at class level that were discovered to be important. The findings may very well challenge a number of assumptions underlying some existing primary school practices. They should certainly be of interest to anyone wishing to understand how teachers and classrooms can better promote children's learning.

Class Level 'Givens'

We found consistent evidence that a change (or several changes) of class teacher during the school year could have a detrimental effect upon pupils' learning and upon their non-cognitive development. Thus, the experience of a change of class teacher during the school year was negatively related to effects in the cognitive areas. For those pupils who had experienced two or more changes in one year (or one change in each of two consecutive years) it appeared to be particularly damaging. Conversely, schools where few pupils had experienced such changes, were associated with positive effects in both attitudes and self-concept.

Class Size

Amongst the given variables affecting classes, the average class size, which ranged from 15 to 34 in the first year, was related to mathematics progress. Pupils in schools with smaller classes made more progress though this only reached significance in the first year. Schools where classes had an average of 24 or fewer pupils generally made better progress than schools with larger classes, in particular, those with 27 or more pupils. This result is important because the majority of previous studies have generally found class size to be unimportant in explaining pupil achievement (see Simpson, 1982). It is likely to be due, in part, to the fact that this study examined progress rather than attainment. Also, most studies which have examined the impact of class size have examined the effects on achievement in language-based areas, rather than mathematics. When account is taken of other factors, the impact of class size increases. Thus, because mathematics progress was related to voluntary status, when this factor was controlled (by means of partial correlation analysis) the relationship between class size and mathematics progress was increased and was also significant in the third year ($r = 0.37$ year 1 and $r = 21$ year 3). In addition to a relationship with pupils' mathematics progress, we found that smaller class sizes were related to beneficial effects upon a number of other areas too, particularly the non-cognitive.

Class Level Policies

Many variables connected with the way teachers taught were also related to pupils' progress and development during the junior years. The results of the Junior School Project show that the methods and strategies adopted by the teacher in the classroom and the nature of her or his communication with pupils can be of great importance in aiding effectiveness.

Communicating with Pupils

There was strong evidence that those teachers who spent greater amounts of time communicating with pupils about the content of their work had a positive effect upon progress in all the cognitive areas. In addition, many of the non-cognitive areas benefited from this focus on work too. The amount of teacher time devoted to giving pupils feedback about their work also had a positive association with progress in a number of areas.

Conversely, where teachers spent a larger amount of their time not communicating with pupils or where they spent a higher percentage of their time communicating about routine (non-work) matters, the impact upon pupils' cognitive and non-cognitive development was negative. Progress was also improved in classes where pupils were involved in their work and where a high level of industry was observed. It appears, therefore, that high levels of teacher-pupil communication, a clear focus upon matters directly concerning work, and a high level of pupil industry all help to promote learning and non-cognitive development.

Pupil Noise and Movement

High levels of pupil noise and of pupil movement around the classroom were correlated negatively with progress and development. This is not to say that the absence of pupil talk and movement was necessarily beneficial. In fact none of the classes observed were completely quiet and all allowed freedom of pupil movement to some extent. It was clear, however, that high levels of noise and of movement were not associated with progress. These two factors were themselves related to less teacher time spent communicating about work, and with lower levels of pupil involvement with work.

Class Interactions

The amount of teacher time spent interacting with the class (rather than with individuals or groups) had a significant positive relationship with progress in a wide range of areas. In contrast, where a very high proportion of the teachers' time was spent communicating with individual pupils, a negative impact was recorded. Two points, however, should be stressed. First, interacting with the class did not necessarily mean whole class teaching. In fact, measures of the extent to which a whole class teaching approach was adopted were very weakly and not significantly related to progress. Rather, it was the proportion of interactions involving the class, rather than any attempt to teach the whole class as one unit, that seems to have been associated with beneficial effects. Second, from analysis of the observational data, it was found that the majority of teachers' interactions were with individual pupils (over 60 per cent, on average). However, some teachers more frequently introduced topics to the whole class, entered into discussions with them, and made teaching points to everyone. This was the case whether children were working individually, or in groups on different tasks, or on the same activity. Such class interactions appeared to be effective in promoting pupil progress. Effects tended to be positive where the teachers spent around a quarter or more of their time in communication with the class as a whole. This finding is in broad agreement with those reported by Galton and Simon (1980).

The association between the proportion of class interactions and pupils' progress may reflect the greater amount of attention received by members of the class through this mode of teaching. This is probably because, when all, or nearly all, of a teacher's time is spent communicating with individual children, each child can receive only a relatively infrequent number of such contacts in any school day, even though the teacher may be extemely busy. On average, pupils received only 11 individual contacts with the teacher in any one day. Given that those with poor behaviour or particular learning difficulties tended to receive a higher number of contacts, other children would tend to receive fewer than the average. The skill of the teacher, therefore, lies in achieving a balance of class, group, and individual communications which will maximise the amount of contact she or he has with each pupil without robbing those contacts of all individualised content.

Mix of Curriculum Activities

There was much variation between classes in the proportion of time during which all the pupils in a class were working on the same curriculum area in sessions, whether they worked alone, in groups, or as a class. A larger proportion of sessions spent on single activities (for example, everybody working on language, though sometimes on different language topics, or on the same topic but at different levels) was related positively to pupils' progress. For a few of the outcomes it was even beneficial for two curriculum activities to be running concurrently. In contrast, where teachers made more use of sessions devoted to a mix of curriculum activities (working in three or more curriculum areas) at the same time, a significant negative impact on progress was found.

It is possible that the frequent use of mixed sessions may have an adverse impact because teacher attention and energy becomes divided between children working in a variety of curriculum areas. Alternatively, the organisation of mixed activities within one session may require higher levels of teacher organisation and management skill if it is to prove effective. These possibilities are discussed at greater length in the next section.

Our results suggest that it may be more effective for a teacher to keep a fairly narrow focus within individual sessions. However, an identical approach in all lessons is neither possible nor desirable. Therefore, it seems that teachers should maintain flexibility in their approach, adopting different forms of organisation, in response to the class and the curriculum area, but bearing in mind the difficulties inherent in using a high proportion of mixed-curriculum sessions.

Stimulating and Well-Organised Teaching

There was evidence that the more time teachers spent asking questions the greater the positive effect upon progress. Furthermore the more teachers were able to make use of higher-order questions and statements (those designed to elicit problem solving, reasoning or imaginative responses from children) the better the progress made. This finding indicates clearly the beneficial effect of intellectually challenging teaching, a feature which relates to teachers' expectations of their pupils. Not surprisingly, the efficient organisation of classroom work, so that there was always plenty for pupils to do (irrespective of the mode of organisation), tended to promote a number of favourable attitudes. In addition, when the work itself was interesting and the lessons bright and stimulating there were clear positive relationships within a wide range of outcomes. Telling or reading stories to children proved to be important too. The more time teachers were able to spend on this activity, the greater the effects upon a number of areas including, interestingly, oracy. Finally, when more time was spent by teachers listening to pupils read, individually, a link was evident with greater progress in writing, and better attitudes in a number of areas.

Pupil Responsibility for Managing their Work

When the pupils' day was given a structure or framework by the teacher such that children were given single tasks to undertake over fairly short periods of time such as a lesson or an afternoon, and were encouraged to manage the completion of the tasks independently of the teacher, the impact was positive for a range of cognitive and non-cognitive outcomes. However, when pupils were given a large measure of responsibility for managing a programme of work over a whole day, or over lengthy periods of time, the effect upon progress was found to be negative in a number of areas. It may be that such large responsibilities were too onerous for many children of the junior age range to undertake effectively without adequate support and guidance. It should be remembered that, even in the third year, nearly 40 per cent of the sample said that they tended to have difficulty in concentrating on their work. In addition, we found that when pupils were given a high degree of choice as to the content and nature of their work activities, the results tended to be poorer pupil progress. The level of inter-pupil co-operation encouraged was important too. Very high levels were associated with poorer effects in both cognitive and non-cognitive spheres. However, there was some indication that in these two areas — pupil choice and co-operation — the effects upon oracy were distinctly positive. This may perhaps be due to the need for a certain degree of communicative competence when negotiating with others and when making choices.

Pupil Groupings

There was some evidence that where pupils worked on the same task as other pupils of roughly the same ability, or when all pupils worked within the same curriculum area but on different tasks at their own level, the effect upon progress was positive. In contrast, where all pupils worked on exactly the same task the effects were negative. This suggests the importance of teachers being sensitive to the varied abilities of pupils and of the need to provide work at appropriate levels of difficulty.

Textbooks

For mathematics there was evidence that, in the later junior years, when teachers followed textbooks closely the result was a positive effect upon progress, not only in mathematics itself, but also on pupils' attitudes to this curriculum area. Interestingly, no such relationships were identified for the use of language textbooks and progress in or attitudes towards language work.

Praise and Criticism

There was a significant negative association between the amount of time teachers spent making critical comments and pupils' progress in a range of areas. Conversely, time spent on praise or neutral feedback about behaviour was related to positive effects. A positive attitude to the class on the part of the teacher was important too. It related positively to progress in mathematics and to several of the non-cognitive outcomes. It seems, therefore, that positive reinforcement and firm but fair classroom management is more effective than a reliance on control through criticism. Furthermore, the positive climate created through the teachers' attitude and use of praise is also beneficial.

References

GALTON, M. and SIMON, B. (1980) *Progress and Performance in the Primary Classroom*, London, Routledge and Kegan Paul.
SIMPSON, S.N. (1982) Statistical Assessment of School Effects Using Educational Survey Data. Ph.D. thesis, University of London.

Young Children's Attainment and Progress in School

(From Tizard, B. *et al.*, 1988, *Young Children at School in the Inner City*, London, Lawrence Erlbaum Associates, pp. 167–76, 181–3.)

Child en's underachievement at school has been a concern of educational researchers for ov r twenty years. This study has built on previous understandings and has added new c mensions to analysis of the issue. It followed the attainment and progress of children from thirty-three inner city schools as they moved from nursery class to junior school, and attempted to explain why some children made more progress than others, given what, on the surface, might appear to be common school experiences.

Children brought skills from home to school which were found to relate to achievement but, as in the ILEA Junior School Project cited in the last extract, children's progress was also found to be affected by the teacher and the nature of the curriculum. The researchers questioned the level of teacher expectations and the breadth of the curriculum considering each to be possible depressants of attainment and progress. Gender and ethnicity were also found to relate to children's learning.

This extract summarizes the main findings linking classroom experience to attainment and progress. It sets the discussion in the context of the national curriculum, assessment and testing and the possible consequent changes which might affect classroom and curriculum organization.

Factors Related to Attainment and Progress in the Infant School

Pre-school Attainments

At the outset we wish to distinguish between attainment, that is, achievement at a particular point in time, and relative progress, that is, the difference in progress made by children who had similar educational attainments at school entry. If all children progressed at the same rate, then those who were doing best at school entry would continue to be doing best at the end of infant school. We found that this was, to a considerable extent, the case, and that the strongest predictor of attainment at age seven was the amount of 3R knowledge that the children had before ever they started school. In the case of reading, the strongest predictor of reading ability at age seven was the number of letters the child could identify at age four-and-three-quarters. The range of reading and maths knowledge at age four, even within a largely working-class sample, was very great. Whilst a few children could read, many did not know the basic conventions of written language. Some children could write their names neatly, others could only produce an unformed scribble. Those children with a head start tended to maintain it on the whole.

This relationship between early and later attainment is not necessarily causal. For example, it cannot be assumed that it was *because* children had some knowledge of letters at age four that they read better than their classmates at age seven. Another factor, such as the child's interest in books, or belonging to a 'literary' kind of family, could have been the cause of both the early and the later attainment. In order to establish whether or not this is the case, it would be necessary to show in a controlled experiment that teaching letters to four-year-olds, irrespective of their interest in books, family characteristics, etc. leads to improved reading attainment later. Bryant and Bradley have carried out such experiments with letter sounding with six-year-olds. They showed that children aged six to eight who were taught letter sounds and taught to analyse the sounds in words read significantly better at age eight than children who had not received this help (Bryant and Bradley, 1985).

We ourselves would guess that knowledge of letters and other early reading skills do bear a causal relationship to later attainment, for two reasons. Firstly, although children can certainly make some progress in reading without recognising the shape or sound of individual letters, learning them involves paying attention to the structure of words, which is one component of reading. Secondly, those children assessed by the reception teacher as having some early reading skills would be likely to be given reading books earlier than the other children. Unless the teacher then gave a great deal of extra attention to the children with fewer skills, the gap between the children which was present before they started school would inevitably be reinforced. It should be added that teachers can hardly be blamed for this situation, since they are not trained or encouraged to set goals for low-attaining school entrants. Indeed, in our interview with the reception-class teachers only a fifth of them described academic progress as one of their two main aims. The majority of reception teachers seemed to believe that socialisation (by which they meant instilling classroom discipline and encouraging good relationships with other children) must take priority in the first year. Yet, our evidence suggests that the reception year is particularly important for progress.

We certainly would not recommend on the basis of our study that parents and teachers should concentrate on teaching letters *at the expense* of other reading-related activities. Learning to read is a complex process, involving not only recognising letters and words, but also being able to extract the meaning of a written passage. Reading aloud to children is an important way to assist this process, by arousing their interest in, and enjoyment of, books and motivating them to learn to read. But the evidence certainly suggests that as one aspect of learning to read, teaching letter sounds is likely to be helpful. There is little evidence that parents' attempts to teach reading and writing to pre-school children will interfere with, or even hold back, children's progress, and whether or not teachers approve, parents will go on making these attempts. The supposed ill effects of such teaching is the first of the current myths about infant schooling that we would wish to contest.

Since the extent of pre-school children's literacy and numeracy was so strongly related to later attainment, we tried to establish where the children had obtained their knowledge. It was not possible by this stage to discover what individual school entrants had been taught in the nursery class, but in our interviews with the nursery teachers we asked them what 3R knowledge and skills they expected children to acquire before they left the nursery. Whilst there was considerable variation amongst the teachers, in general they put little emphasis on teaching literacy and numeracy, and their expectations in these areas were often low. For example, a third of the nursery-class teachers told us that they did not expect children to be able to count above five when they left the nursery, whereas in fact we found that on average the children could count to at least ten. And only a third of the nursery teachers expected their children to know the names and sounds of any letters by the time they left the nursery, whereas we found that on average the children could identify five letters.

All the nursery classes had a plentiful supply of books, and the staff regularly read to the children. But simply introducing children to books in a happy atmosphere does not ensure that they will make a connection between meaning and print, or have any understanding of written language. We found that on leaving the nursery less than half of the children understood that in a picture book it is the print that is read, rather than the pictures. Those children whose parents did not teach them anything about written language often did not learn this in the nursery class either. We should make it clear that we are not advocating that nursery-class children should be sat down with reading primers. In an observational study in children's homes, one of us showed how some mothers of four-year-olds teach number concepts through board and card games, counting biscuits, coins, etc., and embedded learning to read and write in real tasks like writing to Granny, or signing a birthday card (Tizard and Hughes, 1984). The basic conventions of written language can be taught by pointing out whilst reading aloud that print goes from left to right, and down the page, and by directing children's attention to the words and numbers in their environment. It is these kinds of activities that nursery teachers should, we believe, emphasise more. Again, it needs to be stressed that the nursery teachers in our study were following the advice of inspectors, sometimes against their own inclinations. Since we began our research, a trend towards more emphasis on early literacy and numeracy has taken place in ILEA nursery classes.

Factors within the home appeared to make an important contribution to pre-school children's 3R knowledge. Social class has been found to be an important factor by other researchers. We had few middle-class parents within our sample, but we found that those mothers with higher educational qualifications tended to have more literate and numerate four-year-olds.

The associations between the parent's educational practices and pre-school literacy were even stronger, especially the extent to which parents read to children and provided them with books, and also taught them about letters. But much the strongest association was with the child's own ability to define words, which no doubt reflects both innate ability and the extent to which parents talked about words and their meaning with their children. Again, we need to point out that, in order to show that these associations are causal, controlled experiments of the effects on later reading attainment of, for example, reading aloud to pre-school children, would be necessary.

Factors Within the Infant School

School attainment at age seven was not inexorably determined at school entry. In statistical terms, pre-school test results explained about half of the variation in top infant test scores. Although by and large those children who did best at age four did best at age seven, some children did better than would have been predicted from their pre-school scores, whereas others did worse. From an educational point of view, it is important to know what parents and teachers were doing that was responsible for a relative acceleration or slowing of progress. We found that, whereas parents had a big influence on the level of pre-school attainments, factors in the school were more important once the children started at infant school.

The two major factors in the school associated with progress were the range of 3R curriculum taught to the children, and the expectations that teachers had of them. One further factor, the particular school the child attended, was also, to a lesser extent, associated with progress. All three factors were interrelated, but all had an independent association with progress. This means, for example, that irrespective of which school a child attended, or whether or not their teacher had high expectations of them, children's attainments were higher if they had been introduced to a wider 3R curriculum.

We found that the amount of progress the children made depended to a significant extent on the school they attended. The difference was most marked in writing, but it was still significant, of the order of about five points on a standardised test, in reading and maths. For reading, the difference between schools was most marked in the reception year. During this year children in some schools made considerable progress, whereas in others, children with a similar level of knowledge of reading at the beginning of the year made very little progress. Since the correlations between early and later reading attainments became more marked at the end of the reception year, these findings suggest that the reception year offers an important opportunity to give special assistance to the lower-attaining children. In our opinion, a school reading policy for this important year is essential.

In the case of maths, we found no difference between schools in the amount of progress children made in the reception year, but marked differences in the middle and top infant years. These findings are not surprising, given the very small amount of maths teaching that we observed in the reception year in almost all the schools. Many teachers would object that we have underestimated the amount of maths that was going on in the reception year, since children learn a great deal of maths whilst playing in the sand tray, or with Lego. They would argue that experiences of this kind are needed before children are ready for number work. However, evidence is accumulating that children enter school with much more understanding of basic mathematical concepts and skills than is generally recognised. Many four-year-olds can judge the relative size of numbers, count objects, add and subtract small numbers, and understand the inverse relation between addition and subtraction (see review in Young-Loveridge, 1987; Hughes, 1986). Building on these skills, for example, by the use of games with playing cards, dice, etc., seems likely to be at least as fruitful as sand and water play for the development of mathematical skills. This would seem to be a promising area for collaboration with parents.

Several research studies before ours have suggested that the reception year may be of special educational importance. One US researcher discovered that children who had been taught by a particular first grade teacher, Miss 'A.', had higher educational qualifications and higher status jobs as adults than did adults who had been taught as children in parallel classes in the same school. It was said of Miss 'A.' that: it did not matter what background or abilities the beginning pupil had; there was no way that the pupil was not going to read by the end of grade one ... She invariably stayed after hours to help the slow learners ... and could remember each pupil by name even after an interval of 20 years. The researchers found no evidence that parents had been able to select Miss 'A.'s' class for their children. The initial boost that she seemed to give to the children's confidence and attainments was present at the end of elementary school, and the researchers argue that this left the children with an advantage throughout their educational career (Pederson, Faucher, and Eaton, 1978; see also for another study of a reception teacher, Rist, 1970).

Although we have said that children in different schools made different amounts of progress, we have some evidence that in fact the differences were between classes rather than schools, that is, it was the individual teacher (as in the case of Miss 'A.') who made a difference to the child's progress. As to why children made more progress in some schools or classes than others, we only have clues, rather than conclusions, from our findings, because we did not set out to study differences between schools and teachers. But since we found that the 3R curriculum taught varied between schools, and was associated with progress, we suspect that it played an important role in producing these differences.

Up to now, rather little interest has been shown by educational researchers in the infant-school curriculum, that is, exactly what 3R skills and knowledge children are taught at each stage. Yet it is clear that attainment and progress depend crucially on whether children are given particular learning experiences — they cannot be expected to tell the time, for example, unless someone has taught them. We found a wide range between schools or classes in what children of the same age were taught, and this could not be accounted for by the intake of the school.

Within classes, we found a consistent relationship between the teachers' expectations of individual children at the beginning of the year and the range of the 3R curriculum they were introduced to. This was true even when controlling for the children's initial skills. That is, of two children with similar skills at the beginning of the year, the one judged by the teacher to have higher academic potential than the other would be introduced to a wider range of 3R knowledge during the year. It might be argued that this simply means that the teacher was a good judge of which child would in fact be better able to cope with a wider curriculum, but our findings suggest that the teachers were influenced by other than strictly academic considerations — for example, we found that their expectations were influenced by their opinion that a child was 'a pleasure to teach'.

Teachers have expectations not only of individual children, but of the class as a whole. The only way we were able to glimpse these in our study was by asking teachers why they had not introduced certain curriculum items to *any* of the children in their class. Whilst some teachers answered that these items were too difficult for children of this age, others said that they were too difficult for the children in this school. Yet we know that in other schools, with a similar intake, teachers had introduced these items. We suspect that low expectations are an important cause of the low level of attainment in many of the schools we studied. Our sample of children were, on average, well below the national norms in reading and maths, and by the end of infant school 25 per cent were definitely poor readers. (These findings are not necessarily true of ILEA as a whole.) We found no evidence that the children caught up in the junior school. At the end of the first year in junior school both reading and maths scores were highly correlated with those of the year before, and the poor readers had made relatively little progress.

Low attainment in the schools was certainly not caused by a general state of chaos or confusion in the classroom. In three-quarters of our observations, we found children busy working, or organising work, and disruptive or aggressive behaviour in the classroom was rare. Nor was it the case that the children spent a great deal of time playing; the proportion of classroom time devoted to play ranged from 14 per cent in the reception year to 2 per cent in the top-infant year. It does, however, seem to us likely that the low level of reading attainment in the schools was related to the small amount of time that the children spent reading. In our observations we found that only 4 per cent of the working time in top-infant classes (roughly eight minutes a day) was spent by the children in any kind of reading, and quite a lot of this time was taken up with rapidly flipping through books.

This figure is, of course, an average. In some classes none of the children did any reading during the days we observed them; others averaged twenty-seven minutes per child. In nearly all these latter classes, instead of trying to hear each child read, the teachers had arranged for children to read to each other in pairs or in small groups (Farquhar, 1987). It seems important to evaluate whether this approach does, in fact, improve reading skills and the enjoyment of reading, and if it does, to bring it to the attention of more teachers.

If, as we believe, the expectations of the teachers were too low, a crucial issue for future investigation is to establish how expectations can be raised in a largely working-class area. Initially, it is obviously both desirable and feasible to raise the expectations of teachers in low-achieving working-class schools to those of teachers in higher-achieving schools in similar areas. A more ambitious, and very important, project would be to see just how high one can reasonably set expectations in a working-class area — is it possible by this process to achieve the standards of a middle-class school? The question is one of great importance in primary education, since if teachers' expectations are low, children will inevitably leave infant school with a handicap.

There was a serious mismatch between the level of the children's attainment at age seven and the expectations of the parents, especially the black parents. About a half of both the black and white parents told us that they would like their child to go to a university or polytechnic, and over a third of the black parents wanted their child to get a professional job. These are perfectly reasonable aspirations, no doubt shared by the teachers for their own children. Yet only 12 per cent of all young people entered full-time higher education in 1984, and 70 per cent of students accepted for university come from social classes 1 and 2 (Great Britain, 1986). Since very few of the children in our sample came from this social background, they would have to make very much more progress at school, if they were later to enter higher education than was the case at present. Of this the parents seemed unaware. Only a minority had received feedback about the standard of their children's work, the majority seemed satisfied with the schools, and 70 per cent were satisfied with the progress their children had made.

One way to raise attainments, currently being advocated by government, is to impose a centrally controlled curriculum, and monitor standards by external assessment of the children at the age of seven. Most British infant teachers are deeply opposed to these proposals. They fear the loss of autonomy entailed, and also the consequences of teaching to the test. That is, external assessment would be likely to result in teachers coaching children for the test, to the neglect of their wider aims, such as stimulating intellectual curiosity, encouraging a love of books, and widening children's interests. They also worry that assessment at seven would result in a return to streaming in primary schools.

These are real concerns, which we share. It would be a serious loss if innovative thinking and new educational approaches were discouraged by a government straightjacket. This is especially the case because most of the education that we saw was not very innovative. The great majority of children were, in fact, being taught a rather narrow range of subjects in a fairly traditional way. The second myth about British infant schooling that we encountered is that it encourages learning through 'discovery' or play. We saw very little discovery learning, or working in groups. For much of their time, children worked on their own through maths or writing work cards. We also saw no case for arguing that a core curriculum is necessary for infant schools, or that they should go back to the basics. The curriculum in ILEA infant schools is already focused on the basics. We found that two-thirds of classroom time was spent in 3R activities in the top-infant year, 21 per cent on art and creative work, of which the largest proportion was drawing, crayoning and tracing, and only 3 per cent of the time was spent in free play. There was very little teaching of science, other than nature work, and very little practical work. By the top-infant year maths teaching was mainly written number work, reading was usually taught through the use of 'reading schemes', and a lot of time was spent on what many of the children saw as rather dull writing tasks. The need would seem to be not for more time to be spent on the 3Rs, but for children to be helped to attain a higher standard in them, which we have suggested involves raising teachers' expectations and extending the range of the 3R curriculum they teach.

The objections to external assessment referred to earlier do not apply to assessments internal to the school. We believe that such assessments need not discourage innovation, if devised by the teachers themselves with the aim of seeing whether their objectives had been attained, and of discovering the strengths and weaknesses of their pupils. Assessments of this kind involve the teacher in evaluating her own work as much as the children's achievements. They should be quite frequent, rather than occurring only at the age of seven. Our findings suggest that assessing children's skills soon after entry to school, so that teachers could diagnose the areas in which children need help, would be an important way of raising standards. Such assessments would need to be linked to a much clearer setting of goals by infant teachers than is usual at the present time. Unless teachers have clear objectives of what they intend children to learn during the year, both individually and as a class, they cannot assess whether they themselves, or their children, have achieved these objectives. Setting objectives involves curriculum planning, both for the class as a whole and for individual children. Our study suggests that extending curriculum coverage is an important way of putting higher expectations into practice.

Teachers' objectives do not have to be narrow in order to be assessed. If they are concerned that use of a standardised reading test takes no account of their aim of encouraging a love of reading, for example, it is quite possible to decide on simple ways of assessing whether this aim has been achieved. Such an assessment might lead to a review of school practices, to see whether the school offers opportunities to foster reading habits in children. Is it possible, for example, to give them a chance to curl up with a book and read undisturbed for a reasonable period of time, perhaps in the school playtimes? We think there is a strong case for informing parents of the curriculum plans for the year, and also for enlisting their help in assessment at the end of the year. They would be an important source of information about their child's reading habits, interests, ability to use maths in practical situations, and so on. This process, by entailing teachers sharing their educational goals with the parents, might lead to greater home-school co-operation, and perhaps also to a change in the perspectives of both teachers and parents.

[...]

Ethnic and Sex Differences in Attainment and Progress

One of the main aims of our study was to look for factors that might account for differences in the school attainments of boys and girls, and black and white children. At the pre-school stage, we found no significant ethnic differences in early reading, writing and maths skills, or in scores on the WPPSI vocabulary test. The only sex differences at this stage was that both black and white girls were superior to boys in writing. This superiority continued throughout the infant school. At the end of infant school, there was still no overall ethnic difference in attainment, but the black girls had emerged as ahead of all other groups in both reading and writing, whilst black boys were doing worst. Both black and white boys made more progress than girls at maths, with white boys making the most progress. When we retested the children at the end of the first year of junior school, there were still no significant overall ethnic differences in attainment. By now their was a significant sex difference in reading, with girls definitely ahead of boys.

We suspect that those studies that have found an ethnic difference in the achievement of seven- or eight-year-old children have compared black children with white children who were attending different schools in different neighbourhoods. At a later stage other factors, notably racism in all its manifestations, may play an increasing role in the underachievement of black children.

The Infant-school Experiences of Black and White Girls and Boys

There were a number of indications in our findings that not only the attainments but also the experience of infant school tended to be different for these four groups of children. In our classroom observations at top infants we found that on average white boys spent a greater proportion of the school day doing maths than other groups, and this seemed to be because the teachers allocated more maths tasks to them. In general, white boys were the most work-oriented group. We observed that they both initiated and received a greater proportion of work contacts with teachers than the other children, and had fewer purely social contacts with other children in the classroom. In our interviews with the children, it was the white boys who most often said that they felt happy about going to school in the morning.

In contrast, black boys on average had the smallest proportion of contacts with teachers about school work. We observed that they received most disapproval and criticism from the teachers, and they were most often said by the teachers to have behaviour problems. In our classroom observations, they were the group most often seen to be fooling around, but these incidents were relatively rare. In our interviews with them, the black boys were more likely than the other groups to tell us that they had been punished for being really naughty, and also told off in the playground. They were the group who most enjoyed the long dinner-hour playtime, and most looked forward to the holidays.

None of this meant that they disliked school, or had a poor academic self-concept. They were more likely to say that they looked forward to the new experiences of junior school than the other groups, they enjoyed maths as much as the white boys did, and they were the group who most enjoyed reading to the teacher. Both black and white boys were more likely than girls to assess themselves as above average in all school subjects.

Whereas the black boys tended to get into trouble at school, and to do poorly at reading and writing, but to remain cheerful and self-confident about most aspects of school life, white girls in many ways presented the opposite picture. To an extent, they were invisible to the teachers. As a group, they received less disapproval and criticism from the teachers than did the other children, but also less praise. They were least often said to have behaviour problems. They spent more time in the classroom than other groups on such housekeeping jobs as sharpening pencils and fetching materials. Like the black girls, they were less likely than boys to say they enjoyed maths, and less likely to rate themselves as above average in maths, and of all the groups, they were least likely to rate themselves above average in reading and writing. They were also the least likely to say that they found school interesting. They were the group least likely to say that they were punished for being really naughty, but most likely to complain that they got teased at school.

The black girls, it will be remembered, made the most progress in reading and writing in the infant school, and had the highest attainments in these subjects. They shared with the white girls a tendency to like maths less than the boys did, and to rate their maths achievements lower than the boys did. Like the white girls, too, they were less likely than the boys to say they got into fights at school or told off in the playground. In other respects, however, their experiences were different from those of the white girls. The teachers described them as having at least as many behaviour problems as the white boys, and many more than the white girls, although not as many as the black boys. The black girls themselves told us, almost as often as the black boys did, that they got into trouble for naughtiness. They were as self-confident in their assessments of their reading and writing attainments as the boys were, they complained of being teased no more than did the boys, and they were more likely to think that school was interesting than the white girls did.

There were important respects in which the school experiences of both black boys and girls differed from those of the white children. They were much more likely to be the subject of racial taunts from other children, and they did not have the experience of being taught by someone of the same ethnic group. Throughout the infant school, none of the black children had a black classroom teacher (although a few classes had a South Asian teacher), whereas the white children were generally taught by white teachers. Further, only four of the thirty-three schools had a black classroom helper. It was also true that hardly any boys had the experience of being taught by a man — there was only one (white) male teacher in our study. It is difficult to know whether or how the degree of ethnic and sex match between the four groups of children and their teachers affected their behaviour and progress. The best match between teacher and child was for the white girls, who had the fewest behaviour problems but seemed to enjoy school least and have the least self-confidence.

Because we had very few middle-class children in our sample, we do not know the extent to which these generalizations would hold good in a more socially diverse group. It may be, for example, that middle-class white girls tend to be more self-confident than working-class white girls, or that middle-class black boys have fewer behaviour problems than working-class black boys. Our findings do suggest, however, that it can be very misleading to generalise about children of different ethnic groups without taking sex into account, or vice versa. From this point of view, the recent ILEA decision to analyse public examination results by ethnic group and sex is a welcome one.

References

BRYANT, P. and BRADLEY, L. (1985) *Children's Reading Problems*, Oxford, Basil Blackwell.

FARQUHAR, C. (1987) 'Little read books', *Times Educational Supplement*, 8 May.

GREAT BRITAIN, CENTRAL STATISTICAL OFFICE (1986) *Social trends* (1986) No. 16. A Publication of the Government Statistical Service, London, HMSO.

HUGHES, M. (1986) *Children and Number*, Oxford, Basil Blackwell.

PEDERSON, E., FAUCHER, T.A. and EATON, W.W. (1978) 'A new perspective on the effects of first grade teachers on children's subsequent adult status', *Harvard Educational Review*, 48, 1, pp. 1–31.

RIST, R. (1970) 'Student social class and teacher expectations: The self-fulfilling prophecy in ghetto education', *Harvard Educational Review*, 40, pp. 411–51.

TIZARD, B. and HUGHES, M. (1984) *Young Children Learning*, London, Fontana.

YOUNG-LOVERIDGE, J.M. (1987) 'Learning mathematics', *British Journal of Developmental Psychology*, 5, pp. 155–67.

The Effects of Streaming in the Primary School

(From Barker-Lunn, J., 1970, *Streaming in the Primary School*, Slough, NFER, pp. 272, 272–3, 273–4, 275, 276.)

The passage below reports the major findings of a longitudinal research study into the effects of streaming — an organizational device very pervasive in English primary schools in the fifties and early sixties. Paradoxically, its findings were published at a time when they were increasingly irrelevant, since by 1970 the incidence of streaming had declined dramatically. Nevertheless, its findings need to be borne in mind by anyone advocating the reintroduction of streaming or other forms of ability grouping in the context of the National Curriculum and national testing and assessment.

The aim of this study was to examine the effects of streaming and non-streaming on the personality and social and intellectual development of junior school pupils.

The major part of the research was concerned with the follow-up of approximately 5,500 children through their junior school course. This involved seventy-two junior schools: thirty-six streamed and thirty-six non-streamed. The pupils were initially tested at seven years old, in 1964, and then annually until 1967 when they were in their final junior school year.

The instruments of measurement were tests and questionnaires designed to assess pupils' performance and attitudes in nine different areas: (i) attainment in reading, English, number concept, problem and mechanical arithmetic (ii) verbal and non-verbal reasoning (iii) 'creativity' or 'divergent thinking' (iv) interests (v) school-related attitudes (vi) personality (vii) sociometric status (viii) participation in school activities and (ix) occupational aspirations.

Information was also obtained on teachers' attitudes to streaming and other educational topics and on their classroom practices and teaching methods. . . .

1. One of the most important findings concerned the role of the teacher. Teachers within streamed schools were more united in both their views on educational matters and their teaching methods, in contrast to non-streamed schools where there was a wide divergence of opinion. Only about half the staff in non-streamed schools could be called 'non-streamers'. The others held attitudes more typical of teachers in streamed schools. This finding was important, for this group of teachers appeared to create a 'streamed atmosphere' within their non-streamed classes. . . . As this could well result in modifying and thus masking the true effects of an organizational policy of non-streaming, all analyses were carried out in terms of two teacher-types: Type 1 held attitudes and used teaching methods typical of non-streamed schools and Type 2 was typical of streamed schools.

The typical 'streamer' can probably be described as 'knowledge centred'. For these teachers the emphasis was on the acquisition of knowledge and the attainment of set academic standards; they were particularly interested in and concerned for the bright child. They concentrated on 'traditional' lessons and gave more emphasis to the '3 Rs'. Competition was encouraged, and the eleven-plus selection test and streaming were approved of as a means of adapting to individual differences. These teachers believed in firmer discipline and their classroom atmosphere was more formal.

By contrast the approach of the typical 'non-streamer' was more 'child-centred', with a greater concern for the all-round development of each pupil. Their teaching tended to place more emphasis on self-expression, learning by discovery and practical experience. They were likely to encourage a co-operative environment in which pupils worked together in groups and helped each other over difficulties. A more 'permissive' classroom atmosphere, in terms of less discipline and a greater tolerance of noise, was preferred. These teachers disapproved of streaming and the eleven-plus test because of the differentiation implicit in such procedures.

2. Comparisons between streamed and non-streamed schools revealed that there was no difference in the average academic performance of boys and girls of comparable ability and social class. The effect of being taught by a particular teacher-type also appeared to bear little relationship to academic progress, but any effect may well have been blurred by pupils changing from one teacher-type to another in consecutive years.

3. 'Divergent thinking' tests indicated that a higher level of this type of thinking was associated with non-streamed schools when pupils were taught by 'typical non-streamer teachers'. It is suggested that the higher scores were not so much a direct outcome of the form of school organization but were rather due to the teaching techniques used and the more 'permissive' atmosphere created by these teachers.

4. There was no evidence that children of different social classes did academically better or worse in either type of organization. But the findings did indicate that children of lower social class origin 'deteriorated' in reading performance over the junior school course relative to children of higher social class. Also there was a tendency for teachers to over-estimate the ability of higher social class children and under-estimate the ability of lower working-class children. One outcome of this in streamed schools could well be an unwarranted allocation of some lower working-class children to too low an ability stream, particularly where the teacher's judgement is the criterion for allocation. In non-streamed classes, on the other hand, teachers may develop an 'expectancy' towards the performance of their pupils which will tend to be lower than the actual potential of the lower social class children and higher than the potential of the upper class children. Teachers' under-estimations of the abilities of lower working-class children may well be a determinant of the children's decline in performance....

10. The results, in general, indicated that neither school organization

nor teacher-type had much effect on the social, emotional or attitudinal development of children of above average ability, but that they did affect those of average and below average ability.

11. Children of *average* ability were particularly influenced by teacher-type in the development of their teacher-pupil relationship and academic self-image, and, in these two areas, pupils who were taught by 'typical non-streamers' in non-streamed schools were better off than their counterparts in streamed schools. The poorest attitudes were held by pupils taught by 'typical streamers' in non-streamed schools.

12. Boys of *below average* ability also had the most favourable teacher-pupil relationship with typical non-streamer teachers in non-streamed schools....

20. The whole of the research indicated a greater union in the objectives of teachers in streamed schools and a tendency for many teachers in non-streamed schools to hold attitudes or implement policies at variance with the avowed policy of their school. The children's academic performance, in the main, was unaffected by their school's organizational policy or their teacher's attitude to streaming, although the attainments of children who were promoted or demoted were certainly affected. The most striking finding was that the emotional and social development of children of average and below average ability was strongly affected by streaming or non-streaming and by teacher's attitudes....

Health and Stress in the Classroom

(From Pollard, A., 1985, *The Social World of the Primary School*, London, Holt, pp. 26–7.)

Of the many constraints and pressures bearing upon teachers' classroom decision-making, their daily state of health and well-being is one that cannot be ignored. Andrew Pollard concisely illustates the issue here, drawing from his research into the social world of the primary school.

Another aspect of concern which was frequently discussed by teachers in the schools studied was that of their health. On a day-to-day basis the health of teachers obviously does affect their work. They discussed getting particularly tired towards the end of the week and at the end of term; they sometimes had colds, headaches or other minor ailments; and they sometimes had more serious health problems. These factors formed a teacher-interest which would be defended even in the classroom. For instance:

Teacher at Moorside Middle School   I just didn't feel like it today, I think it's that 'flu, so we've done some stuff off the board.

Teacher at Ashton First School   Gosh I'm tired. I think we'll have to do some crayoning ... then at least I can sit down ... I can hear a few readers too.

Teacher at Moorside Middle School   You'd better take it easy; your voice sounds a bit ropy. Get them to do some worksheets or something.

A relatively common problem like backache could have significant consequences too. For instance, in infant schools the question of whether to see children's work at the teacher's desk or whether to circulate often focused on the issue of how particular teachers could manage bending down for long periods. Signs of stress are also common:

Teacher at Moorside Middle School   This is the second day I've got a headache. I'm fed up with all the noise. I'm just glad we can do silent reading now.

Indeed this problem of stress has attracted attention among teachers' professional associations (NAS and UWT, 1976) and researchers (Kyriacou, 1980) and there is no doubt that the avoidance of stress was an important influence on what teachers did in their classrooms. Turning a blind eye occasionally is not just a class management technique: it also relates to whether the teachers feel able to assert themselves at particular signs of mischief or distraction. They may decide to conserve their energy for more serious crises.

References

Kyriacou, C. (1980) 'Coping actions and occupational stress among school teachers', *Research in Education* 24, pp. 57–61.
Nas/Uwt (1976) *Stress in School*, NAS/UWT.

Developing Teaching

(From Calkins, L.M., 1983, *Lessons from a Child*, London, Heinemann, pp. 37–8.)

A separate extract from this study considers the effect on the quality of children's
learning which was brought about by changes in teachers' classroom practices. The
author and researcher, Lucy Calkins, worked alongside the class teacher, Pat
Howard, supporting her as she introduced writing workshops and conferences into
her primary curriculum. Teacher change and development here are not monolithic
events. They constitute thoughtful and careful steps forward, with the teacher building
upon, and consolidating, skills and confidences. In the process, Pat Howard
moves between quite different, and contradictory, curriculum styles, holding on to
what is secure and established in her teaching, whilst reaching out to secure new
possibilities for her children.

The extract illuminates further the issues of how and why teachers develop their
classroom practices in the way they do, and links in with questions raised by the
Desforges and Cockburn study cited earlier.

Butterflies grow through metamorphosis, but for human beings, change is
usually not so sudden. Instead, it happens in bits and pieces, in spurts and
plateaus. Pat Howard had not changed overnight. She still gave spelling
tests every Friday; she still taught social studies through dittos and textbooks. Her children still read Basal readers rather than library books.
Although desks were arranged in clusters rather than rows and children's
projects lined the edges of the classroom, many things had not changed. The
day was still compartmentalized into separate subjects; the curriculum still
followed textbooks; and the children still worked silently much of the time.
Writing was the exception, not the new rule. Mrs Howard's teaching had
become a combination of contrasts — of teacher-directed and child-
centered, of skills-in-context and skills-in-isolation.

These polarities never went away, not that year, anyhow. The visitors
who came to see Mrs Howard's classroom often commented afterward to me
that it was strange to see children learning through interaction, through
pacing their own work, through using skills in the context of writing ... and
yet to see this against the backdrop of a chalkboard full of references to
workbooks, Basal readers, dittos.

I used to wish the polarities would ease away, that child-centered
learning would replace teacher-directed instruction. But Pat had a firm
grounding in traditional approaches to teaching — and I was not around to
support changes during her social studies, science, and reading classes.

Although I would have preferred it had Pat made a radical and complete transformation, visitors to the classroom were heartened to see that a

traditional teacher, well-steeped in textbooks, workbooks and prepackaged curricula, could lead such a successful writing workshop. In fact, the assistant superintendent from the Guilderland, New York, school system recently recalled her visit to Atkinson, saying, 'What impressed me the most was not Mrs Giacobbe's wonderful first grade — we all know there are remarkable teachers who can do remarkable things.' Then she added, 'What impressed me most were the other classrooms, where I saw very traditional teachers doing very remarkable things.'

In truth, Pat Howard's grounding in teacher-directed instruction was probably part of the success of her writing workshop. Because she was accustomed to being an integral part of her student's learning, she was never tempted simply to set children free. This was important, for by late October the children didn't need their teacher in the way they had earlier. They chose their own topics, regulated their own pace, and were audiences for each other. They didn't need Mrs Howard to prod and cajole them into writing or to silence them with the approaching click of her heels. How easy it would have been for Mrs Howard to bask in her success, and then to correct math papers during the writing workshop! But she had never been an advocate of the 'set children free' philosophy. And so — quite unconsciously — she set out to find a new place for herself in the writing workshop.

Two factors seemed to shape the new identity which emerged. One was Pat Howard's participation in the research. I suspect that the content of what she learned from the youngsters was less important than that she was learning from them. She approached children wanting to understand their thinking. 'What problems are you trying to solve?' she'd ask. 'How did you go about doing this?' 'What questions are puzzling you?'

These are unusual things for teachers to ask. We are more apt to seek solutions than problems, and to see our role as delivering answers rather than as posing challenges. Yet the research had given Mrs Howard a new appreciation for the thinking behind not only their writing, but all the children did. One morning Pat brought in a picture her six-year-old daughter had drawn. 'Look at it closely,' she urged as she showed it to me. 'What do you notice?'

Before I had chance to study the picture, Pat pointed out that underneath the crossed out section, she could see the hint of letters TRKO TRT. 'See!' she said with excitement. 'The guy is saying trick-or-treat and he's ringing this doorbell' (and she pointed to the door) 'and this is the candy bowl with the pieces of candy.' In a similar manner, Pat and I squinted to read the crossed out sections on the children's drafts and speculated about the thinking between their lines. And so it was quite natural that, during writing time, Pat moved around the classroom asking children to tell her about their writing and nudging them on to new challenges.

There was another factor which influenced Pat's teaching that year. Because we worked so closely together, she began to share not only the research project, but also my interest in writing. Sometimes I'd read portions of a rough draft to her, and tell her about my conferences with Don Murray. I told her also about our writing group at the University of New Hampshire. On Tuesday evenings, fifteen of us met together to hear each other's work-in-process and to offer suggestions to each other.

'What kind of suggestions do they make to you?' Pat sometimes asked, and then I'd realize that actually, help usually came in the form of questions. Mostly by asking questions — like 'How do you feel about your draft?' 'What are you trying to get at?' 'What will you do next?' 'What discoveries are you making?' and 'How can we help?' — people helped me articulate what I wanted to say in an article, how I felt about the draft, and what I planned to do next.

And so, in an indirect way, the writing community at the University of New Hampshire became part of Pat's thinking and teaching. She tried her hand at writing too — little pieces, written to share with her students. From me and from firsthand experience, she developed a feel for the writing process.

Both our research and her own involvement in writing, then, had a part in shaping Mrs Howard's new role as a writing teacher. She wanted to engage the children in their writing and to give them the time, support and tools to explore and develop their craft. She spent most of the workshop time moving between the desks, working with individuals and with impromptu clusters of children. Watching her, I was reminded of the circus stunt man who sets plates spinning on the ends of long sticks and then steps back to watch. When a plate begins to wobble, the circus man moves over and with his fingertip he gives the plate more spin, then steps back again. 'Keep it up,' Mrs Howard would say. 'Craig, are you working?' 'Renee, why don't you read it to Diane?' 'Jeremy, can I help you?' With light touches, she kept her plates spinning. These brief conferences made it possible for longer conferences to also take place.

Teachers' Problems with Children's Problems

(From Desforges, C. and Cockburn, A., 1987, *Understanding the Mathematics Teacher*, Lewes, Falmer Press, pp. 115–21.)

Under severe pressure in the classroom, a teacher's capacity to make accurate judgements may become impaired. Drawing further on their research into teachers' thinking, Desforges and Cockburn noticed that, in some circumstances, the teachers in their study ceased to think clearly about children's learning needs, resorting instead to strategies that were inappropriate and ineffective. The authors suggest that these 'pathologies of reasoning' may, in part, be a consequence of information overload, given large classes of children and complex curriculum organization and management. There may, also, be other explanations, relating to teachers' beliefs about how children learn, beliefs which are not always borne out by classroom evidence. The research highlighted disjunctions between certain teacher beliefs about children's learning, and subsequent teacher behaviour in the classroom.

The study draws our attention to the paradoxes and ambiguities that pervade classroom life, and to the inordinately difficult managerial challenges daily facing class teachers.

Once the teaching action starts it has been shown that the quantity of information the teachers have to handle and the rate at which it must be processed increase dramatically. Particular moods, events and especially children's responses — each in themselves potentially difficult to deal with — come in a welter of complex interactions. In routine lessons teachers consider all this as fast and furious but relatively normal and containable. Experience and good management puts them in a position, as they see it, to react profitably. In open discussion the predictability of children's responses is low and the probability of having the appropriate material to hand to capitalize on the children's contribution is even lower. In consequence dilemmas proliferate in the teachers' minds. Their comments on their thinking during these interactions reveal doubts and hesitations. What they do not reveal is an awareness of the increasing mismatch between their thinking and their behaviour.

At all levels of activity the teachers' essential humanity to children was manifest. Unfortunately, at levels of intense information processing, another aspect of humanity begins to take its toll. It has been well established that in novel situations humans cannot successfully process very much information at once. If problems come in quick succession and decision times are short, human reasoning tends to exhibit certain well known and — in pedagogic terms — unfortunate characteristics. Laboratory studies of problem solving under stress and real world studies of airline pilots, surgeons, policemen, fireman, businessmen and others in emergencies show that thinking exhibits some or all of the following characteristics. There is a narrowing of the range of possible responses considered; there is a failure to notice certain events, or if noticed, a failure to realize or act on their significance; there is a persistence and repetition of some behaviours in the face of failure and there is a reluctance to test hypotheses or hunches. Ideas which might normally be seen as speculative are seen, under time constraint, as certainties and evidence which contradicts these 'certainties' is simply denied. These pathologies of reasoning have direct, and sometimes dire, consequences for behaviour. Apparently 80 per cent of airline crashes are due to pilot error — frequently in cases where the pilot has had plenty of warning from his instruments that all was not well. It appears that interpretations of these warnings, under stress, exacerbate rather than alleviate the predicament.

In the much more mundane circumstances of laboratory problem solving it has been reported that,

> In some of our research we were forcibly reminded of pathological phenomena which are not normally found or looked for in psychological experiments. Repetition, asseveration, self contradiction, outright denial of the facts and ritualistic behaviour became quite typical in some tasks ... these symptoms were reflections of reasoning under mildly stressful conditions ... (Wason and Johnson-Laird, 1972)

Lest it be thought that anything dastardly was going on in these experiments it is worth noting that the tasks were relatively straightforward. In one task, for example, undergraduates were told that the three numbers, two, four, six conformed to a simple relational rule and that they were to discover this rule by generating successive triads of numbers. Each time they were told whether their triad conformed to the rule. The somewhat obsessive behaviours described above were frequently seen in response to this task. The researchers were not implying that their subjects were pathological — only that under these apparently simple circumstances their behaviour had some resemblance to pathological thought. The work of Wason and Johnson-Laird is consistent with a great deal of research on problem solving which shows that if people are left unaided with a problem, their thinking frequently shows 'fixity', that is to say, a tendency to persist with unsuccessful approaches and a denial of or blindness to alternatives. Their behaviour may show all the characteristics of stupidity or ignorance. Time pressure is known to exacerbate all these effects.

It is not surprising that all these features were evident in the behaviour of the teachers studied. The less routine and familiar were the children's responses, the more the teachers' behaviour became fixated. The crucial thing to emphasize is that there is nothing remotely unusual in this. It simply illustrates that the teachers are human.

The teachers frequently rushed to interpret children's responses and did not pause to check or test their interpretations. In one instance, Mrs F. was explaining how to complete sums of the following type:

She noticed that Vicky was writing '6' at the end of every arrow and concluded, 'She is clueless, absolutely clueless. There is no understanding at all there.' A post-task interview showed that Vicky had a good grasp of addition but did not grasp what the card required.

The rush to interpret correct answers was even more evident and more frequently in error. Time was often spent practising a procedure until the teacher was satisfied that the children understood the underlying idea. In her attempt to get children to understand subtraction Mrs D. had them read out subtraction 'number stories' from diagrams like those shown in figure 15.

After some initial hiccoughs all the children were able to say, 'four take away one leaves three' in response to this diagram. Mrs D concluded that they, 'had got a good grasp at last'. In fact post-task interviews showed that just fifteen minutes later and without Mrs D.'s conducting they could not reproduce their behaviour.

Also seen was the repetition of unproductive teaching behaviour in response to a child's failure. In the following example Mrs B. was trying to get Michael to read out the number symbols to five:

Mrs B.: Now Michael. What number is this (points to '5')
Michael: Number two.
Mrs B.: Number?
Michael: Number ...
Mrs B.: You count. (She points to the numbers as Michael says them)
Michael: One, two, three, four, five.
Mrs B.: What number is that? (pointing to '5')
Michael: Number four.
Mrs B.: You count again (points)
Michael: One, two, three, four, five.
Mrs B.: What number is that? (pointing to '5')
Michael: Number four.
Mrs B.: Start again.
[The cycle continued three more times until Michael said 'two' as Mrs B. pointed to '5']
Mrs B.: Well what number is that? (pointing to '2')
Michael: Number two.
Mrs B.: Well does that number ('2')look like that number ('5')?
Michael: [no response].

Figure 15   Sets for subtraction number stories

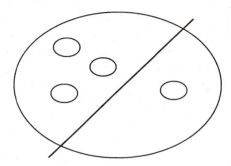

Obviously Mrs B. was fixed on a routine that was going nowhere. One repetition of the cycle would be understandable; five repetitions seem distinctly unprofitable. Why did the teacher so persist? Her own account of her thinking during these events shows that she was surprised, even dismayed, by Michael's responses. She felt, *'surely* he would see...' that having said 'five' when pointed to '5' he would say it again when she pointed again. And 'surely' after two or three repetitions this would 'click'. Mrs B.'s behaviour was sustained by a very powerful view of Michael's problem as a learner. He was seen to be inattentive. This was not considered a hunch to be tested. It was treated as a certainty. The problem, in Mrs B.'s eyes, was to focus Michael's attention on the salient cues. A lot of the moment-by-moment evidence available to Mrs B. was entirely consistent with this view. The video tape shows Michael's eyes did wander. He fidgetted a lot. A non-participant observer might easily have interpreted that as signs of stress or discomfort. But that amounts to the same thing — inattention.

Eventually Mrs B., sustaining the same hypothesis of inattention, decided on a different tack and took Michael to a set of number symbols cut out in sandpaper and had him trace round them with his finger observing that, 'If I cannot get to him through his eyes and ears I will have to go through his fingers.'

One hypothesis that Mrs B. did not entertain was the possiblility that Michael had a very shaky grasp of quantity in this range. Even had she got him to say 'five', on this hypothesis it would have been a largely meaningless achievement. In fact the pre-session interview suggested some such interpretation of Michael's competence. He could recite numbers to five but he could not count off more than three objects if they were of the same type. He could not select three objects from a group. He could not match symbols to quantities in this range. What Mrs B. was asking Michael to do was not only to count to five (which he could) but also to realize (because it was never pointed out) that the symbols related to the words said. This he could not do. Had Mrs B. known more about Michael's competence before this task she might not have expected him to attempt it. Indeed, without a lot more concrete experience of quantity, success for Michael on this task at this stage would have been merely barking at print.

It would appear that the teacher did not know about Michael's strengths and weaknesses in regard to this task and was unlikely to find out given her hypothesis about his failure to attend. Given also that there was plenty of evidence consistent with her hypothesis — evidence seen as confirmatory — alternative explanations were unlikely to be conceived, let alone tested. The force of Mrs B.'s hypothesis was such that she did not even consider the strategy of leaving Michael alone in this instance. His attention had to be locked-on one way or another. She was dismayed that a tried and tested strategy of repetition had not worked. This was unusual in her experience. Whatever it does for children's understanding, repetition usually gets them to say the right answer. Once she had got over her dismay at the failure of her first tactic she showed some inventiveness in adopting another (albeit within the same strategy). However, Michael's basic problem remained untouched and increasingly untouchable as his teacher narrowed her aim to that of getting him to say the right thing at the right time.

What is noteworthy about this instance is that it was commonly seen (in response to children's errors) in all its main features including the narrowing of the teacher's aim, the repetition of a failing tactic and the absence of an attempt to step back and take a longer look at the problem or to test the basic hypothesis on which the teacher's behaviour was based. In short the teachers, in response to novel behaviour by the children evinced all the characteristics of dull and uninformed people. The more open the teaching, the more novel was the children's behaviour and — in train — the more problems were perceived and disappointments experienced.

That these teachers were certainly not dull has been demonstrated repeatedly in these pages. When given the opportunity to comment on the recordings of each others' sessions they showed all the flexibility and insight necessary to generate and test alternate views on children's contributions. Their limited thinking in action must be attributed in part to the press of events. To adopt fresh lines of approach several notions must be grasped rapidly if continuity, attention and interest are not to be lost. The necessity for a change must be perceived. A new angle must come to mind and a justification must come with it. Otherwise there would be little point in the change. This is a very tall order indeed particularly if the reader recalls what the teacher can never forget — the teacher and child are never alone in the classroom.

The press of events however, cannot be the sole reason for the teachers' responses in these circumstances. From the whole range of events happening at any moment, the teacher makes her selections and we may presume that these selections are based on preoccupations that the teacher brings with her to the situation. These preoccupations were not identified as such by the teachers we studied. They did not emerge spontaneously nor were they forthcoming in response to our questions. We are therefore left to speculate as to what ideas, under circumstances of time stress, lure the teachers away from their principles and into fixations.

One such notion seems to be that once an activity has started it must be completed. In the above example, Mrs B. seemed unable to step back and leave Michael to give herself time to think.

This unwillingness to step back might in turn be bolstered by the notion that children are extremely vulnerable both in terms of their confidence and in their capacity to be led astray by error or wrong ideas. Teachers' references to the need to sustain children's confidence permeated our discussions. Of course at the level of general principle this is unimpeachable. But at the level of practice, as Mrs F. pointed out, to sustain confidence it is extremely difficult not to jump in and help at the first sign of a child's hesitant glance. As the teachers recognized, the price of confidence can be dependence but it is a price often paid in the maelstrom of classroom exchanges in which teachers give in to the human instinct to help in preference to their own pedagogic strictures. Confidence in this view demands a good result quickly.

Confidence is not the only issue at stake. It would seem that the teachers had the idea that children can be easily misled into false notions and inappropriate routines. Mrs G.'s unwillingness to explore her children's examples of sphere is an instance of this principle in operation. She recognized the fertility of some of the children's ideas but '... passed over discussion for the sake of the rest of (the children)'. If a teacher holds the view that wrong or unusual ideas can be very misleading then she must endeavour not to start them (*q.v.* Mrs G.) or, if started, to sort them out as soon as possible (*q.v.* Mrs B.). Both responses are premised, logically, on the view that there are 'wrong ideas' or that there are dangerous routes to 'right ideas'. Now clearly, these teachers did not hold either of these views.

It seems that children's ideas are indeed very difficult to manage and they rarely got on the agenda in the classroom because the agenda is already crowded by something that is easier to manage, namely the mathematics scheme. And in fact the schemes do imply that there are right ways to operate and proper uses of terms to be shared. It seemed to us that once the teacher is committed to using the schemes as published — and there are many attractions to this option — she might well feel committed to the behaviours and the mental life we have reported here.

Reference

Wason, P.C. and Johnson-Laird, P.M. (1972) *Psychology and Reasoning: Content and Structure*, London, Batsford.

Craftsmanship and Artistry in Teaching

(from Nias, D.J., 1989, *Primary Teachers Talking: A Study of Teaching as Work*, London, Routledge, pp. 197–201.)

Teaching is, according to Jennifer Nias's research, a complex and skilled activity, calling for a highly developed ability to hold in balance a multitude of conflicting demands and tensions. In this, it endorses many of the insights offered by the Desforges and Cockburn study (pp. 50, 148).

The author shows that to 'feel like a teacher' is to learn to live with dilemma, contradiction and paradox. She also argues that separating the personal from the professional experience of primary teaching is virtually impossible since teaching, as work, becomes an expression and realization of one's sense of self.

Her research was based upon the personal accounts of a group of primary teachers who were interviewed at the beginning of their career and, subsequently, several years later in mid-career. In this extract, the author writes of the wide-ranging and subtle skills which the capable professional develops as they achieve mastery in teaching. Seen at its best, it can look deceptively simple. Yet it is this apparent simplicity which, the author argues, helps to identify the most competent teachers and which, further, offers professional fulfilment.

Primary teaching is, then, an occupation which requires the ability to live with, and handle constructively, a multitude of dilemmas, tensions, contradictions, uncertainties, and paradoxes. As the all-party Select Parliamentary Committee Report on Primary Education (Education, Science and Arts Committee, 1986, 1, 2) reported:

> [Our comments] are made in the context of ... our high regard for the skills of good primary teachers and our recognition of the complexity of their work.

This ability to work productively with complexity depends in turn upon the exercise and refinement of highly developed expertise in four areas, the first three of which make possible the fourth.

First are interpersonal skills. Some of these are almost intuitive, such as the 'pedagogic tact' described by Van Manen (1984, p. 2), a quality of 'sensitivity, founded in love, which enables one to do what is pedagogically the right thing for a child'. Others are based on the ability to acquire, store, retrieve, and interpret accurately information about all the children in a class (Doyle, 1986). Together, they enable teachers to win the confidence of, control, laugh with, listen, and talk to children of all ages.

Second, there are the pedagogic skills of observation, interpretation, organization, management, and communication (see, e.g. Smith and Geoffrey, 1968; Jackson, 1968; Bennett *et al.*, 1984; Doyle, 1986). Together these require, as Desforges and Cockburn so clearly illustrate, personal resources, qualities of insight, hard work, and the capacity to act as a 'ruthlessly efficient quarter-master' (Desforges and Cockburn, 1987, p. 55).

Underlying, and in some senses, enabling both these sets of skills is the ability to adapt to circumstances and constraints through the use of 'coping strategies' ('a type of patterned and active adaptation to a situation by which an individual copes', Pollard, 1982, p. 155). Pollard (1985) describes in detail various ways of adapting used by teachers and pupils to obtain a 'working consensus' in the classroom which will protect and enhance the self-interests of both. 'Open negotiation'and 'manipulation', in particular, require of the teacher a high degree of practised ability in observation, interpretation, and sensitive responsiveness. The resulting 'negotiated system of behavioural understandings' (Pollard, 1985, p. 160) enables both teacher and pupils to safeguard their interests, reduces the stress under which they work and allows teaching and learning to proceed with the minimum of disruption and the maximum goodwill. To survive, then, teachers must also be expert classroom negotiators.

Each of the three sets of skills that primary teachers use in classrooms is impressive to watch in action. However, it is when they are operated together or 'orchestrated' (Woods, 1987a, p. 135) that competence becomes craftsmanship. Shifting swiftly between instruction and affection, management and laughter, teachers 'display a superb feel for moving back and forth between familiarity, liking, caring, warmth and a more detached teacher-like stance' (Lieberman and Miller, 1984, p. 120). To this highly-developed capacity to switch instantly and smoothly between the personal and the professional, experienced practitioners add other abilities: for instance, the ability to handle variety and complexity; to juggle priorities; to resolve dilemmas; to process densely-packed information reaching them simultaneously on many channels; to respond to it with sensitivity and accuracy; and to adjust their intentions, plans, and actions without disrupting themselves or others. This composite skill has been noted and admired by many classroom observers (e.g. Jackson, 1968; Smith and Geoffrey, 1968; Kounin, 1970; King, 1978; Berlak and Berlak, 1981; Lieberman and Miller, 1984; Pollard, 1980, 1982, 1985; Hartley, 1985; Duke, 1986; Desforges and Cockburn, 1987; Woods, 1987). It has also been noted in studies of inter-adult relationships in primary schools (Nias, 1987b; Nias *et al.*, 1989). Although each of these studies has a slightly different focus, they all single out for special attention a capacity to do what is most often described as 'balance'.

Now what is truly remarkable about experienced primary teachers' pedagogic 'balancing' is not so much that they achieve it, but that they do so in the face of unremitting pressures towards disequilibrium. The craft of such teachers is epitomized in their capacity to bring their own emotions and the social systems within which they work into harmony and then to refuse to be disrupted, unbalanced, torn asunder, blown off course, of put out of step (one can use many metaphors, all or them appropriate) by the historical, social, emotional, philosophical, or practical tensions which form the context and backdrop of their work.

There are acknowledged pleasures in the exercise of craftsmanship, and the successful performance of this complex, demanding act of balancing might in itself explain the fact that accomplished classroom practitioners often feel purposeful and satisfied. To handle smoothly the essentially conflictual nature of their work is an expression of practised abilities in which they can justly take pride. The resulting sense of equilibrium may also account for why they feel 'whole', 'natural' and 'in control'. However, this is not the whole story, for successful balancing also brings its own affective rewards; a finely-tuned, well-equilibrated relationship between teachers and pupils is, for all its tensions and intricacies, a warm and even a loving one. The intrinsic pleasures of skilled performance are complemented by the giving and receiving of affection. Teaching offers its 'joys' and 'thrills' (Jackson, 1968, pp. 134, 137) as well as its sense of mastery.

Some people would go further than this, however, claiming that teaching is an art rather than a craft (e.g. Eisner, 1979; Stenhouse, 1980; Lieberman and Miller, 1984; Woods, 1987). Certainly, the creative endeavour needed to transcend its dilemmas, contradictions and paradoxes can result in the exhilaration, intense joy, even 'ecstasy' (Woods 1987, p. 142) of the artist:

> People who have not taught can have little idea what it is like to have *taught well* [author's italics], to be buoyed up and swept along by the response of students who are learning. One reaches for metaphors: chemical reactions, currents, setting alight, taking fire. But however difficult to describe . . . it is something that most teachers . . . have, at least some of the time. (Connell, 1985, p. 127)

Now Connell's description is not unlike that of William James, in which he writes to his wife of the moments in which he feels most deeply and intensely active and alive [when] there is a voice inside which speaks and says, 'This is the real me!' (quoted in Erikson, 1968, p. 19). Perhaps it is in the precious moments when primary teachers become creative artists that they transcend the contradictions of the job and achieve the 'peak experience' of which Maslow (1973, p. 177) writes and in which they, like James, become aware of their full identity.

The notion that primary teachers achieve 'balance' through the exercise of a complex and demanding skill, which at times becomes a creative act, puts a different complexion upon the often-repeated accusation that they are middle-of-the-road, moderate, realistic, pragmatic (see, e.g. Waller, 1961; Lortie, 1975; King, 1978; Connell, 1985; Pollard, 1987), preferring consensus to extremism, compromise to controversy, the immediate to the remote, the concrete to the abstract. To be sure, some of them do answer this description: in any craft-based occupation some people perform less well than others, and teaching is no exception. The skill of balancing requires attributes and qualities — for example, adaptability, flexibility, good information-processing abilities, swift reflexes and responses, physical and emotional energy, perseverance, concentration, self-control — which not everyone possesses in equal measure or all the time. But there is no escaping the need to keep the primary classroom in equilibrium. Consequently, some teachers achieve a type of balance which satisfies them and their pupils by reducing the number of components with which they have to juggle, or by simplifying the relationship between them. Others slow the whole process down or deal with only one part of it at a time. Whatever the strategy they select to retain control over the act of teaching, it may (and sometimes does) lead to a sluggish, unresponsive form of equilibrium characterized by dullness, inertia, complacency, or stagnation.

But it is easy to confuse the calm counterpoise of an experienced teacher with mediocrity. It is a truism that a good craftsman or woman makes the job seem easy. The balance and rhythm which many teachers achieve, in the face of considerable and growing difficulties, can readily be mistaken for stagnation or complacency. Judgements about the skill of teachers should therefore be made only by those who understand the subtleties and nuances of what they observe. Moreover, teachers put 'off balance' by, for example, a particularly disruptive child, an acerbic colleague, a shortage of essential resources, or a deep sense of professional frustration, are likely to search for a new equilibrium which contains but does not redress the cause of the imbalance. Over time, such adjustments may render the craft performance of skilled practitioners heavier, less responsive, and more sluggish. Furthermore, since to 'feel like a teacher' is to feel 'in balance', and this sense in turn carries with it great affective rewards, one can speculate that teachers who believe that they can no longer — for whatever reason — achieve the difficult feat of holding tensions in balance and transcending contradictions, may choose to leave the profession, either literally or by withdrawing their interest and commitment from it. When either of these developments takes place, the education system is deprived of its most skilled and experienced practitioners.

References

BENNETT, S.N., DESFORGES, C., COCKBURN, A. and WILKINSON, B. (1984) *The Quality of Pupil Learning Experiences*, London, Lawrence Erlbaum Associates.

BERLAK, A. and BERLAK, H. (1981) *The Dilemmas of Schooling*, London, Methuen.

CONNELL, R. (1985) *Teachers' Work*, London, Allen and Unwin.

DESFORGES, C. and COCKBURN, A. (1987) *Understanding the Mathematics Teacher: A Study of Practice in First Schools*, Lewes, Falmer Press.

DOYLE, W. (1986) 'Classroom management and organization', in WITTROCK, M. (Ed.) *Handbook of Research on Teaching*, New York, Macmillan.

DUKE, D. (1986) 'Understanding what it means to be a teacher', *Educational Leadership*, 44, pp. 27–32.

EDUCATION, SCIENCE AND ARTS COMMITTEE (1986) *Select Parliamentary Committee Report: Achievement in Primary Schools*, London, HMSO.

EISNER, E. (1979) *The Educational Imagination*, London, Collier Macmillan.

ERIKSON, E. (1950) *Childhood and Society*, New York, Norton.

ERIKSON, E. (1968) *Identity: Youth and Crisis*, London, Faber and faber.

HARTLEY, D. (1985) *Understanding the Primary School*, London, Croom Helm.

JACKSON, P. (1968) *Life in Classrooms*, New York, Holt, Rinehart and Winston.

KING, R. (1978) *All Things Bright and Beautiful: A Sociological Study of Infant Schools*, Chichester, Wiley.

KOUNIN, J. (1970) *Discipline and Group Management in Classrooms*, New York, Holt, Rinehart and Winston.

LIEBERMAN, A. and MILLER, L. (1984) *Teachers: their World and their Work*, Alexandria, Va.: Association for Supervision and Curriculum Development.

LORTIE, D. (1975) *School Teacher: A Sociological Study*, Chicago, University of Chicago Press.

MASLOW, A. (1973) *Further Reaches of Human Nature*, Harmondsworth, Penguin.

NIAS, J. (1987) 'One finger, one thumb: A case study of the deputy head's part in the leadership of a nursery/infant school', in SOUTHWORTH, G. (Ed.) *Readings in Primary School Management*, Lewes, Falmer Press.

NIAS, J., SOUTHWORTH, G. and YEOMANS, R. (1989) *Staff Relationships in the Primary School: A study of Organizational Cultures*, London, Cassell.

POLLARD, A. (1980) 'Teacher interests and changing situations of survival threat in primary school classrooms', in WOODS, P. (Ed.) *Teacher Strategies: Explorations in the Sociology of the School*, London, Croom Helm.

POLLARD, A. (1982) 'A model of classroom coping strategies', *British Journal of Sociology of Education*, 3(1), pp. 19–37.

POLLARD, A. (1985) *The Social World of the Primary School*, London, Cassell.

POLLARD, A. (1987) 'Primary teachers and their colleagues', in DELAMONT, S. (Ed.) *The Primary School Teacher*, Lewes, Falmer Press.

SMITH, L. and GEOFFREY, W. (1968) *The Complexities of an Urban Classroom*, New York, Holt, Rinehart and Winston.

STENHOUSE, L. (1980) 'Curriculum research and the art of the teacher', *Curriculum*, 1(1), pp. 40–4.

VAN MANEN, M. (1984) 'Action research as theory of the unique: From pedagogic thoughtlessness to pedagogic tactfulness'. Paper presented at American Educational Research Association Conference, New Orleans.

WALLER, W. (1961) (new edn) *Sociology of Teaching*, New York, Russell and Russell.

WOODS, P. (1987) 'Managing the primary teacher's role', in DELAMONT, S. (Ed.) *The Primary School Teacher*, Lewes, Falmer Press.

3 Teachers as Researchers

Research as a Basis for Teaching

(From Stenhouse, L., 1985, 'Research as a basis for teaching', in Rudduck, J. and Hopkins, D. (Eds) *Research as a Basis for Teaching: Readings from the work of Lawrence Stenhouse*, London, Heinemann, pp. 124–6.)

Most teachers are on the 'outside' of educational research in three senses. Firstly, their questions and concerns are not usually the focus for traditional reseach. Secondly, teachers are not usually actively involved in conducting traditional research. Rather, they are the objects of it. Thirdly, research findings are often inaccessible to school practitioners. Teachers have little time to study research in depth unless it is part of a formal course of study. Thus, it is difficult for research to contribute to teachers' learning and to development of classroom practice.

Concerns about this divide between research and teachers gave rise to the 'teacher as researcher' movement. In this, attempts have been made to fashion a style of research that centres on teachers' own concerns, that gives teachers control over the research process and, at the same time, contributes to teaching development. This has become known as action research, sometimes called classroom enquiry, and is a style of research in which change and practical outcomes are sought.

The first extract in this section from the late Lawrence Stenhouse, often referred to as 'the father of teacher research', outlines the way in which classroom research and teacher development can, and should, be interwoven with the cause of classroom improvement.

Just as research in history or literature or chemistry can provide a basis for teaching those subjects, so educational research can provide a basis for teaching and learning about teaching. Professional skill and understanding can be the subject of doubt, that is, of knowledge, and hence of research.

In education what might such research look like?

In this country, since the 1950s, the received doctrine has been that the core of education for teaching lies not in research in education, but in the application to education of the conclusions of research in the 'contributory disciplines' of philosophy, psychology and sociology. Most of those teaching these disciplines to teachers have not been able to share a research base with their students, who are clearly quite unlikely to become philosophers, psychologists, or sociologists, since they are on professional courses for teachers. All too easily philosophers, psychologists and sociologists, whose researches are problematic in their own fields, become — only sometimes against their wishes — authorities in courses for teachers.

An alternative to the constituent disciplines approach is to treat education itself — teaching, learning, running schools and educational systems — as the subject of research. This alternative is not characterized by a neglect of disciplines, upon which it draws eclectically, but rather by the fact that what is drawn from the disciplines and applied to education is not results or even the theories which give shape to each discipline, but methods of enquiry and analysis together with such concepts as have utility for a theory of education. The problems selected for enquiry are selected because of their importance as educational problems, that is, for their significance in the context of professional practice. Research and development guided by such problems will contribute primarily to the understanding of educational action through the construction of a theory of education or a tradition of understanding. Only secondarily will research in this mode contribute to philosophy, psychology or sociology. And this principle of applied research is, I think, appropriate *mutatis mutandis* in all the professional schools of our universities.

How can I best make clear the implications of such a position? Let me take as a point of departure an example of research and training which I take to be sub-professional.

In Ohio State University I visited the Disaster Center, a research and development unit concerned with making more effective the response of the emergency services to disasters. There I saw in a laboratory an exact replica of the Columbus, Ohio, police nerve centre. Police staff were released to man their familiar positions while simulations of disasters were fed through their information channels and their responses were studied. While I was watching, a simulated airplane crash on a Columbus surburb was enacted. It was cleverly contrived. News that the wife of one of the men on the switchboard had just given birth to a son was fed through as a distractor. Information that the deputy superintendent's family had been badly injured when the plane hit his residence invited the team to override public priorities with private ones. Research and training were well integrated. The task was to find the best procedure, to test it against interference and then to enable the emergency team to react smoothly and automatically without needing to pause for thought or run aground on difficult judgements. The laboratory situation was a godsend. You cannot keep crashing planes on Columbus as a research strategy.

If we were to take this as a model for educational research, then we should provide laboratories which simulate classrooms. Desks carefully carved with graffiti might be assembled, walls might be hung with the Fall of Icarus and centrespreads from *The Teachers' World*, fans could pump in the scent of sweat and damp clothes mixed with chalk dust. But what of the pupils?

We deal in education — as with medicine or law or social work — with human action which cannot be channelled through headphones. We need real pupils, and we cannot properly engage them in doubtful experiments or even in placebo treatments.

In short, real classrooms have to be our laboratories, and they are in the command of teachers, not of researchers. This is the characteristic of professional schools: the research act must conform to the obligations of the professional context. This is what we mean by action research. It is a pattern of research in which experimental or research acts cannot be exempted from the demand for justification by professional as well as by research criteria. The teacher cannot learn by enquiry without undertaking that the pupils learn too; the physician cannot experiment without attempting to heal. As the Tavistock Institute put it: 'No therapy without research, no research without therapy' (Smith, 1979).

Such a view of educational research declares that the theory or insights created in collaboration by professional researchers and professional teachers is always provisional, always to be taught in a spirit of enquiry, and always to be tested and modified by professional practice. The teacher who founds his practice of teaching upon research must adopt a research stance to his own practice: it must be provisional and exploratory.

It is this that marks him out as a professional, as compared to the Ohio police emergency team: for while the object of the disaster simulations is to allow them to respond effectively without pausing for thought, the object of educational research is to develop thoughtful reflection in order to strengthen the professional judgement of teachers.

Reference

SMITH, D. (1979) 'Action Research and the Ford Teaching Project! A Strategy for Educating Classroom Practice'. Unpublished MEd dissertation, University of Liverpool.

Action Research: A Definition

(From Elliott, J., 1981, *Action Research: A Framework for Self-Evaluation in Schools*, Cambridge Institute of Education, p. 1.)

A Definition

Action research might be defined as:

The study of a social situation with a view to improving the quality of action within it.

It aims to feed practical judgement in concrete situations, and the validity of 'theories' it generates depends not so much on 'scientific' tests of truth, as on their usefulness in helping people to act more intelligently and skillfully. In action research 'theories' are not validated independently and then applied to practice. They are validated through practice.

Action Research in Action

(From Bassey, M., 1986, 'Does action research require sophisticated research methods?', in Hustler, D. *et al.*, *Action Research in Classrooms and Schools*, London, Allen and Unwin, pp. 18–9, 21–4.)

Michael Bassey has done much to promote teacher action research in a range of professional learning contexts. Here, he explores some of its characteristics. Through fictionalized teacher accounts he gives a flavour of the way in which action research might fit the expressed classroom concerns of teachers, and might inform teachers' practical decision-making. In this, he gives some sense of how the style and rhythms of this kind of research link closely to the circumstances of the classroom.

One of the characteristics of action research is that it is research which people get on with and do quickly. As such it can be contrasted with academic research. The academic world enjoys the intellectual delights of rigorous thinking about minutiae and is able to devote long periods of time to it. Thus an MPhil student will spend usually about two years of full-time study to gain the research degree, and a PhD student longer. But a school teacher with a classroom problem which might be illuminated by research methods is likely to have only a few hours to devote to the search for a solution.

One of the handouts used on our Primary Generalist BEd at Trent Polytechnic is adapted from the writing of W.G. Perry and entitled 'Discoveries of the Obvious'. It includes this paragraph:

> My fifth discovery was that I am not a watcher of the world, but an actor in it. I have to make decisions and some of them have to be made now. I cannot say 'Stop the world and let me get off for a bit, I want to think some more before I decide.' Given so many differences of opinion among reasonable people, I realise that I can never be sure that I am making the 'right' decisions. Yet because I am an actor in the world, I must decide. I must choose what I believe in and own the consequences and never know what lay down the roads I did not take.

Academics are watchers of the world: teachers are actors in it. Teachers make decisions and search for 'right' decisions. Sometimes research enquiries may help in the search for 'right' decisions. Sometimes the research evidence is in a published report which teachers can relate to their own classrooms, but other times they need to obtain the evidence themselves for every classroom is unique and one teacher's solution may not be appropriate for others.

The actions of classroom teaching can be expressed in this way. Classroom teaching entails assessing the educational needs of children, identifying intentions for what you hope they will achieve, locating suitable resources and working out appropriate strategies whereby the intentions may be achieved. The acts of defining needs, intentions, resources and strategies all entail decisions which although involving value-judgements, can be illuminated by empirical data. And the collection of empirical data implies research.

[...]

I consider that there are two kinds of pedagogic research, i.e. meaning research that attempts to improve the quality of teaching and learning. One kind attempts to produce general statements about teaching and learning. Thus Neville Bennett in *Teaching Styles and Pupil Progress* and Maurice Galton, Brian Simon and Paul Croll in the ORACLE reports, base their conclusions on surveys of relatively large numbers of teachers and pupils and try to draw general conclusions. I describe this kind of research as 'search for generality' and although there is much of interest to teachers in these studies, I find little that gives guidance to the individual teacher in the day-to-day work of the classroom. The other kind of pedagogic research I describe as 'study of singularities', which means accounts of the happenings in single classrooms. It may be the description of a particular piece of teaching, with an explanation of why the teacher works in this particular way, it may be an account of an experiment in which pupils learn in some way which the teacher has not tried before; it may be the results of interviews with the parents of one class on what the children tell them about life in school. In each case there is no attempt to generalize the findings beyond the classroom, but there is recognition that there may be aspects of the results which stimulate other teachers to try something similar. The York Street School examples on the following pages are of this latter kind: they are studies of singularities. I have invented them to illustrate a number of points about classroom action research.

The York Street School Action Research Reports could only be produced in a school where the staffroom is supportive of this kind of professional enquiry. The snide comments that 'Martha's obviously after the deputy head's job' or 'Penny ought to get on with it instead of fretting about' would kill this sort of initiative. Years ago these responses might have been common, but today many teachers are prepared to share their experiences with colleagues and to learn through staffroom discussion.

The reports illustrate a number of points about classroom research by teachers.

The issues under study were classroom issues identified by the teacher as worthy of investigation — queues and fidgeting. This should be an essential feature of any classroom action research — that the issue is one of concern to the teacher. But they have another essential feature — in both cases there was a reasonable expectation that investigation would lead to some improvement in classroom practice.

York Street School

ACTION RESEARCH REPORT 23   12 February 1983

Classroom Queue

I was concerned about the length of the queue at my desk of children wanting their assignments marked or seeking assistance with their work. I discussed it with the class (3rd years), the children agreed that too much time was being wasted in the queue, and we decided on two kinds of monitoring. During individual work periods one of the children would keep a record every four minutes of the people at my desk (we used an egg timer) and I would keep a record of why each child came to me at the desk. Each morning first thing I would announce the average queue length for the previous day.

After the first week it became clear that of the 30 people in the class 8 were spending much more time than the rest in the queue and so I discussed with them the importance of their learning to be independent and self-sufficient. Also I changed the routine for handing work in (two wire trays at the other end of the room instead of piling it on my desk).

By the end of the second week the queue had shrunk from an average of six people to an average of two. We agreed that the study had been worthwhile and decided that if the queue grew long again we would repeat the monitoring.

I don't think that either my pep talk to the persistent queuers, or the wire trays, explain the change. My guess is that it was due to class interest in shortening the queue. But the experiment achieved what I wanted it to do, and the children obviously enjoyed being on the 'inside'.

Martha

Both reports are written on one side of a sheet of A4 paper and would have been run off on the school duplicator. Both reports convey part of their message through a line drawing. Also the reports are written in the first person vernacular without any pompous academic forms such as 'in the opinion of the present writer'. They are chatty, but brief and to the point.

In both cases it is clear that the children have been 'on the inside' of the research. Martha's children knew she was trying to shorten the queue and Penny's children knew that Marian was counting how much they fidgeted. The academic researcher may snort and say. 'No wonder that the children's behaviour changes since they knew what was expected of them.' But to the action researcher this is immaterial if the situation is improved. Democratic involvement of as many people as possible is an important feature of action research.

The only reference to the educational literature is to Penny's source of inspiration. There is no tedious reference to queueing theory or to physiological explanations of fidgeting. Action researchers use the literature only to the extent that there is something significant and germane to the issue under study; they do not genuflect to Pavlov and Piaget in order to impress their readers!

Most writers on action research see it as (1) seeking improvement in the action, (2) democratic in its involvement of the participants (not 'research

York Street School

ACTION RESEARCH REPORT 24   3 May 1983

Story Telling

Elaine Moss's article in *Education 3–13* (edited by Colin Richards, 1978) on 'story telling' inspired me to carry out an experiment on my first year junior class.

For story time over the last fortnight I had chosen *Charlotte's Web* by E.B. White. Instead of reading aloud every chapter, I read alternate chapters but told the in-between ones. This meant quite a bit of work each evening in preparing the chapters which were to be 'told'. I put a few notes on a postcard so as to get the sequence of events right.

In order to monitor the effect on the children I asked Marian (the nursery assistant) to join us and count the number of 'fidgets'. She used a hand counter for this and sat with it hidden in her lap. We had a few trial runs beforehand at recording the level of fidgeting. Obviously there is an arbitrary element in deciding what constitutes a 'fidget', but we found that Marian's counts over several days accorded with my subjective impression of the children's fidgeting. On the first trial run I told the children that Marian was joining us to listen to the stories and that she was also going to see how much they fidgeted — but we made no further reference to this. (I hope this was ethical!) I also told the children that I was going to experiment with reading and telling the story and that afterwards I would ask them which they preferred.

These are the results over ten days. The height of the histogram represents the number of fidgets; 'R' means that I read and 'T' that I told the story. The difficulty is in measuring fidgets, but Marian and I both thought she was recording consistently. It would seem that, apart from the first day, my story telling held the children's attention more than my reading aloud.

In a show of hands on day 10, 18 of the children voted for 'telling' as better and 12 for 'reading' as better. Some of their comments were interesting: 'It sounds more like you were there' (pro-telling); 'I was worried that you might miss something out' (pro-reading).

Penny

subjects'), and (3) reflective. The latter point is not brought out clearly in these reports so let us expect that after three months, these two teachers would be writing further reports on the basis of careful reflection and discussion with colleagues of the issues involved.

Suppose that other members of staff in the school also started to study the problems of classroom queueing. It could become a school issue, with a staff working party meeting regularly to consider progress. This could eventually lead to a more extensive paper which might be submitted to a teacher's journal for publication. I add this comment simply to establish the view that action research reports are not 'necessarily limited in scope!

Teaching as Finding Out

(From Armstrong, M., 1981, 'The case of Louise and the painting of the landscape', in Nixon, J. (Ed.) *A Teachers Guide to Action Research*, Grant McIntyre, p. 15.)

These words of Michael Armstrong serve as an introduction to the following extracts in which teachers give account of their own classroom enquiry, and of the consequent changes in thinking and practice.

How are we to understand the growth of understanding? Most attempts by students of human development have been made outside the classroom, in laboratories and clinics, or in the studies and libraries of universities and research institutes. Or if research has taken place within classrooms, it has been conducted by outsiders who have played little part in the daily life of the class, least of all in teaching. Participant observers have not, for the most part, been observant participators. It is commonly assumed that the requirements of objectivity oblige us to eliminate teaching from the list of serviceable research techniques. The unfortunate consequence is that we thus deprive ourselves of a powerful, if rarely articulated, source of evidence and insight as to the nature of intellectual growth. For part of the art of teaching consists in eliciting, analysing and seeking to make more reflective the thought and action of others: consists, that is to say, in asking children questions, discussing their ideas, exchanging experience with them, finding out what they know and how they think, watching them grow. There is a self-consciousness implicit in this aspect of a teacher's activity that makes those teachers who manage it successfully — however fitful and fragmentary their success — students of those they teach as well as their teachers. Participant observation is characteristic of their method and inseparable from it.

Learning About the Classroom Through Diary Keeping

(From Enright, L., 1981, 'The diary of a classroom', in Nixon, J. (Ed.) *A Teachers Guide to Action Research*, Grant McIntyre, pp. 37–8, 42–4, 51.)

A common form of data collecting, used by many teacher researchers, is the reflective diary. In extracts from Lee Enright's article, we see how a primary teacher used this device for recording a range of impressions from daily classroom experience. Analysis of these data provided the teacher with a new and critical look at children's learning capabilities.

The Diary of a Classroom

Any teacher embarking upon an action research project faces the problem of when, how and what to record: before, during or after the lesson; emotions, facts, dilemmas or surprises. This problem was particularly acute in my case because my research was a response to general, but nevertheless urgent, concerns. These centred on the way in which children use ideas to solve problems for themselves, how these ideas might be shared through more effective group discussion, and how the teacher might collaborate with the pupils in the learning that goes on in the classroom.

Since, at the outset of the research, I was not at all sure what data would help me explore these questions, I decided to record as much detail as I could about everything that happened in my class. During the first half of the summer term of 1978 I began to keep a diary. I wrote this up daily, a task which required between two and three hours every evening. Maggie Gracie, who was the deputy head of the school, also taught my class and was able to take an active part in the research. She read through my entries regularly and added her own comments where she felt necessary. Her moral and professional support proved invaluable.

The following year I repeated the diary. I had moved with my class up into the third year and it seemed an opportunity not to be missed to repeat the exercise with the same group of children a year later. Moreover, several questions remained from the previous summer. In particular I had become very interested in the part played by talk and discussion in learning and I wanted to examine what happened in my class. Because it still took two to three hours each night the diary was again restricted to the first seven weeks of the summer term. Nevertheless, in that short time I still managed to fill five A4 files.

It is now two years since I wrote the first diary and one year since I wrote the second. Reading through them produces a variety of sensations; some of the events I can hardly remember, while others are recalled in detail by a single sentence. The person writing the diaries could almost be someone else; someone who was obviously very excited by what was happening and who had the good fortune to work in an atmosphere of support and encouragement. All the data given here comes straight from my diaries; some are quoted directly, others are paraphrases. . . .

Three boys — Mark W, Martin O and Roy — had great success through ignoring the conventional restrictions involved in monoprinting. On the first occasion. Mark W and Roy asked if they could use two colours instead of the standard one colour — hence monoprint. I said I did not think it would work unless they could really mask off one area from the other. Some time later they showed me a beautiful duoprint for which they had used blue and brown.

The next day Roy had really caught the bug with this work. His first print used three colours, but was not as successful as his duoprint — probably because he did not press hard enough. However, he carried on, saying that how he would do one with four colours.

> Roy prepared what he called his 'Shepherd's Sunset': Martin O was allowed to help achieve the artistic effect. The sky was blue first, then some white was added with a finger and mixed slightly. Red was added in spots, and then all the colours were mixed until Roy was happy. We got two prints off the board, both of which are very pleasing.

This episode made me realise that however 'crazy' or impracticable children's ideas may appear, they often produce work which is of very high quality. This incident encouraged me to be more accepting of apparently inapplicable ideas, and thus encouraged the children to come up with them. Children in my subsequent classes have benefited from this approach, and I have also found it works with other members of staff in my teaching team.

Knowing when and how to intervene often poses problems when teachers are trying to encourage children towards finding their own solutions. Maggie and I came to the conclusion that when the problem is one that teacher has no immediate answer to, it is perfectly reasonable to join in with the children's speculation.

It should be made quite clear to children, though, that your speculations are just that — they are not directives. It is also true that if children know that they are free to ignore your suggestions, the intervention becomes less crucial.

> Tracy, Sarah T and Theresa asked if they could use a flower press. I said there wasn't one belonging to the school. I thought Fiona owned one, but it turned out that she had left it at home. Did they fancy making one? They did! Unfortunately, we had no butterfly

nuts in school either, but they improvised a way of putting pressure on their flower samples.

They put them between thick sheets of corrugated card and jumped up and down on them! This certainly flattened the flowers, but a) it didn't dry them sufficiently, and b) jumping up and down with both feet landing on the same spot repeatedly is, in Sarah T's words, 'Knackering!'

At this point, I remembered Maggie's brick collection. She has been collecting examples of unusual or 'limited edition' house bricks, and these are kept in her office. I sent the girls to ask if they could borrow some bricks.

Theresa, Tracy and Sarah T collected their flowers from Maggie's office today. Because of the week's half-term holiday, the flowers were pressed for nearly a fortnight. The girls were very pleased with the result. They said they weren't going to put them in their books. They wanted to mount them on something. While they were still sorting them out, I noticed the store of polystyrene in the corner of the Art Area, which adjoins the Science Laboratory where we were working.

I went over to look for a decent sized piece, and found one which had two circles and two rectangles cut out of it. I took it in and suggested they arrange some sugar paper in the spaces (the rectangles and circles were all in rectangular recesses), but Sarah T said they could put the sugar paper at the back of the holes so that it would show through — brilliant! I left them to it.

Once you begin to accept that children are adept at solving their difficulties, it is easy to become over-excited and start concentrating on your own feelings. This never occurred to me until I started to look at myself as a teacher by keeping the diary. For instance, on one occasion some boys in my class faced the problem of how to make arrows go further. I became too excited to think about the effect I was having on their discussion, which was tape-recorded and then transcribed for inclusion in my diary. However, as soon as I listened to the tape, I began to realise what I had done. Russell had made thirteen contributions, Stuart had made seven, Mark K three, and I had made twenty-four — more than all three boys put together. I had also interrupted six times. I had not realised just how easy it is to dominate children's conversation and discussion. Now I find that I can learn about children's ideas by listening and by using eye contact to bring in other members of the group. Before I heard this tape and transcribed it, I hadn't understood that being excited and positive about what is being discussed can be just as damaging as holding 'discussions' held along the 'leading questions' lines....

I wrote the diaries while working full time in the classroom. I would argue that it is not necessary for a teacher to withdraw from teaching before carrying out useful research. Much that is valuable can only be carried out by the teacher who is working in the class. Keeping the diaries forced me to look more closely at myself, the children and our interaction. It has made me think twice about the things I say and do in the classroom. Further, the research enhanced my understanding of problem solving, handling discussions and teacher participation generally; and it helped me to gear my teaching to the needs of the individual children.

I believe that children learn best through enactive experiences, and the logical extension of this is that teachers do the same. I found two distinct advantages in action research: it enabled me to discover more about myself as a teacher, and I experienced a mode of learning I can incorporate into the work I plan for the children.

Discovering About Discovery Learning Through Classroom Enquiry

(From Hulse, Y., 1988, 'Discovering discovery learning', in Conner, C. (Ed.) *Topic and Thematic Work in the Primary and Middle Years*, Cambridge Institute of Education, pp. 11–13, 16–17, 18.)

Yvonne Hulse's article shows quite clearly the meshing of teacher development and classroom research. As the focus of enquiry, the teacher decided to think more closely about topic work, an aspect of her curriculum that she felt needed improvement. As a result of asking questions about children's learning in topic work, and of using observation to explore those questions, the teacher became involved in an important learning process. The study raised questions about planning, organisation, responding to children's curiosities, classroom interaction, teaching style, and the nature of discovery learning. We also see how the curriculum developed in response to the insights raised for the teacher by her classroom enquiry. In this, curriculum development became a continuous process, determined by the interplay between teacher, child and regular professional reflection.

Understanding the process of cognitive development and reflecting on its implications concerning my own teaching practice, I began to realise that I was discovering for myself the substantiality of discovery learning.

The Plowden Report states that in discovery learning the 'essential elements are enquiry, exploration and first-hand experience' (Para. 669). Taking these factors as a simple means of identifying discovery learning, my intention was to investigate their presence in the topic work I have observed.

All the observations were done at random. The groups of children were unspecified in advance. The exercises were done as the opportunity arose within the 'normal' classroom pursuits.

The aim of this article is to attempt to unravel some of the mysteries of learning that happened during the course of one term specifically in relation to topic work. It is an account of *discovering discovery learning*. As teacher, I was discovering with the children. We learned many things together.

For the course of the summer term the whole school had been given a broad brief. Our topic work was to fit under the heading of 'Living Things'.

> Traditionally, the only science taught in primary schools was nature study ... there is hardly any material more suitable for study for young children than living forms. (Plowden, 1967, Para. 663/4)

And I had lots of ideas. We could grow things. We could use this as a basis for lots of observation drawing. We could make graphs. We could ... and then I realised that perhaps it wasn't what the children wanted or even needed to know. I put it to them.

The children are aged between five and seven and were intrigued by the unusual request. What would you like to find out about? A great debate followed and I confess that I forced a compromise solution.

Whales were dismissed — we did that last year. Snakes were a possibility as were bees. Eagles were put under the broader heading of 'Birds of Prey'. I homed in on the birds of prey. I knew I could get hold of the taxidermised variety from the local museum and it was always possible to get 'the man with the owls' to pop in. And just think of the art work we could do: charcoal drawing, pastels, needlework, pottery. I was brimming with enthusiasm, but was I guilty of steering the children in the direction that I wanted to go, to the place where I was confident of success. I think I probably was. I knew I intended to consider owls rather than eagles.

The term started. The stuffed owls peered out with unblinking eyes from their glass cases over my handiwork on the pinboards. The children were impressed briefly but flitted on to more important issues concerning events at home and peer group relationships. I let them go. We needn't rush. We had a long term ahead. The owls would wait until the children were ready.

A few days later we were off almost by accident. Two little girls had been enrolled as Brownies. They wanted to know which of our owls was a Brown Owl. It was the only one we hadn't got, but the discussion had begun. We identified the owls and looked very closely at them. I discovered that the children had gathered a fair amount of knowledge concerning the birds and they gave specific indication of having read the information I had provided. They knew which board to turn to and yet I had not consciously witnessed their attention to the displays. Was this the emergence of some of the elements essential to discovery learning? I was encouraged to continue my investigation, but I was still not completely sure what I was seeking. The children made drawings of the owls. Some enjoyed it but to others it seemed a chore. I realised that perhaps we didn't do enough observational work. I needed to encourage them to look more carefully and to be more accurate in their representations. Yet I had not to dismiss any of their attempts.

All of our work was progressing according to my original schedule and yet my usual reservations were there. My instinct told me that the children's curiosity and reverberant enthusiasm was still untapped. The teacher needs to know how to elicit the right responses. I realised my quest was partly to begin to seek out and understand how to reach the abundant source of learning potential in my keeping.

The dissection of some barn owl pellets proved to be the first key. The pellets had been treated for fleas but the children were warned about keeping their fingers away from their mouths as the pellets possibly carried worms. These instructions fascinated them and the children were constantly reminding each other to wash their hands. We used an enormous heap of paper towels that day. The pellets themselves received a mixed welcome. The element of exploration was apparent from the start. Sarah didn't like the look of them; Hayley didn't like the feel. For Ian and Daniel, exploration gave way to enquiry as they found a tiny skull and wondered what animal it had belonged to. As they continued to explore they gained confidence in their penetration of the pellets. Experience taught them to be gentle so as not to break the bones. Sarah's exploration began with the help of a pencil but ended there some ten minutes later. Carlie took Sarah's departure as her opportunity. She had been enquiring about the boys' explorations from the sidelines and now she seized her chance to gain her own first-hand experience. Her initial experience of the pellets' texture left her unsure of the exploration but delight quickly followed from the discovery of the first bone.

The boys continued to find pleasure as they explored the pellets and uncovered bones. When Daniel found the first rodent skull, he couldn't contain his excitement. Others came to enquire and Daniel was more than willing to share the experience verbally with them.

As the pile of bones grew larger, the group redirected their attention from the pellets to a closer inspection of their recent discoveries. There were comparisons, identifications, hypotheses, all components of enquiry. Their enthusiasm was contagious and self-supplementing, leading to further enquiry, exploration and first-hand experience. It was an experience they were eager to communicate amongst themselves, to visitors and even to the school in an assembly. . . .

As I watched the children, I became aware that enquiry happens often in their movements and gestures: fascinated faces, pointing, whispering behind hands, wriggling up on to knees, giggles, nervous raising of hands. The children were caught in an experience they wanted and needed to explore. They had opportunities, too, to display their knowledge absorbed from previous experiences and were delighted at Mr Spires' surprise at their descriptions of the contents of pellets. Their excitement at learning new facts was obvious. The children's eyes moved with the owls. Their emotions were brought to life as they sympathised with the tawny owl's injury. Just by watching the owls, Christopher observed differences and enquired: 'Why has the tawny owl got bigger eyes than the barn owl?' Jody wanted to know: 'Why does he (tawny owl) turn his head right round like that?' And enquiries of long ago were remembered: 'Is that a brown owl?'

Enquiries as to why the owls' flight should be silent came from the experience of feeling the draught made by the barn owl's wings yet not hearing anything at all. Although told about the wing feathers being barbed it wasn't until they explored and experienced the incredible softness of the feathers by stroking the barn owl that they understood why the owl was so silent in flight. They explored reasons for the necessity of this silence and enquired about its relevance to other birds.

Mr Spires' visit inspired some written work including letters of thanks.

At the end of term I was to be further encouraged. Although we had covered the work on owls in a very informal and almost haphazard way, when given a free choice of writing a number of children chose to make their own book about owls.

Not all the work we did was so helpful. After Mr Spires' visit I arranged an activity to extend the development of physical science. It proved extremely difficult to observe and impossible to write down coherently. The work was done by one group and I was left with such a frustration that I abandoned the notion very quickly. I had taken the idea from the silent flapping of the barn owl's wings. We could explore the properties of sound and movement when 'flapping' different materials and objects. On examining the evidence that I did salvage from the observation, I began to comprehend the confusion. The pattern was decidedly different.

Exploration was evident. The children seemed almost relieved to disappear in search of items even though they seemed unsure of their purpose. Previous experiences helped to verbalise their findings by making comparisons: 'Like the wind', 'A jingle sound like bells'. But of enquiry there was very little to see. What there was seemed almost an emotional petition to comprehend what was being asked of them. I realised that perhaps I hadn't understood it either. How could I expect them to understand? How could I communicate something that I had failed to formulate properly for myself? The children did their best. They didn't fail me, I failed them. I discovered the truth. True discovery learning should be initiated and carried through by the learner. The teacher's role is to come alongside, to encourage, to direct only when asked. I must learn not to interfere, just guide. . . .

I personally enjoyed my own discovery learning and it has left me with an eager anticipation of more. I am looking forward to developing the topic work in my own classroom, as I begin to understand more fully the goals I have for myself and for the children, as well as helping them to achieve the goals they set themselves.

Reference

CENTRAL ADVISORY COUNCIL ON EDUCATION (England) (1967) *Children and Their Primary Schools*, (The Plowden Report), London, HMSO.

Responsibility in Learning

(From Fraser, A., 1987, 'Sometimes they know themselves better than we do maybe'. Unpublished MA thesis, University of East Anglia, pp. 17–31.)

As part of a research-based long course of study, Alister Fraser chose to monitor development of the classroom 'council' or 'meeting'. This had been established by a class of third and fourth year juniors in response to the children's request for more involvement in decision-making. In this, the children chose, for discussion, the topics that seemed to be of relevance to them. They also evolved, over a term, formal procedures for conducting their debates and made significant contributions to schoool organization and the curriculum.

The study gives a qualitative, close up view of learning as it took place in the classroom. As with Yvonne Hulse's study, (p. 174) the teacher's own understanding developed alongside that of the children. In this extract, the teacher analyzes aspects of one of the meetings, both as it happened and, later, away from the classroom action. The children had been discussing responsibility in school at their previous meeting. After ranging over a number of topics, they took up the subject of responsibility again, at a much more mundane level than their teacher had wished. But later reflection offers new interpretations and forces the teacher to question his own assumptions about the children's learning style and their preferred starting points.

The study implicitly raises a key question about what it might mean to start from the child's experience in learning. It also shows how small scale classroom research can challenge and change a teacher's previous conceptions.

As the weeks and months have passed since the meeting began, I have been increasingly aware of a discrepancy between what I see as suitable subject matter and what the children seem happy with. When I look back through my notes taken during each meeting, I am quite horrified to see the number of entries such as:

Great sense of disappointment.

The meeting has limped through the last half hour and is positively dull.

Is the meeting nothing more than a forum to air grievance?

I get a feeling of annoyance. Why can't they get off these details and on to something more interesting?

I find this meeting getting very dull. They seem happy enough with it though.

I am finding it very difficult to bear with the content of this meeting; the constant side-tracking, the bickering.

I feel they see the door but are unable to go through. The way forward seems so glaringly obvious but they miss it every time.

Why do I feel so irritated by this meeting? I want them to get off this trivia and on to something more weighty.

I have asked myself why this should be so. How could it be that my agenda is so very different from theirs? What is it that I expect from these meetings that the children apparently either do not want or do not need? After all, THEY choose what they talk about, THEY decide when a subject is to be closed or continued; I have to assume that they talk about the things that they want to and that matter to them.

I decided to look a little more closely at this particular issue. I have taken the meeting of 16 December 1986, one with which I was particularly disenchanted, and have set a transcript of parts of it against my field notes. I follow this with an analysis of the data.

December 16 1986

A cold classroom. The blower heater makes such a din the children have vote it be switched off whilst they have their meeting.

Donna: Last week we discussed the stock cupboard, children's party, the letter to be sent to Mr B., responsibility...
Paul: Did you send the letter to Mr B., Michelle?
Michelle: Yeh, I have
Paul: Oh and also, I think the party for the children went very well.
Chair: Michelle
Michelle: Well Paul, yes I have written it but I've got to take it down to Mrs S. and I've got to check it's alright.

I find it difficult to say what I am feeling. Last week's meeting was really interesting. They were talking about responsibility and proposed it be carried on this week. I have a sense of expectation of good things to come.

Chair: Any other business? Michelle
Michelle: I have had a couple of complaints ... well, one to be precise, but I'm not going to name the person who has complained, but Charles has been teaching the younger ones, the children in Mrs P.'s class to swear and fight.
Charles: I didn't swear!
Chair: Deborah
Deborah: If it's still OK with the meeting, I think Charles ought to go in the middle and explain himself why and...

> *Paul:* I don't think that's a very good punishment because, I mean, you just go up to the middle, 'Oh I'm sorry I've done it. It won't happen again.' You go back to your place and it doesn't matter. I mean it doesn't matter a bit. And also Charles ... I've never heard Charles swear before in front of one of the little ones but he has been scrapping with Ian Clark, I know.
>
> *Donna:* Paul it's not just going in the middle saying, 'Oh I'm sorry I won't do it again.' You explain yourself why you did it in the first place.
>
> *Michelle:* But that's the trouble. We went through that last time ... we nearly brought people up here ... nearly every meeting and it was getting to be just good fun to go in there and say, 'I'm sorry I did it, it won't happen again.' And things like that. And Charles, it can't be a very good game if you're teaching the younger ones to fight. And if you weren't teaching them to swear how come I've got a complaint from Ben that you were?

The subject moves around to Charles playing at fighting games with the Infants and the meeting disapproves. I can't see any future in this topic. I feel myself getting rattled by it.

> *Zak:* One, Michelle, Charles does not swear to the little ones and two, OK the game was a bit rough but the little ones enjoy it. I mean, they haven't got hurt.
>
> *Paul:* Yes, but it's not whether they enjoyed it or not, it's bad for them. And also, I've never ... I disagree with Ben because I've never before heard Charles swear to a little one anyway.
>
> *Chair:* Debbie
>
> *Debbie:* Just because they haven't got hurt before, they may get hurt now if you keep carrying on bashing them around and throwing them on the floor.
>
> *Zak:* The game we are playing is not a fighting game it is friendly.
>
> *Paul:* But fighting is still fighting and it'll teach them to actually bully littler people than themselves
>
> *Donna:* Friendly or not, Zak, they still get hurt.

Charles deserves everything he gets — just give it him and let's move on. I am finding it difficult to sit through all this laborious subject matter.

> *Chair:* Paul.
>
> *Paul:* So what are we going to do about Charles then?
>
> *Chair:* Deborah
>
> *Debbie:* Let's just let him go in the middle and let him explain why he does it and if he does it again then we could think of something then, 'cause every time people have gone up in the middle it has always stopped.

I feel my mind wandering outside the classroom. There is a smell of burning wood from the cottage next door and it brings back memories of a childhood trip to France. I vaguely wonder if any of these children will remember this scene in twenty-five years time.

> *Paul:* I think that if you are going to play with the little ones you should play nicely. And I propose we close the subject for now as this is the first time you've been told.
>
> *Debbie:* A minute ago, Paul, you wanted to decide what we were going to do about it. Now you want to close the subject.
>
> *Chair:* All those in favour of Paul's proposal which was . . .
>
> *Paul:* . . . that we close the subject and tell them not to do it again and to play nicely with the little ones.
>
> Chair: All those in favour raise one hand . . . Carried! Any other business?
>
> *Debbie:* I want to counter-propose that Charles goes in the middle . . .
>
> *Michelle:* You can't counter-propose that Charles goes in the middle 'cause you've just . . .
>
> *Chair:* . . . The subject is closed!
>
> *Michelle:* You've just proposed . . .
>
> *Chair:* Michelle, the subject is closed!
>
> *Michelle:* No! She can counter . . . she can counter-propose if we re-open it or we don't close the subject or whatever it is!

The mechanics of their meetings are so tedious — but the children don't seem to mind. Debbie is her usual back-biting, aggressive self.

> *Cathy:* Last week on Thursday I was playing netball and I saw one of the little ones on the window sill in the Infants toilets. I think it was Jonathan or his brother.
>
> *Victoria:* Mr F., can you bring that up in Assembly again?
>
> *Mr F.:* No, I don't think so. We can go on like this for ever can't we? No, you've got to come up with some better solutions.

It always seems to me that the meetings are at their worst when the children set themselves up as policemen. Is autonomy in children about nit-picking? Is this pursuit of autonomy not worth all the trouble we are giving it? There's a lot of interaction here but to what end?

> *Michelle:* But why do we need to find out who it is? Why can't we just find a solution to stop them. All we're doing is gabbling on about whether it was Jonathan or not! We're not getting anywhere.
>
> *Paul:* I propose that three people go down to Mrs S. and Mrs P. and remind the infants of the dangers of climbing up.
>
> *Chair:* All those in favour raise one hand . . . Unanimous.

Their deliberations are long-winded and laborious but it has to be said that they do seem to get there in the end.

Donna: I know it's something a bit stupid but yesterday at breaktime there was some people writing on the blackboard, 'Donna for Simon.' And they've been spreading it around the school for weeks and it's not fair on me!

Paul: Or Simon!

Michelle: Whoever is doing whatever you're doing writing on the board about Simon fancies Donna, is another form of bullying!

Victoria: Who was writing 'Simon for Donna' on the board?

Voices: Kim! Kim! Charles! Cara!

Victoria: Why? Why do you have to write that? Does it matter if he fancies her? There's no need to go spreading it around the board.

Simon: I don't!

Zak: No, but Simon said, 'Go ahead, you can write it on the board. It's soon rubbed off.'

Deborah: Even if he did say you can go ahead it don't mean to say you have to!

Interesting, Victoria asks the question, 'Why?' about someone writing on the board. She wasn't concerned about punishing the guilty party but wanted to know the reasons it was done. Debbie, aggressive as ever, ruins the moment; it is almost as if those children who are ready to move on in their moral development are held back by those who are not.

Why am I getting so irritated by much of the subject matter? Last week the meeting ended on a high note. They had really got into the subject of responsibility. Some of them didn't want to finish the meeting. It ended with a proposal to continue the discussion this week. What has happened to it?

But are not the things they are dealing with now important to them? Does the subject-matter really matter? Isn't the process of this meeting enough in itself?

I'm cold and irritated, tired and not really involved in this meeting. My mind is on something else and I just can't find it in me to get involved. I dimly hear the meeting taking care of itself. THEY don't seem to be bored; quite the contrary, the meeting has a very good-humoured atmosphere.

Kevin: Peter tells me Ryan had a box of Maltesers in the toilet!

[Laughter]

Cathy: If he was eating them in there it is quite unhealthy to eat in the toilets!

[Laughter]

Ryan: We weren't eating them in the toilets, Peter, they were in my bag and we were eating most of them at lunchtime.

Debbie: I've got two things to say. One, you shouldn't be opening your Christmas present at school 'cause they are for Christmas ...

Ryan: It would have melted!

[Laughter]

At last I hear them beginning to take up the idea of responsibility from last week. I feel my spirits rising.

> *Peter:* Last week weren't we supposed to ... in this meeting to go back on to responsibility?
>
> *Michelle:* Oh yes. It doesn't matter whether we proposed it or not because I'm just opening the subject. Can we talk about responsibility please?
>
> [Long pause]
>
> *Victoria:* What did we talk about last week 'cause I've forgotten?
>
> *Kevin:* We were talking about responsibility ... like Richard fell over and we got onto that subject and dodgeball.
>
> *Paul:* I think we've finished with the dodgeball. We were actually on responsibility not whether we should play dodgeball at breaktime.
>
> [Long pause]
>
> *Paul:* What we decided about dodgeball last week was that nobody got hurt and the ball had gone over once and that was when it was getting very silly and people were punching it as high as they could.
>
> *Debbie:* Can't we get off the subject of dodgeball. I think we all know how to play it and we've gone all through that last week.

They just can't get into it. Many false starts but they do not succeed in taking it on board. They seem unable to take it on in the abstract and need a practical focus.

> *Peter:* Wasn't it proposed that there were to be no ball games in the playground?
>
> *Victoria:* But the trouble is now we've got no ball games on the playground. There's nothing to do.

I find myself experiencing a lot of difficulty in refraining from taking over. Responsibility and things like that is what they should be talking about! This is why I started the meetings off in the first place!

> *Michelle:* Look we're not on to ball games. We're on responsibility!

Amazing, they just do not seem able to enter an abstract area like this without a context to take them into it. They were really fired up last week by this very issue and now they cannot rekindle it. Responsibility is a dead duck this week and my spirits flag.

I listened to the tape recording of this meeting several times and on each occasion I was transported back experiencing the same feelings of frustration and irritability. I read through my field notes and they had precisely the same effect. Having transcribed the meeting and having inserted my field notes at the appropriate points, I am now not so sure that I was justified in feeling the way I did. The very act of listening to carefully and writing down what was said has helped me to an understanding that was precluded by the nature of my immediate reactions.

It was altogether too pat to reach the conclusion that my irritation and disenchantment was the result of a mismatch between what I considered suitable subject matter and what was suitable from the children's point of view. Going beyond that, I now realise that it is with myself and not the children that I ought to be irritated. Irritated, for not seeing that the children were very much concerned with the very issues that I wanted them to be considering. On the surface the meeting was about the naughtiness of Charles, graffiti on the blackboard and ball games. Underlying all that was consideration of fundamental issues such as social interaction, self-knowledge and understanding, crime and punishment and so on. There was no discrepancy between my agenda and theirs. The only difference was in the way I wanted them to tackle it and the way they actually did. The vehicle should have been unimportant in the sense that I should have been aware that the issues were, in fact, being addressed; but at the same time it was critically important to the children. Without it they could not handle the abstract ideas. What I think I have stumbled upon here is an example of the difference between stages of cognitive development. The children needed the practical context in order to address abstract ideas. Margaret Donaldson (Donaldson, 1978) uses the term 'disembedded thought' to describe thinking that is not operating within the supportive contexts of meaningful events:

> It is when we are dealing with people and things in the context of fairly immediate goals and intentions and familiar patterns of events that we feel most at home. And when we are asked to reason about these things, even verbally and at some remove from them, we can often do it well. So long as our thinking is sustained by this kind of human sense, and so long as the conclusion to which the reasoning leads is not in conflict with something which we know or believe or want to believe, we tend to have no difficulty.

They needed the context of Charles playing with the younger children as a way of thinking about punishment; they needed the context of the graffiti on the blackboard to consider the notions of bullying and social interaction. And as a teacher I ought to have been more aware of that.

The matter of their apparent inability to discuss responsibility is interesting and seems to fly in the face of what I have just said. After all, discussion had already taken place, and at some length, the week before. A context had already been established. Why therefore were they unable to rekindle the sort of passion with which it had been tackled only seven days earlier? I can think of only three possibilities. Firstly, they felt is had already been done to death and it really was just flogging a dead horse; the immediacy of the moment had passed. Secondly, it was just too much like hard work! Christmas was just around the corner and end-of-termitis had set in. Thirdly (and I shudder every time I re-listen to the tape recording) they were only too aware of the sighing and general looks of disapproval and disenchantment that were emanating from their teacher! Yes, I wanted them to discuss responsibility but I wanted it couched in my reality and not dodgeball or whatever.

But there is more than one lesson to be learned here. If I had set myself the task of devising a lesson on 'bullying,' for example, I wonder if in my wildest dreams I would have used the context of a few children scribbling things on the blackboard about another couple of children, to get the message across? I doubt it very much. Even if I had, would it have had any authenticity for the children? And it makes me wonder just how inappropriate a lot of our teaching really is. How many of our lessons are set in contexts that we think are appropriate but come nowhere near the child's world. And does the teacher/children/classroom mix provide an appropriate learning environment? Margeret Donaldson (Donaldson, 1978, p. 82) has this to say:

> ... you cannot master any formal system unless you have learned to take at least some steps beyond the bounds of human sense, and (that) the problem of helping children to do this in the early stages of their schooling — or even earlier — has not been properly recognised and is not usually tacked in any adequate way.

Moreover, we talk about releasing children from the egocentricity of early childhood; I wonder how much of the irritation I felt was because my own agenda was, on the surface at any rate, being thwarted — teacher egocentricity in action!

Reference

DONALDSON, M. (1978) *Children's Minds*, London, Fontana/Collins.

Studying Classroom Organization

(From Groarke, J. *et al.*, 1986, 'Towards a more open classroom', in Hustler, D. *et al.*, *Action Research in Classrooms and Schools*, London, Allen and Unwin, pp. 81–6.)

Action research at its best becomes a long term analytical process rather than an occasional professional event. Here we see the teacher working through systematic action research steps, from identification of a problem to a second stage revised action plan. As Michael Bassey pointed out in an earlier extract (p. 165), the teacher researcher has to work at a quicker pace than most traditional classroom researchers, since, in order for the enquiry to be of value, it aims to feed classroom decisions which demand practical action. The process, therefore, cannot be too ponderous. In this, the reader will be able to sense the difference in style between this work and some of the large scale qualitative research cited earlier.

I decided to study the organization of my classroom and its effect on the quality of learning for several reasons. First, I knew that in order to provide the best possible learning situation I needed to make some systematic study which would give me insight into the present organization and how it affected the structure of learning. Secondly, having taught previously in large junior schools where streaming and setting were the norm, I felt that I needed to revise my ideas and practice to suit the needs of a mixed ability class in a small primary school. Thirdly, I wanted to find out which methods worked best for me, so many (apparently) conflicting theories and exhortations as to how best to teach were, to say the least, confusing. There were other, subsidiary reasons stemming from the three broad ones above. In particular, my worry that children seemed to be wasting a lot of time in activities peripheral to or unrelated to the work which I wanted them to be doing.

My previous experience was of two large 'three form entry' junior schools which were considered 'formal' in that there was a timetable which had to be adhered to and class teaching resulted in all children in a class working at the same subject at the same time. Both schools were streamed: one by ability, the other by age with sets for language and maths. My appointment to a smaller, one form entry primary school with mixed ability classes meant that I had to consider making changes which from the start included arranging my own timetable. In order to meet the challenges of this new situation I started an inservice course which led me to investigate my teaching and embark upon classroom action research.

During my first two terms at the school (I started in January) I became more and more dissatisfied with the way in which I was running my class. I had grouped the children by ability for maths and English work but then more or less allowed them to proceed individually. They had to complete certain maths and/or language tasks before they went on to project work or art and craft. Many of the other lessons were class lessons in which I attempted to teach the class as a whole. I was still 'bound' by the restrictions placed upon me by my previous schools and by my lack of knowledge as to the alternatives available and I felt that I was not getting to the heart of the problem for the children at both ends of the ability range. So, at the start of the new academic year (1980), I decided that I needed to make a definite break from the way in which I had been teaching for the previous five years. I did not want to rely solely on intuition — I felt that more objective evidence was required upon which to base any changes I might make. Hence my interest in classroom action research when it was introduced during one of the lectures at college.

(1) General Idea

Any previous changes in the organization of my classroom had been made on the basis of guesswork, experience or intuition. Any subsequent changes I wanted to make should be made on the basis of a close examination of what was actually going on in the classroom. The changes which would be made should aim to relieve the pressures on me (e.g. with all children doing maths there was a constant demand for my attention — for help, for marking, for telling children what to do next ...) so that I could stand back from time to time to see what was going on and thus use my time to best advantage. The changes should also result in a better match of the task to the child, obviating the boredom of the more able children and the frustration of the less able.

(2) Reconnaissance

I wanted to use a portable cassette recorder to 'listen in' to what was going on in a target group of children. Before doing this I told the children what I was going to do and that it was for my 'night school'. They accepted this without question as many of their parents go to night school. To accustom them to the presence of the tape recorder I left it around (recording) for several weeks. This ensured that, by the time I came to make the recordings which I would transcribe the novelty had worn off and the children would be behaving quite naturally.

I observed and recorded the target group for half-hour periods during which I made written observations of five-minute intervals, noting down what each child in the group was doing. As an aid to my memory, and to give a more general impression of the classroom, I kept a daily diary in which I jotted down anything which might give me a clearer insight into the workings of the classroom.

One or two problems arose which I had not foreseen. First, it can be very difficult trying to observe a group of six children at regular intervals when there are thirty others in the room — just as you are about to write down your third observation a mini-crisis develops at another table! Second, small portable cassette recorders pick up a lot of unwanted noise as well as the interaction of the target children. Perhaps more sophisticated equipment would have overcome this; as it was, it made transcribing the tape recordings very difficult at times. A valuable insight into the workings of my classroom was obtained from an observer with wide experience of primary schools who helped me to realize that certain aspects of the classroom could be investigated more deeply.

My findings were interesting because, although (to my surprise) most of the talking (which I had assumed to be 'time-wasting') was 'on task', it tended to be very superficial. The children were not really involved in their work. They appeared to be interested only in completing the task in hand. Some of the children were rushing to finish work to get on to 'more exciting' tasks. The children with difficulties were penalized as they could not finish their tasks (in maths or language) and get on to art and craft or project work and they were relying heavily on other children nearby to help them. Instead of motivating them to complete their English and maths, this method of organization seemed to be counter-productive (i.e. realizing that they would not finish in time, they gave up and became bored and disruptive).

(3) **General Plan**

I would abandon the system which had specified maths/language tasks followed by more creative work and introduce a 'rotating timetable'. This would, I hoped, relieve the pressure on me and also the pressure on the children. They would know that, at the end of a particular group period, they would change activites, so that even if they disliked what they were doing they knew that there would be an end to it in the not-too-distant future. They would all get a turn at art or topic work, as well as maths or language.

(4) **Action Steps**

(a) Reorganize furniture and materials. I made several resource-cum-work areas in the classroom, starting with a library area and an art area, then introducing a maths area and a project area. I tried to arrange the desks and chairs so that there was a variety of environments available — large group, small group, pair and individual.

(b) Reorganize the timetable. Instead of subject areas I wrote 'group work'. During these periods the children would be doing one of the specified activities with their group. The times were quite long (on average one hour), though I still had to accommodate class lessons such as PE, music, games.

(c) Reorganize the curriculum so that each of the six groups had a particular curriculum area to work at. These were: language, maths (number work), practical maths (measuring, etc.), project, art and craft and music. Subsequently, when the school adopted a better-balanced maths scheme the number work and practical maths were integrated and I added creative writing.

(d)   Organize the children into groups of approximately six. These were friendship groups so they were mixed ability groups. The maths and language work, however, was set according to ability. So, for example, for six children working at language during one 'group work' period only two or three might be doing the same work.

(5) **Monitoring and Implementation + Effect**

I immediately noticed a reduction in the pressure on me, the children and (something which I had not considered, though it seems obvious now) the materials. If only six children were engaged in language work at any one time it did not matter if we only had twenty-nine dictionaries, for example: previously it could have caused problems. I also found that the curriculum had broadened for the children at the lower end of the ability range. Whereas before it had taken them so long to complete their maths and language task that they could rarely spend any appreciable time on other areas of the curriculum, now they spent the same amount of time as everybody else on the different curriculum areas. The time spent changing from activity to activity was not as long as I had feared.

(6) **Reconnaissance**

Although this system worked far better than the previous one I had used, it was not without its drawbacks, as I found after a few months. I was still keeping the diary and so I decided to narrow the focus again on to a small group of children to confirm or contradict the conclusions I had drawn from the wider observation. I used the same techniques as before (with the same inadequate equipment!) and my findings were as follows:

(a)   the system was too inflexible. One hour might be too long (far too long!) for a group to practise percussion instruments in the stock room; it might be too short for a group engaged in research for a topic.

(b)   Some children needed a lot of supervision and encouragement from me or they would sit back and let the time pass until they could get on to something else.

(c)   My time was still not being used to best advantage. I found that I was repeating instructions to group after group after group; the same problems kept cropping up as each group came to work at a particular 'subject' so I would have to leave the group I was with to come and explain.

(d)   I was still tending to mis-match tasks to certain children.

(7) **Revised General Idea**

I would achieve more flexibility by altering the organization.

(8) **Action Steps**

(a) I revised the timetable so that there were a large number of shorter (approximately half-hour) group periods in a week.

(b) I gave the children more responsibility for organizing their work in that they could decide when they would do a particular activity (as long as they did a certain number during the course of a week). This means that they could spend half an hour at something then change, or they could carry on and spend an hour, an hour and a half, two hours, depending upon their interest and the demands of the task. The children kept their own daily record of what they had done. These were collected by me every Friday so that I could see how much time each child was spending on the various activities to ensure that there was not too much emphasis on one area of the curriculum at the expense of others.

(c) I devised a timetable for myself, distinct from the children's, showing the 'group work' periods as blanks, during which I could work with a particular ability group, or friendship group, or with an individual. This was to be as flexible as possible, being filled in from day to day.

(9) **Monitoring of Implementation + Effects**

This system produced a good response from the children who seem adapted to it and made good use of its flexibility. It seemed to make the best use of their time as they had quite a large degree of control over its use. I was able to spend more time with individual children or with small groups, and so I was able to discover their needs and cater for them. The work I set the children tended to be a better 'match' and therefore there was a better chance of its seeming meaningful to the children who would then complete it. So in changing the organization of my class I had also improved the motivation of the children. The atmosphere in the classroom was more relaxed and informal, but the quality of the work and the attitude towards the work had improved visibly.

The study highlighted ways in which I needed to grow as a teacher and helped me to become aware of certain steps I could take to achieve this. When I moved to a new school as deputy head I found myself in a situation where I had to re-examine my practice, taking into account the different ethos of the school, the different expectations of parents, children, colleagues and the head and the previous experience of the children. I could not start at this new school where I had left off at my previous school, but because of my experience of action research I was able to undertake close scrutiny of *this* classroom and make the changes I thought necessary much more quickly and confidently then would otherwise have been the case.

I still keep a daily diary and value the cassette recorder (with all its limitations) as an 'ear' into what is happening in the classroom. I anticipate that this kind of questioning will continue throughout my teaching career — nothing ever stays the same, the teacher changes, the children change, and consequently one's perception of oneself in the classroom changes. I now know that there is a process by which I can investigate my classroom and initiate improvements in my practice whenever I perceive the need.

Reflective Teaching in Action

(From Southworth, P., 1987, 'Happy talk', *Cambridge Journal of Education*, 17, 3, pp. 156–8.)

Though not specifically designed as a formal action research study, this account from a classroom teacher documents the reflective processes she went through in providing for the needs of an elective mute in her class. The journey starts with a review of previous support offered to the child and his family — the 'reconnaissance' stage characteristic of the formal action research process (Elliott, 1981, page 1). The article then gives insights into the teacher's thinking and how this was related to the practical decisions she made and implemented. The paper documents a constant weaving in and out of reflection, judgements, action and revision of judgements as the teacher responded to the developing situation.

The work displays all the hallmarks of 'reflective teaching' outlined in a separate extract from Andrew Pollard's book (pp. 210–11).

It was after the interview, I felt very pleased with myself on securing a permanent position in Cambridgeshire. The head teacher and I walked into what was going to be my classroom. 'Oh by the way,' he casually said, 'you'll have an elective mute, Clem.' My stomach did a quick somersault. I knew the problems, as I had taught one before. The conversation took another direction and no other mention was made of the child. Owing to a variety of reasons, Clem's previous teacher and I had little time for discussion before she left for overseas.

During the weeks before I started at the school in September 1986 I thought a little about Clem and his 'problem'. I hadn't seen him in the classroom or read his records so I had very little to draw on. What I did have, however, was my experience of teaching Amanda, another elective mute, about six years previously. There were slight differences in the situation; Amanda was silent only in the school building. Other than that, she was like any other child. From what I had understood Clem would neither talk to strangers nor communicate in the school playground.

When Amanda came to me after a year in school I suspect I had the same feelings as anyone else who has had to deal with a 'mute' — 'I'll make her talk'! Over the next twelve months I tried every tactic I could think of. I was kind, I was firm. I withdrew privileges but to no avail. I spent hours trying to get her to talk but I just became more and more frustrated and exhausted with it all. Amanda did talk the following year, but by then I was at another school so I didn't know how it was achieved.

What I learnt from Amanda was that my intentions of 'success' had generated my own feelings of failure. I now know mutes will talk. What is needed by the teacher is patience, and an acceptance that you may not be the one they talk for. Also I think it is important that as far as possible one treats them as 'ordinary' class members. With those reflections in mind I started the new school year.

In the first week of term I read the detailed file on Clem. There were copies of reports from teachers, headteachers, educational psychologists, and speech therapists. There were also copies of letters not only written and received by those already mentioned, but from the DEO, the school doctor and nurse, the educational welfare officer and lastly Clem's parents. I was amazed. I recall no support from outside agencies at all for Amanda when I worked in Lancashire.

It would take far too long to go into every aspect of Clem's school record. One or two points are perhaps worth noting. He was first seen by the educational psychologist six months after he had started school. It was recommended he should stay at the school and have extra 'assistant' time. (I don't know if the latter ever came about!) From that time his case had been kept constantly under review. From the parents there had been a continuous dialogue with the school but little physical presence. There had also been complaints by them about other children 'picking' on Clem. I detected a wariness on their part towards all the outside agencies who had become involved with Clem and understandably they were worried as to the outcome of all this attention. The prospect of Clem talking in the near future didn't look good; he had been known to make animal noises to a few children but no recognisable conversation had ever been recorded in his three years at school.

There were two items inside the file that I decided to continue. These were a 'book' for home/school communication and a 'tape'. The 'book' had been in use for a year, instigated at the suggestion of the educational psychologist, and was working well. The 'tape' of Clem's reading made at home and regularly returned to school was a more recent introduction the previous summer term. Again this seemed to be working well.

In the second week of the Autumn term I introduced myself to Clem's parents via the 'book' using as informal a style as possible, and I sent the tape home.

After a few weeks Clem was having trouble with his reading so I decided to tape the next story so he could listen and follow the story before reading it himself. I also taped a brief 'introduction'. Two weeks later in the 'introduction' I asked Clem if he would allow me to play his reading tape to the class so they could hear what his voice was like. The following day at lunch time I played back the tape. The sentence 'I give my permission for you to play this to the class' sounded out. I was delighted. That afternoon Clem was out of the classroom for a while so it gave me the opportunity to have a 'pep talk' with the rest of the class. I pointed out that Clem was very shy, that this was a big step for him. We then started to record ourselves reading. When Clem came back into the classroom it was quite natural to play his recording as well, although his brought spontaneous applause from the class.

By the middle of October things seemed to be going well. The 'book' told me that Clem trusted me but also that he had spoken to a couple of his brother's friends for the first time. I didn't, however, place a great deal of hope on the latter statement as I had heard exactly the same sentiments expressed about Amanda. We were playing Clem reading daily and the class reminded me if I forgot! Clem's mother had also made contact personally. On one occasion towards the end of October she had been one of several parents who had taken up the invitation to come into school and sample the school lunch. This was an ideal opportunity for me to sit and chat to her and more importantly for Clem to see us together. She was obviously very anxious about Clem and I tried to encourage her to relax about him, easier said than done!

In mid November via the 'book' I heard that Clem had a puppy. I asked him on the tape if he would tell us about the puppy that night after his usual reading session, then the class could hear all about it. In common with many classrooms we often have informal talk sessions and this seemed an ideal opportunity to involve Clem in one of these.

The following day we played the tape and at the end of the session I drew Clem close to me and asked him if he would nod or shake his head in answer to the children's questions about the puppy. This he did, but it restricted the questions somewhat! The next course of action was to ask him to 'mouth' the answer and to my amazement he did. Taking a chance, I asked if he could make the same sound as his puppy. Hey presto, out came a 'woof' — I felt the same as when my son said his first word! I didn't push him any further then and the conversation took another avenue.

Shortly afterwards we had to go into the hall for a talk by the railway police. When we were returning to the classroom Clem's best friend came rushing up to me to say that Clem had said 'I wouldn't want to be electro-cuted'. That was it, the dam had burst. I spoke to Clem; he replied not directly but into my ear. At playtime some of the class went rushing to tell the reception class teacher the news. She had, of course, taught Clem and I suspect was rather sceptical about this information. However, she spoke to him and he replied in the same way he had to me. From then on we couldn't stop him! Gradually he stopped the whispering in your ear. What a thrill it was to see him joining in assembly and chatting in the playground. In the classroom he didn't know when to be quiet and yet I didn't want to stop him! So a happy ending to Clem's story. Now I've almost forgotten he didn't speak. He is still quietly spoken and may never be an extrovert but he seems so much happier. The children have always been very patient with him but were highly delighted when he did speak.

Why did he start to speak? I don't think we can really say. Was it that the puppy provided him with something about which he really wanted to com-municate? Was it the fact that his mother and I made contact and she became more relaxed about him? Was it the tape and hearing his own voice in school? Was it the handwritten book establishing a more personal approach than typewritten letters? Was it my lack of 'tension' about the situation? Or was the time just 'right'? Perhaps each of these had some bearing on the final outcome; I don't know, I'm not an expert. All I know is what worked for Clem and perhaps if you ever have an 'elective mute' the approach outlined here may work for you.

Reference

ELLIOTT, J. (1981) *Action Research: A Framework for Self-Evaluation in Schools*, Cambridge Institute of Education.

The Effect of Teacher Enquiry on the Child

(From Pickover, D., 1984, 'Recognising individual needs', in Thompson, A. and L. (Eds) *What Learning Looks Like*, London, Longman for Schools Council, pp. 81–3.)

An in-depth, small scale observation study by the teacher can be the beginning of complex and long-term change for children and classrooms. Through child observation and study, new understandings and feelings can develop for the teacher. These may have a profound effect upon the way she views the child, her capacity for diagnosing needs, the provision she makes, and the effect this has on the child's motivation, learning and sense of worth. This extract from Di Pickover's article illustrates this well. As for Pam Southworth (pp. 192–5), curriculum development is not a mechanistic and pre-determined process. At its best, it can evolve from the developing quality of the teacher's understandings and sensitivities, as she moves through stages of data gathering, reflection, discussion, sharing and re-formulation. In much the same way that Stephen Rowland articulates (pp. 199–202), the power of small scale teacher research to bring about improvements in classroom practice are well demonstrated.

As my observations continued I became very interested in the importance of listening to pupil-teacher exchanges. What could I learn by paying more attention to the important issues in a child's world? The example of William, a 9-year-old member of my group, serves to show that teacher and child can learn so much together when they begin to recognize one another. The story has no end as the learning is still taking place.

Before I listened to William, I saw him as a child who seemed indifferent to school and recognized that there was probably little about school he would relate to. His home and school life are different in many ways.

For several weeks, William brought to school wildlife sketches, carefully drawn pictures of the woods and fields about our village. His collection included pictures of his pole cat, his ferret and his dog. There were pictures of foxes and pheasants. I looked with some interest at the pictures but thought little more about his offerings as they slid to the bottom of his locker. He continued to bring along pictures yet still I continued to ignore the message. William had few friends in the group and his life-style is different from that of many of the children. However, other children in the group began to support his interest before I did and soon brought along their own books and pictures about wildlife to share with him.

One day, by chance, I asked the lady who delivered the meat to the school kitchen if pheasants were available at her shop. Some days later, a brace of pheasants arrived. I hoped, through William's interest, to continue to promote his improved social standing in the group. I videod the scene, as

William, now the centre of intense interest and excitement, shared with the group his knowledge of pheasants and his experiences on the highways and byways about our village. From this beginning, that is the point at which the children and then the teacher first took real note of William's interest, many things have changed for him. He is now a valued reference point in the school for his knowledge about wildlife. The wider school community, for example, the teachers, the cook, the village policeman, all now have a positive point of contact with him. At lunch-time one day, another teacher helped William to write a letter to the local gamekeeper, as he wished to incubate some pheasant eggs at school. The school secretary rang the local museum for stuffed exhibits as William's exhibit had reached an advanced stage of decay.

His own family supported his interest and revealed their own love of the countryside. My 'Match and Mismatch' group were interested in William's development and offered their own suggestions, including titles of fiction books related to his interests, and before long William began the story of *Danny, the Champion of the World* by Roald Dahl.

William talked about and sketched, and plucked and dissected his pheasant, and enjoyed the attention he received and his new found social status. And he was not disruptive. At 2.40 one afternoon and close to home time, William (under no known pressure) announced that he would like to write a story and in what remained of the afternoon he began his tale about 'The Lucky Poacher.' The following extract comes from the beginning of William's story.

> 'Watch out Jim,' said Dave, 'Here comes the keeper. Let's hide the guns, nets and ferrets in the land drain and hide in that hedge.'
>
> The keeper went past them so they got out and went home. The next week Dave went to Jim's house and Jim had some pole cats. Jim picked one up and said, 'This is a good one I got five rabbits with it Sunday. We will take this one tonight. There will be no keeper about because he's playing darts at the pub so we can take the dog and guns and lamps.'
>
> The night came and there was no keeper about so they went into the woods. They found a rabbit hole so they put the pole cat down and quick as a shot a big rabbit ran out. They shone the lamp on it and let the dog go. After a few minutes the dog came back with the rabbit. Dave put it in his pocket. They went on after they had got out the pole cat. All of a sudden they heard a grunting. They hid in the hedge. Then they saw what they thought was the keeper. It was a fox walking in the dry leaves.

The pages that followed provided a fascinating story from a child who previously had struggled with every line he wrote. William must have wanted to share his interest in wildlife for a long, long time. One day I thought to look through his record folder — a large envelope into which teacher and child put pieces of work throughout the child's school life. A glance through it showed wildlife entries in pictures and stories and paintings, small but significant entries which had been put into it at fairly regular intervals.

My observations of William and of the other individuals in my group have helped me to listen more carefully to children. Listening, in the end, to William has helped me to change his whole approach to school life. His wildlife work goes on. So too do my classroom observations. I hope that by investigating and reflecting upon my own practice, I might better understand the needs of the individuals with whom I work and act in their best interest.

Classroom Enquiry as a Way of Understanding Learning

(From Rowland, S., 1986, 'An approach to understanding children', in Hustler, D. *et al.*, *Action Research in Classrooms and Schools*, London, Allen and Unwin, pp. 29–31.)

Stephen Rowland is firmly of the belief that study of one's own teaching and classroom is the most effective way by which a teacher can come to understand how children learn. His own research, referred to in a previous section (pp. 47–9) convinced him of this. Here he talks of the insights which the teacher researcher can gain from in-depth study of children's learning. Such study can be valuably complemented by sharing and testing ideas with fellow professionals in order for teacher researchers to extend and enrich their subjective theories.

Teacher research tends, by nature, to be bound to the context of individual schools, classrooms or children, given that one of its main purposes is to improve teaching. It is a study of particular cases, rather than of many. This sharing and challenging of individual subjective ideas can add significantly to the validity of the theories which emerge from small-scale study, and can make the research more generally valuable to other teachers.

Classroom Enquiry as a Way of Understanding Learning

Throughout these comments I have referred to the need to be continually interpreting children's activity — their actions, their language, their writing and so forth. However, given the real classroom situation, with thirty or more children often engaged in a wide variety of activities and only one teacher, much of our interpretation is done very rapidly and on the spur of the moment. The speed with which we have to make decisions on our feet often allows little time for cool reflection. For this reason, the interpretations we make in the classroom are likely to be based upon rules of thumb and everyday assumptions about the children and the subject matter which we use uncritically. A more careful investigation of what children's activity really means requires not only time but a certain 'intellectual space': an opportunity to reflect, preferably with others, and to develop and share insights into the children's concerns, skills and understandings. Certainly, we cannot reflect with this degree of intensity upon all the children's work, nor even upon a major proportion of it. Nevertheless, the in-depth study of selected samples of activity from our classrooms can lead us to challenge, modify and at times radically alter those assumptions from which we work when we interact with children in the classroom. It can help us build an understanding of the learning process and of the concerns of children which are expressed and developed through that process. We must develop such understanding if we are to realize our role as educators rather than merely as purveyors of knowledge.

It is this attempt to study in depth, or analyze, selected samples of children's activity and work from the classroom that I call Classroom Enquiry. I use the term 'Enquiry', rather than 'Research', because what we are doing differs from normal academic research in several fundamental respects. Our enquiry starts with our experience of the children and their activity. This experience is necessarily subjective. It is quite obvious that any two observers — and especially any two teachers — presented with the same classroom event will perceive different things. For example, a piece of writing that strikes one teacher as showing a poor grasp of grammatical conventions, for another may be evidence of ingenuity in self expression.

This essentially subjective way in which we interpret children's activity has been considered by many educational researchers to be something to be avoided at all costs. 'Unreliable' accounts by teachers are dismissed in favour of such devices as observation schedules which list categories of behaviour to be noted and ticked off at regular intervals, and questionnaires and tests whose results can be readily subjected to statistical analysis. Such attempts to gain understanding again reflect a view that knowledge about the world — our knowledge about the children as well as their knowledge — can be mechanically broken down, or reduced, into 'bits' without regard to the subjective experience of the observer or the observed.

On the contrary, explanations of the learning process itself must be concerned with the children's intentions, their intepretations and the thinking they bring to bear upon their activities. It is these non-behavioural aspects of classroom life to which we must gain access. Such access cannot be achieved by an observer who is separated from the children both physically and psychologically by the research tools used to measure behaviour. As teachers, however, with our close involvement with children and our professional skills which are intended to enhance our understanding of them, we are in a privileged position. The inner thoughts and intentions of children will never be quite open to us and we shall always have to speculate. But we are, nevertheless, in a position to relate closely to children, to prompt their thinking and thereby to begin to reveal it.

Our own writing plays an important part in this process of revealing the children's understanding, of sorting out our ideas about it. One can only get so far by thinking alone. With children's writing in mind, Bruner (1966, p. 105) described writing as 'a calculus of thought for ill-informed problems — problems, that is, without unique solutions'. For the enquiring teacher, writing is not so much a means of recording data — although it certainly has that function — or even of communicating ideas, as much as it is an important part of the process of reaching closer understandings; understandings which are always provisional and are the subject of further reflection.

However, once we accept that it is our subjective experience and reflections upon that experience that provide the richest material for our enquiry, there are serious difficulties we have to meet. How sure can we be that our interpretations of the children's activity will not merely reflect our prejudices, our personal framework of values? Will not the understanding we thereby gain serve to confirm our position rather than challenge it?

In order to meet these difficulties we have to think carefully about how we can share our descriptions and interpretations of classroom activity with each other. Whereas conventional research seeks to minimize the subjectivity of the observer and make generalizations from as wide a sample as possible, classroom enquiry capitalizes upon the different viewpoints of teachers in order to evolve deeper understandings of the particular. We therefore have to construct opportunities for exploring these different perspectives. Our classroom enquiry, then, is not only an individual's reflective analysis of what has taken place, but it also must invite the reflections of others. It goes without saying that this sharing of ideas must be critical, that is we must welcome the expression of contrary viewpoints in an atmosphere that is secure enough for individuals to reason with and reject each other's ideas. The results of such open sharing of our understandings of children's activity will not result in generalized and objective truths about how children learn. To search for these would be a hopeless enterprise. Rather, it aims to produce intersubjective understanding of the complexities of the learning mind and a more articulate language with which to share such understanding. The difficulties we have in understanding how children's minds, and indeed our own minds, grow are arguably not so much the result of a failure to establish the 'true facts' about learning, but more the result of a failure to develop a language and a conceptual framework for interpreting and communicating our experience of learning.

It is our task, through classroom enquiry, rather than the task of the professional researcher, to develop this framework. Traditionally, the functions of production and consumption in educational research have been separated by the institutions of research and schooling. Academic research has produced 'findings'. Teachers have been encouraged to make use of those findings. That we have largely failed to do so reflects not only the difficulties we have in finding the time to interpret research that is often written in a language that is inaccessible to many of us. Nor does it simply reflect an inevitable opposition to the conclusions which such research has reached. Rather, it is based upon our conviction that it is the teachers' and children's experience of the classroom which is authentic, their reflections upon it which are most significant, and that it is in these that our understanding of children in the classroom will be rooted. But that understanding will not develop by itself. It requires our concerted effort to make opportunities of sharing our experience, reflecting upon it and thereby making it more articulate.

Reference

BRUNER, J.S. (1966) *Towards a Theory of Instruction*, Cambridge, MA, Harvard University Press.

Using Observation to Learn about the Classroom

(From Siegen-Smith, N., 1984, 'Talking counts', in Thompson, A. and L. (Eds) *What Learning Looks Like*, London, Longman for Schools Council, pp. 18–20.)

This teacher was a member of the 'Longsearch' group, formed in Hertfordshire by teachers who were interested in researching their own classrooms. The group context has the advantage of offering a fuller exchange of ideas, experience and perspectives than are afforded to the action researcher working alone. As Stephen Rowland suggested (pp. 199–201), collaboration enables the teacher researcher to benefit from the giving and receiving of challenge to their thinking. Such challenge may enrich the analysis and interpretation of classroom data, extending teacher researchers' subjective theories.

In this extract, the teacher talks of small studies undertaken using observation. In particular, the benefits, as well as some of the problems, involved in using the video camera in small-scale research are outlined.

Where I felt that video and audio tapes would be most useful was in capturing what happens when the teacher is not directly involved, when children work together alone. I have only begun to collect evidence, and am particularly interested in developing this area of my observation. It seems that there are two types of task to identity: those that need talk to *get them done* and those which are accompanied by talk. During these collaborative situations, different children take on different roles, for example, craftsman and apprentice, author and critic. So far, what has stood out is that children can and do apply themselves unaided to the task in hand, maintain the application and share ideas with one another to move each other on. One particular example was when three first-year girls were attempting to make a water-clock. They set to obtaining containers, tubes and bricks from a box of available equipment. They could have allowed the water to drip from one container to another, but chose to adopt a syphoning system, even though this had not been discussed with me in the classroom. One child said, 'My dad does his wine like this, I've seen him do it.' Another replied saying she had seen someone do it too. They managed to syphon the water from one container to another and then proceeded to solve the problem of a flow rate that was too fast by blocking the end of the tube with first a paper-clip and then plasticine. It seems that without my presence the task had developed further than I had expected it to go. They recalled their own experiences and fitted them to the task in hand. Had I not observed, I would not have seen a normally quiet, timid girl initiate the syphon idea, nor would I have seen how it was taken on by the other two children.

To return to the idea of children working as craftsman and apprentice, I observed two first-year girls working with clay. One of the girls had been shown by me how to wedge the clay and the importance of cross-hatching in order to join pieces together. The child who had not had the benefit of this group explanation became the apprentice to the other girl who patiently explained all that had been shown her. I also recorded on video two boys who were reading each other their writing. One adopted a quite mature style of questioning, asking his partner, 'What do you think of this?' and 'How do you think you could make this better?'

What is important, I feel, is to establish a framework which provides for this variety of context, where children can contribute to their own learning, can lead the teacher down unconsidered avenues, can themselves become critical of their own work and can work with their peers towards common goals.

Two other observations illustrate how the physical environment and material resources affect the way children learn.

Having spent many hours collecting and displaying materials in my classroom, it seemed appropriate to determine whether they do in fact stimulate children, suggest lines of inquiry, inspire tentative language. While team-teaching a group of mixed first- and second-year children, my partner and I had decided to display a selection of animal coverings. This included various types of furs, feathers, shells, horns and skins. On the first morning, and at various times in the day, the children stood about in groups discussing the possible origins of the various objects, sharing each other's ideas, comparing the unknown with the known, professing likes and dislikes and suggesting to each other ways in which they might like to paint and draw the objects. Following this initial impetus, ideas and responses were expressed in a variety of media.

More recently in my first-year class, I have been looking to see where children choose to read. What seems to have emerged from this is the need to offer choice and organize the classroom accordingly, making the most of shared areas outside the room too. One child wrote:

I like reading outside because it's nice and quiet and the birds twitter and there's a nice soft breeze and there's no noise to bother me. That's why I like sitting outside.

I feel that there should be room for children to exercise their choice and for these possibilities to be made explicit. Three girls asked whether they could read in a shared cloakroom area with carpet. They took books with them and gradually each changed their books to ones without words. They took them outside and sat beside each other chanting out their own stories from the pictures. The outcome was, 'shall we go and ask her if we can write stories?' The children were moved into writing by the availability of a certain type of book and, it seems, by the possibility of choosing the place to go. The separateness of the place seemed to have enabled them to create a quiet fantasy world where making up stories was easy and natural.

During the two years since I joined the group, I have dabbled with various methods of observation. Working in the early days with a team-teaching partner and group member made it particularly easy to set up and use video equipment. We found that the influence of the video was quite substantial on the children and ourselves; and found it difficult in a large open-plan unit not to engineer situations at particular tables. We found though that the video can and does reveal aspects of learning which could not otherwise be observed. I value the use of audio-cassette recorders, but have found that they too have an effect on the children unless they have become used to having them around. I have managed to observe many interesting and useful things by freeing myself and taking a step back in the classroom and noting what children say and their interactions, responses and initiations. I feel I would like now to go on to use a micro-cassette recorder, which I feel may be more flexible in capturing moments of the classroom which might be critical.

Being a member of a group concerned to observe and make sense of learning has sensitized me to the multiplicity of situations operating within the classroom. It has confirmed and articulated intuitions and encouraged a critical yet constructive scrutiny of my performance:

> What are my responsibilities as organizer of the framework of my classroom?
>
> What is the quality of the interaction, my interventions, collaborative learning, my listening?
>
> Are there contexts for real response?
>
> Have I acknowledged the commitments of the children themselves to their own learning?
>
> Do I inhibit or encourage this commitment?

What I feel I am tentatively aiming towards, as a participant observer, is how to 'steer a path between total abdication and total domination', as well as how to create contexts for learning which capitalize on the resources of the classroom. To have once become a participant observer, one can no longer look or listen with unquestioning eyes and ears.

Reference

Investigating Talk: Guidelines for Teachers' Groups, Schools Council Language for Learning Project, Institute of Education, London University, 1981, p. 27.

Teachers Working Together in School Through Action Research

(From Day, C., 1986, 'Sharing practice through consultancy: Individual and whole school staff development in a primary school', in Holly, P. and Whitehead, D., *Classroom Action Research Network Bulletin*, 7, Cambridge Institute of Education, pp. 121–3.)

As an 'outsider' from the university, Chris Day worked as consultant to the staff group of a primary school, helping them to establish action research in their professional practice. This project had two main purposes for the staff. Firstly, they wanted 'to evaluate individual teaching styles and techniques in order to make the most effective use of teachers' and pupils' time in the classroom'. Secondly, they wanted 'to share their teaching with colleagues in order to gain ideas and assess strengths and weaknesses across the school as a whole'. The strength of the project lay in linking individual teacher development to whole school development.

The full article gives a detailed account of the action research undertaken by each teacher. In this extract, a summary is presented of the main learning outcomes. It also shows how these contributed to understanding at school level.

Individual and Whole School Development Issues

The kinds of teacher learning that occurred are summarized below both in relation to specific classroom practices and pupil learning, and in terms of perceived gains for themselves as professional self-critics; and this summary is followed by staff testimony as to how the individual learning was related to whole school staff development.

The Learning for the Individuals: a Summary of Main Gains in Classroom Teaching identified by Teachers

John

1 Allowing time for children to formulate answers to questions.
2 Identifying a greater concentration span of children working in groups than anticipated.
3 Questioning the use of only 'functional' language by children.
4 Demanding too much of self as teacher in setting up and servicing small group activities.
5 Observing that children's talk in groups, like that of adults, goes off at a tangent.

Eileen

1 Classroom organization is good.
2 Identifying that she did not speak to some children or draw out others enough.
3 Questioning her use of language with children, particularly her questioning.
4 Questioning her organization of activities (in P.E.)

Linda

1 Helped her to see various aspects of her classroom organization more clearly and to make changes for improvement.
2 Identified that she talked too much.
3 Identified that children used much 'incidental' language in small group talk.
4 Identified a problem of 'challenging' the children (in P.E.).
5 Identified that her original teaching method was too stressful and exhausting for her. Changed this and became more effective.

Anna

1 Identified that children coped well with working together as a whole class.
2 Identified that children were learning to wait for her attention.
3 Identified that she needed to pay more attention to individual children.

Maria

1 Reinforced the 'special help' she gave to individual children.
2 Gained a fresh insight into her use of apparatus (in P.E.).
3 Identified that children in small groups do not always use procedures taught previously by teacher.
4 Identified that she sometimes, unintentionally, gave children answers to some points instead of letting them work out for themselves.

Marian

1 Confirmed that small groups worked efficiently.
2 Was surprised to find she 'hurried' some pupils, providing answers for them rather than 'insisting' on them being worked out by children.

3 Identified that she needed to encourage more original ideas.
4 Identified that children need 'extra' help in learning how to use new equipment.
5 Learned that she ought to encourage children to discuss their work as a group.
6 Underlined the importance of 'structured talking' among children working in small groups.

As well as these gains the teachers in their diaries also pointed, unasked, to general gains which they perceived to be of benefit to them.

Summary of Professional Learning Issues

John   — an increasing confidence in his own critical skills
        — 'gained enormously as a classroom teacher'
        — enabled him to improve the quality of his teaching.
Eileen — 'reinforces certain points' and made her think deeply about the issues concerned
        — growth of self-confidence in her own critical abilities.
Linda   — 'more confident, better organized'.
Anna   — 'a great opportunity to stand back and analyze' her teaching and philosophy.
Maria   — after watching the videos she changed her approach to working in and with small groups — with a more satisfactory outcome.
Marian — it is a good way of studying children
        — illustrated 'strengths and weakness of which I am already aware'.

The Learning for the School: One Year Later

'While the scheme was of obvious interest and importance on (the) individual level it would seem to follow that any benefits to be gained by an individual teacher should be transferred to the whole school.'

The result of the meetings between staff, informally during the work with individual teachers — when one would occasionally be invited to view another's lesson on videotape or 'hear' about the experience in staffroom conversations — and formally in the three after-school in-service meetings agreed for the purpose of sharing practice, can be illustrated by comments written a year later by teachers and the headteacher. Teachers found the comments from other members of staff 'very constructive and illuminating' and that the exercise 'fostered even greater co-operation with each other'. As a staff they had been able 'to observe each other's teaching approaches and learn of different methods and techniques ...' and enabled to 'gain an overall appreciation of the learning activities pursued in the school from the nursery through the entire primary age range ...'. They had found the material 'very useful as a basis for staff discussion either on general classroom procedures and techniques or on particular aspects of classroom practice'. They valued the record they now had of 'educational activities which should benefit any new teacher joining the staff'.

Their detailed comments reveal the importance of this sharing experience in terms of their enhanced understandings of the context in which they taught.

Progression and Continuity

All the teachers commented on the value of being able for the first time, to see a context for their own teaching in which they were able 'to discover our aims and objectives collectively, rather than in isolated areas such as nursery, infant and junior'. As a staff they found that their 'unspoken aims were made clear' to their colleagues as well as themselves. The insights gained into what other classes of older and younger age groups were doing 'helped plan more effective work and gain a more consistent approach to learning throughout the school'.

These comments from the teachers illustrate the new insights into the curriculum and organization of teaching:

> As an Infant teacher I very rarely have the opportunity to see a junior teacher organize her day and teach concepts. It was very interesting and enlightening to see how similar her approach was to mine, within an integrated day.

> It was interesting to see how the progress in child development is maintained and encouraged by teacher's caring attitude; the way the work is presented; the objectives and teaching points upon which the work is based; the natural conclusions following each activity and to observe how my own work fitted into the overall scheme.

> As I watched my own recordings I realized that much more value could be gained by involving other members of staff; it gave me a source of reference and it gave them a change to see me at work and to comment favourably or unfavourably, upon what they were watching.

Importantly in terms of the project aims, they identified the contribution of the work in the process of forming school policy:

> ... With this view of activities pursued through the school, we have been aided in our formulation of school policy and examination of any curriculum area or teaching technique we may be omitting.

Those engaged in professional development work have often raised the problem of transferring individual learning to the school context in ways which will influence others. No such problem need arise where the integration of individual and whole school development is contracted in the initial stages of design (Elliott, 1982).

Reference

ELLIOTT, J. (1982) 'Institutionalising action research in schools', in ELLIOTT, J. and WHITEHEAD, D. (Eds) *CARN Bulletin No. 5*, Cambridge Institute of Education.

The Meaning of Reflective Teaching

(From Pollard, A. and Tann, S., 1987, *Reflective Teaching in the Primary School*, London, Cassell, pp. 4–5.)

The notion of reflective teaching, around which this book is based, stems from Dewey (1933), who contrasted 'routine action' with 'reflective action'. According to Dewey, routine action is guided by factors such as tradition, habit and authority and by institutional definitions and expectations. By implication, it is relatively static and is thus unresponsive to changing priorities and circumstances. Reflective action, on the other hand, involves a willingness to engage in constant self-appraisal and development. Among other things, it implies flexibility, rigorous analysis and social awareness.

Dewey's notion of reflective action, when developed and applied to teaching, is very challenging. In this section, we review its implications by identifying and discussing what we take to be four essential characteristics. These are:

1 Reflective teaching implies an active concern with aims and consequences, as well as with means and technical efficiency.
2 Reflective teaching combines enquiry and implementation skills with attitudes of openmindedness, responsibility and wholeheartedness.
3 Reflective teaching is applied in a cyclical or spiralling process, in which teachers continually monitor, evaluate and revise their own practice.
4 Reflective teaching is based on teacher judgement, informed partly by self-reflection and partly by insights from educational disciplines.

A reflective teacher, therefore, is one who constantly questions his or her own aims and actions, monitors practice and outcomes, and considers the short-term and long-term effects upon each child.

Reference

DEWEY, J. (1933) *How We Think: A Restatement of the Relation of Reflective Thinking to the Educational Process*, Chicago, Henry Regnesy.

What is Appealing about Action Research?

(From Cummings, C. and Hustler, D., 1986, 'Issues in action research', in Hustler, D. *et al.*, *Action Research in Classrooms and Schools*, London, Allen and Unwin, pp. 38, 39.)

What then was appealing to us about action research? There are two attactive features in the literature which we would like to emphasize. In discussing these, we will attempt to take up a few of the implications of these features as we tried to take account of them in our preparations. First, action research in the classroom starts with attempts to uncover 'problems' or 'matters of concern' as perceived by teachers, rather than problems as perceived and conceptualized by those not directly involved in the day-to-day business of classroom life. Starting points for much research on education stem from concerns linked with particular educational disciplines, where the problem is first and foremost a problem within some aspect of that discipline, whether it be to do with learning theory, language development or whatever. Research also stems from national considerations and worries, which must be taken on board, but which the teacher in the classroom may find difficult to translate into a 'problem for me'.

Our view certainly is not that action research is 'better' or should replace such research, only that it is different and one central aspect of that difference lies in this focus on 'problems' as perceived by the practising teacher. By 'problem' we could be talking about anything which emerges or forms a starting point: from a niggling worry about how much time some children are spending queuing up for the teacher, or a feeling that more could be done with story-time, to some strong concern as to how the present pattern of allocating children to tables may be affecting progress in particular areas, or a growing lack of conviction about aspects of the teaching style we generally adopt.

[...]

A second feature is that action research cannot be pre-planned or pre-structured in the same way, for example, that traditional experimental procedures demand. As the research develops, so do ideas develop which can lead to action of some sort, which leads to more information and analysis and more ideas and so forth. The goal is not to produce a study which meets, as a major target, the criteria for 'respectable' scientific work and which can stand as a contribution to learned journals. The goal is to illuminate and, if possible, attempt to resolve issues as the research develops. As the name implies, action research involves action, which feeds back into the situation and can lead in unforeseen directions, which are followed up because it seems to the teacher *at that stage of the research* that it is worth pursuing them.

A Teacher's Learning

(From Waterson, M., 1984, 'However do they do it?', in Thompson, A. and L. (Eds) *What Learning Looks Like*, London, Longman for Schools Council, p. 40.)

I think that the most important learning that has taken place during the time I have been a member of the 'Match and Mismatch' group has been my own.

Listening quietly in the evening to the tape of a child who during the day has read with you at your elbow, makes it possible to catch things which you missed when the actual experience was in progress. Perhaps sometimes we are so busy willing a happening that we do not pay sufficient attention. Perhaps it is impossible for us to do so. And if that occurs when only one or two children are involved, how many times does it happen with a class? Using a tape with a child reading, a child you see week after week after week, enables you to obtain a cross-section of that child's development as a reader.

The use of the tape-recorder and the diary not only provides record of some permanency, a source of information for comparison with other findings about that same child or others, but seems to quicken powers of observation and mental note-taking at times when it is impractical to use either method of recording.

Index

The Study of Primary Education —
A Source Book:
Contents of Volumes 1, 2 and 3

Volume 1: Perspectives

A Rationale for Infant and Junior Education
(From Board of Education, 1937, *Handbook of Suggestions for Teachers*, HMSO)

The Formal Establishment of Primary Education
(From the Education Act, 1944)

A Report of Progress
(From Central Advisory Council for Education (England), 1967, *Children and Their Primary Schools*, HMSO)

Progress Refuted: The Black Papers
(From Cox, C. and Dyson, A. (Eds) 1969, *Fight for Education*, Critical Quarterly Society, and 1970, *Black Paper Three*, Critical Quarterly Society)

The William Tyndale Affair: A Cause Célèbre
(From Gretton, J. and Jackson, M., 1976, *William Tyndale: Collapse of a School or a System?*, Allen and Unwin)

Public Debate and Official Response
(From DES, 1977, *Education in Schools: A Consultative Document*, HMSO)

A Brief Professional Appraisal
(From DES, 1978, *Primary Education in England*, HMSO)

'Demythologising' Primary Education
(From Richards, C., 1980, 'Demythologising primary education', *Journal of Curriculum Studies*, 12, 1)

Achievement in Primary Schools
(From the Third Report of the Education, Science and Arts Committee of the House of Commons, 1986, *Achievement in Primary Schools*, HMSO)

Primary Education: Evaluation and Assessment
(From Bolton, E.J., 1985, 'Assessment techniques and approaches: An overview', in *Better Schools: Evaluation and Appraisal*, HMSO)

Towards a National Curriculum
(From DES, 1987, *The National Curriculum 5–16: A Consultation Document*, HMSO)

2 Primary Education: Contrasting Views

Introduction

A   Liberal Romanticism
Basic Assumptions
(From Blyth, W. (Ed.) 1988, *Informal Primary Education Today: Essays and Studies*, Falmer Press)

Informal Primary Education in Action: Teachers' Accounts
(From Nias, D.J., 1988, in Blyth, W. (Ed.) *Informal Primary Education Today: Essays and Studies*, Falmer Press)

Criteria of a Good Primary School
(From Griffin-Beale, C. (Ed.) 1979, *Christian Schiller — in His Own Words*, Black)

'A Recognisable Philosophy of Education'
(From Central Advisory Council for Education (England), 1967, *Children and Their Primary Schools*, Vol. 1, HMSO)

Teaching Through the Arts
(From Marshall, S., 1963, *An Experiment in Education*, Cambridge University Press)

B   Educational Conservatism
Black Paper Basics
(From Cox, C. and Boyson, R. (Eds) 1975, *Black Paper 75*, Dent)

Putting Primary Education Back on the Right Track
(From Froome, S., 1974, 'Back on the right track', *Education 3–13*, 2, 1)

Our Schools: A Radical Policy
(From Sexton, S., 1987, *Our Schools: A Radical Policy*, Institute of Economic Affairs Education Unit)

C   Liberal Pragmatism
The Importance of Planning, Organization and Assessment
(From DES, 1979, *Mathematics 5–11*, HMSO)

Topic Work: Where Are We Now?
(From Conner, C., 1988, 'Topic work: Where are we now?' *Cambridge Journal of Education Newsletter*, 11)

D Social Democracy
The Community School and Community Education
(From Midwinter, E., 1972, *Priority Education*, Penguin)

Education for Life
(From Kitwood, T. and Macey, M., 1977, *Mind That Child!*, Writers and Readers Publishing Cooperative)

Educational Priority Areas
(From Central Advisory Council for Education (England), 1967, *Children and Their Primary Schools*, HMSO)

E An Alternative Perspective
The 'Progressive', 'Elementary' and 'Technological' Traditions
(From Golby, M., 1982, 'Microcomputers and the primary curriculum', in Garland, R. (Ed.) *Microcomputers and Children in the Primary School*, Falmer Press)

3 Primary Education: Philosophical Perspectives

Introduction

Children's Needs
(From Dearden, R., 1968, *The Philosophy of Primary Education*, Routledge and Kegan Paul)

Interests and Education
(From Wilson, P., 1971, *Interest and Discipline in Education*, Routledge and Kegan Paul)

A Critique of Plowden's 'Recognisable Philosophy of Education'
(From Peters, R.S. (Ed.) 1969, *Perspectives on Plowden*, Routledge and Kegan Paul)

Plowden's 'Facts' about Children: A 'Child-Centred' Critique
(From Wilson, P., 1974, 'Plowden aims', *Education 3–13*, 2, 1)

'Child-Centred' Education: A Critique
(From Dearden, R., 1976, *Problems in Primary Education*, Routledge and Kegan Paul)

Principles Governing the Content of Education: A Critique of Progressivism
(From Bantock, G., 1980, *Dilemmas of the Curriculum*, Martin Robertson)

The Beginnings of a Reformulation of 'Progressive' Education
(From Armstrong, M., 1977, 'The Informed Vision: A programme for educational reconstruction', *Forum*, 9, 3)

Primary Teaching: What has Philosophy of Education to Offer?
(From Bonnett, M. and Doddington, D., 1990, specially written for this volume)

4 Primary Education: Sociological Perspectives

Introduction

The Five Basic Roles of the Primary School
(From Blyth, W., 1965, *English Primary Education*, Vol. 1, Routledge and Kegan Paul)

Socialization into School
(From Newsom, J., Newsom, E. and Barnes, P., 1977, *Perspectives on School at Seven Years Old*, Allen and Unwin)

Social Class and Educational Opportunity
(From Floud, J., Halsey, A. and Martin, F., 1956, *Social Class and Educational Opportunity*, Heinemann)

Social Class Differences in Attainment and Ability at Seven
(From Davie, R., Butler, N. and Goldstein, H., 1977, *From Birth to Seven*, Longman)

Factors Affecting Children's Performance in Primary Schools
(From Central Advisory Council for Education (England), 1967, *Children and Their Primary Schools*, Vol. 1, HMSO)

Policy Informed by Research: Proposals for the Establishment of Educational Priority Areas
(From Central Advisory Council for Education (England), 1967, *Children and Their Primary Schools*, Vol. 1, HMSO)

Policies and Practice in Pursuit of Equality
(From Halsey, A. (Ed.) 1972, *Educational Priority, Volume 1: EPA Problems and Policies*, HMSO)

Language and Educability
(From Bernstein, B., 1971, *Class, Codes and Control, Volume 1: Theoretical Studies Towards a Sociology of Language*, Routledge and Kegan Paul)

Continuity or Discontinuity between Home and School Experience of Language: A Critique of Bernstein's Views
(From Edwards, A., 1976, *Language in Culture and Class*, Heinemann)

The Sociological Study of Educational Knowledge
(From Bernstein, B., 1975, *Class, Codes and Control, Volume 3: Towards a Theory of Educational Transmissions*, 2nd ed., Routledge and Kegan Paul)

Visible and Invisible Pedagogies: An Introductory Overview
(From Robinson, P., 1981, *Perspectives on the Sociology of Education: An Introduction*, Routledge and Kegan Paul)

Control, Accountability and William Tyndale
(From Dale, R. *et al.* (Eds) 1981, *Education and the State*, Vol. 2, Falmer Press)

Teachers and Their Pupils' Home Background
(From Goodacre, E., 1968, *Teachers and Their Pupils' Home Background*, NFER)

Primary Education and Social Control
(From Sharp, R. and Green, A., 1975, *Education and Social Control*, Routledge and Kegan Paul)

Classroom Interactions and Pupils' Perceptions
(From Nash, R., 1973, *Classrooms Observed*, Routledge and Kegan Paul)

The Nature of Infant Education: A Sociological Perspective
(From King, R., 1978, *All Things Bright and Beautiful?*, Wiley)

Making Sense of School
(From Jackson, M., 1987, 'Making sense of school', in Pollard, A. (Ed.) *Children and Their Primary Schools*, Falmer Press)

Racism and Sexism
(From Davies, L., 1987, 'Racism and sexism', in Delamont, S. (Ed.) *The Primary School Teacher*, Falmer Press)

5 Primary Education: Psychological Perspectives

Introduction

Psychological Traditions
(From Claxton, G., 1984, *Live and Learn: An Introduction to the Psychology of Growth and Change in Everyday Life*, Harper and Row)

The Implications of Piaget's Work
(From Isaacs, N., 1961, *The Growth of Understanding in the Young Child*, Ward Lock)

Piaget and Education
(From Adibe, N., 1978, 'The many implications of Piaget's work for education', *New Era*, 59, 3)

Piaget Revisited
(From Tamburrini, J., 1982, 'New directions in nursery school education', in Richards, C. (Ed.) *New Directions in Primary Education*, Falmer Press)

The Myth of Piaget's Contribution to Education
(From Boyle, D., 1983, in Modgil, S. and Modgil, C. (Eds) *Jean Piaget: An Interdisciplinary Critique*, Routledge and Kegan Paul)

Comprehending the Task: A Re-Examination of Piaget
(From Donaldson, M., 1978, *Children's Minds*, Fontana)

An Outline of the Contribution of Jerome Bruner
(From Conner, C., 1989, specially written for this volume)

Vygotsky and Education
(From Britton, J., 1987, 'Vygotsky's contribution to pedagogical theory', *English in Education*, 21, 3)

Common Knowledge
(From Edwards, D. and Mercer, N., 1987, *Common Knowledge*, Methuen)

The Technology of Teaching
(From Skinner, B.F., 1968, *The Technology of Teaching*, Appleton-Century-Crofts)

Behaviour Modification: Theory and Practice
(From Presland, J., 1978, 'Behaviour modification: Theory and practice', *Education 3–13*, 6, 1)

Reception and Discovery Learning
(From Ausubel, D. *et al.*, 1978, *Educational Psychology: A Cognitive View*, 2nd ed., Holt, Rinehart and Winston)

Meaningful Learning
(From McClelland, G., 1983, 'Ausubel's theory of meaningful learning

and its implications for primary science', in Richards, C. and Holford, D. (Eds) *The Teaching of Primary Science: Policy and Practice*, Falmer Press)

Freedom to Learn
(From Patterson, C.H., 1977, *Foundations for a Theory of Instruction and Educational Psychology*, Harper and Row)

Self Concept and Motivation
(From Yamamoto, K., 1972, *The Child and his Image*, Houghton Mifflin)

Meeting Special Educational Needs
(From Ainscow, M., 1987, 'The primary curriculum and special needs'. A paper presented to the conference of the National Council for Special Education, April)

Learning Styles
(From Conner, C., 1988, 'Learning styles and classroom practice', in Conner, C. (Ed.) *Topic and Thematic Work in the Primary and Middle Years*, Cambridge Institute of Education)

Children and Their Learning
(From Fraser, A., 1987, 'A child structured learning context', in Dadds, M. (Ed.) 'Of Primary Concern', *Cambridge Journal of Education*, 17, 3)

Identification and Imitation
(From Schaffer, H., 1968, 'Identification', in Lunzer, E. and Morris, J. (Eds) *Development in Human Learning*, Granada Publishing Ltd.)

Learning and the Peer Group
(From Rubin, Z., 1980, *Children's Friendships*, Fontana)

Problem Solving
(From Fisher, R. (Ed.) 1987, *Problem Solving in Primary Schools*, Blackwell)

Real Problem Solving
(From Easen, P.R., 1987, 'Developing real problem solving in the primary classroom', in Fisher, R. (Ed.) *Problem Solving in Primary Schools*, Blackwell)

Matching Tasks to Children's Attainment
(From Desforges, C., 1985, 'Matching tasks to children's attainment', in Desforges, C. and Bennett, N., 'Recent Advances in Classroom Research', *British Journal of Educational Psychology* Monograph Series, 2)

Does Educational Psychology Contribute to the Solution of Educational Problems?
(From Jacobsen, B., 1985, 'Does educational psychology contribute to the solution of educational problems?', in Clazton *et al.*, *Psychology and Schooling: What's the Matter?*, Bedford Way Papers, No. 25, University of London Institute of Education)

Index

The Study of Primary Education — A Source Book: Contents of Volumes 2, 3 and 4

Volume 2: The Curriculum

General Introduction

Compilers' Notes

Acknowledgments

The Study of the Curriculum: An Introduction

1 A Diversity of Views

On Curriculum
(From 'On curriculum', reprinted in Griffin-Beale, C. (Ed.) 1979, *Christian Schiller: In His Own Words*, A and C Black)

The Essence of Primary Education?
(From Marsh, L., 1973, *Being A Teacher*, A and C Black)

A Process Model of the Primary Curriculum
(From Kelly, V., 1981, 'Research and the primary curriculum', *Journal Of Curriculum Studies*, 13, 3)

A Common National Curriculum?
(From Boyson, R., 1975, 'Maps, chaps and your hundred best books', *The Times Educational Supplement*, 17 October)

The Need for Greater Uniformity
(From Froome, S., 1970, *Why Tommy Isn't Learning*, Tom Stacey)

Curriculum Core
(From Lawlor, S., 1988, *Correct Core: Simple Curricula For English, Mathematics and Science*, Centre for Policy Studies)

Is Primary Education Possible?
(From Oliver, D., 1984, 'Is primary education possible?', *Education 3–13*, 12, 2)

Ground Rules for a Community Curriculum
(From Midwinter, E., 1972, *Priority Education*, Penguin Books)

Education, Politics and the Neglect of Communality
(From Lawson, K., 1979, 'The politics of primary curricula', *Education 3–13*, 7, 1)

Bases for the Primary Curriculum
(From Blyth, W., 1984, *Development, Experience and Curriculum in Primary Education*, Croom Helm)

An Enabling Curriculum
(From Blyth, W., 1984, *Development, Experience and Curriculum in Primary Education*, Croom Helm)

A View of the Primary Curriculum
(From DES, 1980, *A View of the Curriculum*, HMSO)

2 'Official' Statements

Responsibilities for the Curriculum
(From DES, 1979, *Local Authority Arrangements for the School Curriculum*, HMSO)

Towards a Framework for the Curriculum
(From DES/Welsh Office, 1980, *A Framework for the School Curriculum*, HMSO)

Policy for the School Curriculum
(From DES/Welsh Office, 1981, *The School Curriculum*, HMSO)

The Organization and Content of the Primary Curriculum: A Note
(From DES, 1984, *The Organization and Content of the 5–16 Curriculum: A Note*, HMSO)

The Primary Curriculum: A National View
(From DES, 1985, *Better Schools*, HMSO)

The National Curriculum
(From DES, 1989, *From Policy To Practice*, HMSO)

HMI's Observations on the Primary Curriculum in England
(From DES, 1978, *Primary Education in England: A Survey by HM Inspectors of Schools*, HMSO)

The Primary Curriculum in Northern Ireland: General Considerations
(From DENI, 1980, *Primary Education*, HMSO)

The Primary Curriculum in Scotland: General Considerations
(From SED, 1980, *Learning and Teaching in P4 and P7*, HMSO)

HMI Observations on the First School Curriculum
(From DES, 1982, *Education 5 to 9*, HMSO)

3 Aims

Who Should Decide?
(From White, J., 1979, 'Aims and curricula: Do heads and teachers have the right to decide?', *Primary Education Review*, 7)

Primary Teachers' Aims
(From Ashton, P., 1978, 'What are primary teachers' aims?', in Richards, C. (Ed.) *Education 3–13, 1973–77*, Nafferton Books; and Ashton, P. 1981, 'Primary teachers' aims 1969–77', in Simon, B. and Willcocks, J. (Eds) *Research and Practice in the Primary Classroom*, Routledge and Kegan Paul)

4 Curriculum Issues

The Primary Curriculum: Perennial Questions and General Issues
(From Richards, C., 1981, 'The primary curriculum: Perennial questions and current issues', *Primary Education Review*, 12)

The Curriculum from 5–16: An HMI View
(From Richards, C., 1986, 'The curriculum from 5 to 16: Background content and some implications for primary education', *Education 3–13*, 13, 1; and Southworth, G. (Ed.) *Readings in Primary School Management*, Falmer Press)

Subjects, Specialist Teaching and Curriculum Overlay
(From Richardson, J., 1987, 'Subject to subjects', *Forum*, 29, 2)

Analyzing the Primary Curriculum
(From Alexander, R., 1984, *Primary Teaching*, Holt, Rinehart and Winston)

Continuity: Goals and Policies
(From Dean, J., 1980, 'Continuity', in Richards, C. (Ed.) *Primary Education: Issues for the Eighties*, A and C Black)

Continuity and Liaison: Primary-Secondary Practices
(From Findlay, F., unpublished manuscript)

Continuity Between Primary and Secondary Schools: A Proposal
(From Thomas, N. *et al.*, 1985, *Improving Primary Schools*, ILEA)

Primary-Secondary Transfer: The Experience of ILEA
(From ILEA, 1988, *Improving Secondary Transfer*, Bulletin 17, ILEA)

Continuities and Discontinuities in the Primary Curriculum
(From Blyth, W. and Derricott, R., 1985, 'Continuities and discontinuities in the primary curriculum,' *Curriculum*, 6, 2)

The Range of the Primary Curriculum
(From DES, 1978, *Primary Education in England*, HMSO)

Curriculum Consistency
(From Richards, C., 1982, 'Curriculum consistency', in Richards, C. (Ed.) *New Directions in Primary Education*, Falmer Press)

Curriculum Diversity
(From Farquhar, C. *et al.*, 1987, 'Curriculum diversity in London infant schools', *British Journal of Educational Psychology*, 57)

Curricular Integration or Differentiation?
(From Dearden, R., 1976, *Problems in Primary Education*, Routledge and Kegan Paul)

Integration in the Curriculum: A Developmental View
(From Blyth, W., 1985, 'Integration in the curriculum: Some observations', in Day, C. *et al.* (Eds) *Prospects for Curriculum*, Association for the Study for the Curriculum)

The Problem of Match
(From DES, 1978, *Primary Education in England*, HMSO)

The Role of Assessment in 'Matching'
(From Harlen, W., 1982, 'The role of assessment in "matching"', *Primary Education Review*, 13)

Proposals for a National Assessment System
(From DES, 1988, *Task Group on Assessment and Testing: A Report*, HMSO)

Who's Afraid of Evaluation?
(From MacDonald, B., 1976, 'Who's afraid of Evaluation?', *Education 3–13*, 4, 2)

An Accountability Model for Progressive Education
(From Elliott, J., 1979, 'Accountability, progressive education and school-based evaluation', *Education 3–13*, 7)

Approaches to Accountability at School Level
(From Becher, T. *et al.*, 1981, *Policies for Educational Accountability*, Heinemann)

An American Perspective on the Evaluation of the Primary Curriculum
(From Eisner, E., 1974, *English Primary Schools: Some Observations and Assessments*, National Association for the Education of Young Children)

School Self-Evaluation: Rationale, Scope and Participation
(From, Rodger, I. and Richardson, J., 1985, *Self-Evaluation for Primary Schools*, Hodder and Stoughton)

Factors Influencing Primary Schools' Effectiveness
(From ILEA, 1986, *The Junior School Project: A Summary of the Main Report*, ILEA)

How Do Teachers Plan?
(From McCutcheon, G., 1980, 'How do elementary teachers plan? The nature of planning and the influences on it', *The Elementary School Journal*, 81)

Curriculum Policy-Making
(From Garland, R., 1982, 'Curriculum policy-making in primary schools', in Richards, C. (Ed.) *New Directions in Primary Education*, Falmer Press)

Achievements in Primary Schools: Key Issues
(From Thomas, N., 1987, 'Achievement in primary schools: The Select Committee's Report', *Education 3–13*, 15, 2)

5 Other Aspects

Principles for Record-Keeping
(From Clift, P. *et al.*, 1981, *Record-Keeping in Primary Schools*, Macmillan)

Some Realities of Classroom Life
(From Jackson, P., 1968, *Life in Classrooms*, Holt-Rinehart)

Curriculum Schemes and Guidelines
(From Alexander, R., 1984, *Primary Teaching*, Holt, Rinehart and Winston)

The Place of 'Discovery Methods'
(From Bantock, G., 1969, 'Discovery methods', *Black Paper Two*, Critical Quarterly Society)

Learning How to Learn
(From Dearden, R., 1976, *Problems in Primary Education*, Routledge and Kegan Paul)

The Autonomy of the Primary School Teacher
(From Taylor, P. and Reid, W., 1973, 'Influence and change in the primary school', *Education 3–13*, 1, 1)

Curriculum Structure and Topic Work
(From Bonnett, M., 1986, 'Child-centredness and the problem of structuring project work', *Cambridge Journal of Education*, 16, 1)

The Curriculum — As Observed in Some Inner City Classrooms
(From Tizard, B. *et al.*, 1988, *Young Children at School in the Inner City*, Lawrence Erlbaum)

The Informal Curriculum
(From Blyth, W., 1984, *Development, Experience and Curriculum in Primary Education*, Croom Helm)

Messages Conveyed by Physical Forms
(From Evans, K., 1979, 'The physical form of the school', *British Journal of Educational Studies*, 27, 1)

Order and the Use of Space in Primary School Buildings
(From Cooper, I., 1982, 'The maintenance of order and use of space in primary school buildings', *British Journal of Sociology of Education*, 3, 3)

Gender Stereotyping: Another Aspect of the 'Hidden Curriculum'
(From Clarricoates, K., 1983, 'Some aspects of the "hidden curriculum" and interaction in the classroom', *Primary Education Review*, 17)

Learning at Home and at School
(From Atkin, J. and Goode, J., 1982, 'Learning at home and at school', *Education 3–13*, 10, 1)

Parents and the Curriculum
(From Tizard, J. *et al.*, 1982, 'Collaboration between teachers and parents in assisting children's reading', *British Journal of Educational Psychology*, 52)

The Primary Curriculum: Towards a World View
(From Blyth, W., 1984, *Development, Experience and Curriculum in Primary Education*, Croom Helm)

Index

The Study of Primary Education — A Source Book: Contents of Volumes 1, 3 and 4

Volume 3:
School Organization and Management

General Introduction

Compilers' Notes

Acknowledgments

Introduction

1 Roles and Responsibilities

Introduction

The Primary Head
(From Alexander, R., 1984, *Primary Teaching*, Holt Education)

Leadership in Primary Schools: The Role of the Head
(From DES (Welsh Office), 1985, *Leadership in Primary Schools*, HMI Occasional Paper)

The Managerial Work of Primary Headteachers
(From Coulson, A.A., 1986, *The Managerial Work of Primary School Headteachers*, Sheffield Papers in Education Management, No. 48, Sheffield City Polytechnic)

Perceptions of Heads in Primary Schools
(From Southworth, G.W., 1987, 'Primary school headteachers and collegiality', in Southworth, G.W. (Ed.) *Readings in Primary School Management*, Falmer Press)

Primary Heads and School Culture
(From Nias, D.J., Southworth, G.W. and Yeomans, R., 1989, *Staff Relationships in the Primary School: A Study of School Cultures*, Cassell)

The Deputy Head
(From Whitaker, P., 1983, *The Primary Head*, Heinemann)

The Role of the Deputy Head
(From DES (Welsh Office), 1985, *Leadership in Primary Schools*, HMI Occasional Paper)

A Deputy Head Observed: Findings from an Ethnographic Study
(From Nias, D.J., 1987, 'One finger, one thumb: A case study of the deputy head's part in the leadership of a nursery/infant school', in Southworth, G.W. (Ed.) *Readings in Primary School Management*, Falmer Press)

Class Teaching, Specialist Teaching and the Role of the Post-Holder
(From DES, 1978, *Primary Education in England*, HMSO)

The Duties of Teachers with Curricular Responsibilities
(From DES, 1982, *Mathematics Counts*, HMSO)

The Role of the Curriculum Post-Holder
(From Campbell, R., previously unpublished paper)

Curriculum Co-ordinators
(From The Third Report of the Education, Science and Arts Committee of the House of Commons, 1986, *Achievement in Primary Schools*, HMSO)

Teachers and Teaching
(From DES, 1985, *Education Observed: Good Teachers*, HMSO)

Moving Towards Partnership
(From Sallis, J., 1988, *Schools, Parents and Governors*: *A New Approach to Accountability*, Routledge)

2 School Organization and Management

Introduction

Managing the School as an Organization
(From ILEA, 1985, *Improving Primary Schools*, ILEA)

Characteristics of Good School Organization
(From DES, 1987, *Primary Schools: Some Aspects of Good Practice*, HMSO)

Curriculum Management and Organization: The Collegiate Approach
(From Wallace, M., 1988, 'Towards a collegiate approach to curriculum management in primary and middle schools', *School Organization*, 8, 1)

The Culture of Collaboration
(From Nias, D.J., Southworth, G.W. and Yeomans, R., 1989, *Staff Relationships in the Primary School: A Study of School Cultures*, Cassell)

Teacher Isolation and School Organization and Culture in the Small Rural School
(From Bell, A. and Sigsworth, A., 1987, *The Small Rural Primary School*, Falmer Press)

Inside Primary School Organization
(From Pollard, A., 1985, *The Social World of the Primary School*, Holt, Rinehart and Winston)

Supply, Temporary and Part-Time Teachers: Partial Members of the School?
(From Nias, D.J., 1989, *Primary Teachers Talking*, Routledge)

Classes: The Fundamental Unit of Organization
(From The Third Report of the Education, Science and Arts Committee of the House of Commons, 1986, *Achievement in Primary Schools*, HMSO)

Vertical Grouping
(From Lee, J., 1984, 'Vertical grouping in the primary school', *School Organization*, 4, 2)

Small Rural Schools and Peer Groups
(From Bell, A. and Sigsworth, A., 1987, *The Small Rural Primary School*, Falmer Press)

The Ages at which Children Enter School
(From The Third Report of the Education, Science and Arts Committee of the House of Commons, 1986, *Achievement in Primary Schools*, HMSO)

Local Education Authority Admission Policies and Practices
(From Sharp, C., 1987, 'Local education authority admission policies and practices', in *Four Year Olds in School: Policy and Practice*, NFER/SCDC)

Special Educational Needs in Infant Classes
(From Lewis, A., 1986, 'Meeting special educational needs in infant classes: A discussion of evidence from HMI reports on individual schools', *School Organization*, 6, 2)

Meeting Individual Needs: Towards a Whole School Response
(From Ainscow, M. and Muncy, J., 1989, *Meeting Individual Needs*, David Fulton)

Parents and Other Voluntary Helpers
(From The Third Report of the Education, Science and Arts Committee of the House of Commons, 1986, *Achievement in Primary Schools*, HMSO)

Parents and Partnership
(From Arkinstall, M., 1987, 'Towards a partnership: The Taylor Report, school government and parental involvement', in Lowe, R. (Ed.) *The Changing Primary School*, Falmer Press)

Parent-School Relationships
(From Tizard, B., Blatchford, P., Burke, J., Farquhar, C. and Plewis, I., 1988, *Young Children at School in the Inner City*, Lawrence Erlbaum)

Schools, Governors and Parents
(From Sallis, J., 1988, *Schools, Parents and Governors: A New Approach to Accountability*, Routledge)

3 Professional and School Development

Introduction

Staff Development
(From Schools Council, 1983, *Primary Practice*, Methuen Educational)

Headship Development
(From Coulson, A.A., 1988, 'Headship development through personal and professional growth', in Clarkson, M.W. (Ed.) *Emerging Issues in Primary Education*, Falmer Press)

Developing Collegiality Through Management Development
(From Wallace, M., 1988, 'Towards a collegiate approach to curriculum management in primary and middle schools', *School Organization*, 8,1)

Staff Relationships and Teacher Education
(From Nias, D.J., Southworth, G.W. and Yeomans, R., 1989, *Staff Relationships in the Primary School: A Study of School Cultures*, Cassell)

Learning in Staffrooms
(From Nias, D.J., 1989, *Primary Teachers Talking*, Routledge)

In-service Education for Teachers of Young Children
(From Abbott, L., 1987, 'In-service education for teachers of young children', in *Four Year Olds in School: Policy and Practice*, NFER/SCDC)

School Development Plans
(From ILEA, 1985, *Improving Primary Schools*, ILEA)

Characteristics of School Development Plans
(From Holly, P.J. and Southworth, G.W., *The Developing School*, Falmer Press)

Issues Arising from School Development Plans
(From Campbell, P., 1987, report prepared for Suffolk Education Authority)

Self-Evaluation for School Development
(From Rodger, I.A.S. and Richardson, J.A.S., 1985, *Self-Evaluation for Primary Schools*, Hodder and Stoughton)

Evaluation for the Developing Primary School: Learning from GRIDS
(From Holly, P.J., 1987, 'Evaluation for the developing primary school', in Southworth, G.W. (Ed.) *Readings in Primary School Management*, Falmer Press)

Teacher Appraisal:Contexts and Elements
(From Day, C., Whitaker, P. and Wren, D., 1987, *Appraisal and Professional Development in Primary Schools*, Open University Press)

Appraisal as Teacher Learning and Change
(From Day, C., Whitaker, P. and Wren, D., 1987, *Appraisal and Professional Development in Primary Schools*, Open University Press)

Learning and Teacher Appraisal
(From Dadds, M., 1987, 'Learning and teacher appraisal: The heart of the matter', in Southworth, G.W. (Ed.) *Readings in Primary School Management*, Falmer Press)

Effective Schools
(From Mortimore, P., 1988, *School Matters*, Open Books)

Index

The Study of Primary Education — A Source Book: Contents of Volumes 1,
2 and 4